JOSEPH J. KUKULAN

The Native's Return

*An American Immigrant
Visits Yugoslavia
And Discovers
His Old Country*

By
LOUIS ADAMIC

Fully Illustrated

Harper & Brothers
New York and London

CONTENTS

PART ONE: HOME AGAIN IN CARNIOLA

   I. *After Nineteen Years*   3

  II. *My Cousin Toné Marries*   35

 III. *Death Waits for My Uncle Yanez*   57

 IV. *We Stay in Carniola*   80

  V. *Mr. Guggenheim and I Become a Legend*   93

PART TWO: THE COAST AND MOUNTAIN REGIONS

   VI. *Southbound*   109

  VII. *A Village of Lonely Women*   115

 VIII. *Montenegro in the Daytime*   125

  IX. *Dalmatia—A Peasant Riviera*   147

   X. *A City Suspended in Space*   178

  XI. *"Here the Clock Was Set Back"*   203

 XII. *The Epic of Kossovo*   223

PART THREE: BELGRADE AND CROATIA

 XIII. *A "Boom" Town*   233

 XIV. *Trouble in Croatia*   266

  XV. *A Peasant Genius*   296

{ v }

XVI. *"Doctor Hercules"*   308

XVII. *I Meet the King-Dictator*   325

CONCLUSION

XVIII. *Back to America*   355

ILLUSTRATIONS

A special section of illustrations drawn from the scenes of this book follows page 232. The page numbers given with the captions accompanying each illustration refer to related passages in the text.

PART ONE

Home Again in Carniola

CHAPTER I

After Nineteen Years

E ARLY IN THE SPRING OF 1932, WHEN I RECEIVED A Guggenheim Fellowship requiring me to go to Europe for a year, I was thirty-three and had been in the United States nineteen years. At fourteen—a son of peasants, with a touch of formal "city education"—I had emigrated to the United States from Carniola, then a tiny Slovene province of Austria, now an even tinier part of a *banovina* in the new Yugoslav state.

In those nineteen years I had become an American; indeed, I had often thought I was more American than were most of the native citizens of my acquaintance. I was ceaselessly, almost fanatically, interested in the American scene; in ideas and forces operating in America's national life, in movements, tendencies and personalities, in technical advances, in social, economic, and political problems, and generally in the tremendous drama of the New World.

Events and things outside of America interested me but incidentally: only in so far as they were related to, or as they affected, the United States. I spoke, wrote, and read only in English. For sixteen years I had had practically no close contact with immigrants of my native nationality. For three years I had been a soldier in the American army. After the war I had roamed over a good half of the United States and had been to Hawaii, Philippines, Central and South America. In the last few years I had become an American writer, writing on American subjects for American readers. And I had married an American girl.

{ 3 }

To Stella I had told but a few main facts about my childhood and early boyhood in the old country; and what little I had told her of my parents, and the village and house in which I was born, had seemed to her "like a story." She scarcely believed me. To her I was an American from toes to scalp.

Now, because of my Guggenheim Fellowship, we were going to Europe.

One day early in April, Stella said, "We'll visit your folks in Carniola, of course." She evidently thought that would be the natural thing to do.

"Of course," I said. "Of course," I repeated inaudibly to myself, then added aloud, "Just a short visit, though— for an afternoon, perhaps."

She said, "I suddenly realized that you told me you have people over there—in Carniola (I like the sound of the name)—and now I'm curious about them—what they're like."

"So am I," I said, though actually, I think, I wasn't; not in any deep, vital sense, at any rate.

None the less, I wrote to my family in the old country that my wife, who was an American and spoke no Slovenian, and I should, in all probability, visit them on Sunday afternoon, May 15th. The ship that we decided to sail on was scheduled to arrive in Trieste on the 14th, and I figured that we might as well get the visit over with the first thing; then we should immediately find a place in the mountains somewhere in Italy or Austria and I should begin to work on my new book dealing with America.

II

Three weeks later, in mid-Atlantic, I said to Stella, "I'm a bit scared of this visit home."

"I thought something was bothering you," she said. "Why?"

"Well," I began to explain, "although in a way it seems

{4}

like the day before yesterday, it's a long time since I left home. I was very young and I think I've changed a great deal—fundamentally—since then. All my emotional and intellectual life now seems to be rooted in America. I belong in America. My old country, somehow, is a million miles away—on another planet—and my old country includes my people."

Stella listened sympathetically.

"Of course," I went on, "I remember my parents as they were before I left home, but now my memory of them is seriously blurred by the idea which abruptly intrudes itself upon my mind, that in these nineteen years, which have been a drastic, turbulent period for everybody in Europe, they, too, must have changed—not merely grown older, but changed, probably, in their characters. This adds to the distance between them and me.

"I have four brothers and five sisters in Carniola. Seven of them were already in the world nineteen years ago. Of the two born since then, I have, of course, no notion, except that their names are Yozhé and Anica, and their ages seventeen and fifteen, respectively. The other seven I remember but dimly as they were in 1913. I was the oldest (three children before me had died). My oldest sister, Tonchka, was thirteen. My oldest brother, Stan, was ten. My youngest brother, Francé, was a little over a year. Now he is nearly twenty-one. Tonchka is thirty-two, married, and has two children. Stan is twenty-nine. Another sister, Mimi, was four when I left. Now she is twenty-three, a nun in a hospital, and her name is Manuela. Why she became a nun is more than I know. Then there is my brother Anté and my sisters Paula and Poldka —barely more than names to me. In fact, I have to strain my memory to tell you their names. And now I'm going to visit them because that, somehow, seems the proper thing to do."

"It'll probably be very interesting," said Stella.

"Probably very awkward," said I. "During the last fifteen years my contact with home has been exceedingly thin. For two years after America's entry into the war I could not write to my people because I was in the American army and they were in Austria. We were 'enemies.' For two or three years after the war my circumstances were nothing to write about to anybody; so I didn't. In the last eight or nine years I wrote home, as a rule, once in six months—a card or a short note, to the effect that I was well and hoped they were all well, too. I could not write much more. For one thing, I could not begin to tell them about America and myself; how I felt about America, what a wonderful and terrible place it was, how it fascinated and thrilled me. They might misunderstand something; something I'd say might disturb them; then I'd have to explain, and so on; there would be no end to writing—to what purpose? At the end they would really know nothing or very little about America or me. One has to live in the United States a long time to even begin to know it. Besides, if I got them interested in America, some of my brothers and sisters might want to come over —and I did not want that. I had troubles enough of my own. And they were possibly as well off in Carniola as they would be in America. . . . Another thing: of late years I could express only the most ordinary things in my native tongue. I could not write in Slovenian of involved matters, such as my life in America.

"At home, of course, they did not understand me, what I was up to in America, why I wrote so little; and they, with their peasant patience and pride (which, as I recall, does not break down even before members of their own family)—they, in turn, asked me for no explanations, and their letters to me were almost as brief as mine to them. They—mother or one of my sisters or brothers—usually answered that they were well, too, thank you. Occasionally they added some such information as that Tonchka had married or had had a child, or that Stan or Anté had had

{ 6 }

to go into military service, or that Mimi had become a nun
—bare facts, nothing else.

"So I don't know what I'll find. I have no idea how they
stand economically. When I left for America my father
was a well-to-do peasant in the village. Now, if one is to
believe American newspapers, all of Europe is in a bad
way, and I don't know what's happened to my people
lately. Then, too, you must remember that I'm coming
from America, and when one returns from America one is
supposed to bring with him a pot of money and help those
who have stayed at home—while all I have is a Guggenheim Fellowship, barely enough to keep you and me in
Europe for a year!"

Stella was optimistic. "Chances are it won't be so bad as
you think. Perhaps your people are as scared of you, what
America has done to you, and the kind of girl you married,
as you are of them and what the nineteen years have done
to them."

"Maybe," I said. I felt a little better, not much, and
not for long.

III

Our ship stopped for a few hours each at Lisbon, Gibraltar, Cannes, Naples, and Palermo. Save in Cannes, everywhere, on getting ashore, we were mobbed by ragged
youngsters, crying, "Gimme! Gimme!" and making signs
that they were famished and wanted to eat. In the streets
(especially in Lisbon) women with children in their arms
approached us and made signs that their babies were hungry. Most of these, no doubt, were professionals, dressed
and trained for begging; but even so it was depressing.

"In Yugoslavia it may be even worse," I said.

On the morning of May 13th we began to sail along
the coast of Dalmatia, once also a province of Austria,
now a part of Yugoslavia. We passed tiny islands and
bright little towns along the shore line, and gradually I

began to feel better. I scarcely know why. Perhaps because the hills ashore looked so much like the hills from San Pedro to San Diego in southern California where I lived for years. Perhaps also because the Adriatic Sea, with the sun on it, was even bluer, lovelier than the Mediterranean.

But even so, I was hardly prepared for Dubrovnik, or Ragusa. From the ship, as we approached it, it appeared unreal. "Like a stage set for a play," Stella remarked. And another American, leaning next to her on the rail, said, "One expects a bunch of actors to appear out there at any moment and begin to sing, 'We are the merry villagers. . . .'"

The boat stopped for three hours and we went ashore. Here we were not mobbed by beggars. Some of the young boys on the pier were almost as ragged as those in Lisbon and in Palermo, but they looked anything but starved or sick. Their grins reached from ear to ear. Their white, strong teeth flashed in the sun. Their faces were brown. Locks of straggly dark hair hung over their blue eyes.

To one of the ragamuffins Stella offered a coin. He looked at her, startled. *"Zashto?* (What for?)" he asked. I explained to the youngster in Croatian (which, to my surprise, I suddenly began to speak with very little difficulty) that my wife wanted to make him a present of the coin. He scowled: *"Hvala liepa!* (Thank you!) No alms!" Then, as if something just occurred to him, his sun-tanned young features lit up. "If you and the lady wish to be friendly and generous," he grinned, "please offer me an American cigarette if you have one and see if I'll take it."

He got several cigarettes; then his mouth and eyes—his whole face—broke into a smile that I cannot describe. *"Hvala liepa!"* he shouted, and dashed off. Several other boys, all shouting, followed him.

I felt grand. "My people!" I said to myself. " 'No alms!' " I could have run after the urchin and hugged him. "My people!" I said, aloud.

Stella laughed. We both laughed.

We walked through the ancient, sun-flooded, and shadowy streets of Dubrovnik, whose history reaches back to the fifth century. Many of the streets were not streets at all, but twisty stairways running from the main thoroughfares up the steep grades. Some of the people we saw were obviously foreigners—visitors or tourists from Austria, Czechoslovakia, Germany, France, and England—but the majority were native Dalmatians of all ages, many in colorful homespun costumes, and Serbo-Moslem laborers from near-by Bosnia and Herzegovina, wearing *opanke*, Serb sandals, with upturned toes and baggy Turkish breeches, close-fitting jackets, and red fezes. On one street we saw two veiled Mohammedan women walking on one side; on the other side were two Catholic nuns. In the doorways sat mothers, giving their breasts to infants. There were swarms of children everywhere.

"Such faces!" exclaimed Stella every few minutes. "Even the homely ones are beautiful, they're so healthy and brown."

In Dubrovnik—unlike in Lisbon, Gibraltar, Naples, and Palermo—no one forced himself upon us to sell us something. Here no guides were offering their services; there were no shifty-eyed peddlers of obscene photographs. In the little bazaars, where business evidently was poor, the men and women in charge of the stores seemingly did not care whether the passers-by stopped to look at and buy their handmade peasant embroidery, jewelry, and earthenware or not. They talked and laughed among themselves, or sat still and dozed in the warm sun.

On the way back to the pier, going down a steep stair-street, we came upon a tall, splendidly proportioned girl, dark-haired and blue-eyed, clad in an agreeably colorful medley of several south-Dalmatian costumes, among which the local Ragusan dress predominated. On her head she balanced a great basket of something or other; perhaps of wash for one of the modern houses above the old town. The basket seemed a part of her. She walked and swayed from her hips. Her arms were bare and firm. One of them she held akimbo. In the other hand she carried a bunch of golden-rain blossoms. She slowed her pace to look at us; possibly Stella's American dress interested her.

I said, "*Dobar dan!* (Good day!)"

"*Dobar dan!*" she returned, smiled—again one of those smiles to which words cannot do justice—and stopped. "Are you *nashki*? (of our nationality?)"

"I was born in Slovenia," I said, "but went to America as a young boy. My wife is American."

"So!" said the girl, eagerly. "An uncle of mine is in America. He is a fisherman in Louisiana, where the great river Mees-sees-seep-pee," she syllabicated, "falls into the ocean." She smiled all the while.

"She is beautiful," said Stella. "What a body!"

I translated, "My wife says you are beautiful and you have a fine body."

The girl's smile widened and deepened, and her face and neck colored. "*Hvala liepa!*" she said. "Please tell your American wife that *she* is beautiful."

I told Stella what the girl had said. Then from the bunch she carried the girl handed her several twigs of golden-rain and, without saying anything, went on up the stairs.

"That is what I call nice," said Stella, looking after the girl. "Such a simple, sincere gesture."

I had a sudden feeling that I would like Yugoslavia, her people; that, perhaps, even my visit home would be more a pleasure than an ordeal.

IV

Fifteen hours later—Saturday forenoon—the ship docked in Trieste.

Before we got off, there came aboard a Slovene gentleman, overwhelming in his eager politeness and courtesy. He bowed, shook my hand, bowed again and kissed Stella's hand. Then he proceeded to inform me, in most precise, formal, and yet not unbeautiful words, that he was the personal representative of the *ban* (governor) of Dravska Banovina (now the official government designation for Slovenia), and that his special duties were to officially welcome us to my old country, to see that at the Italo-Yugoslav border the Yugoslav customs and immigration people would not disturb our luggage or cause us any other annoyance, and generally to see, so far as was within his power, that our stay in the *banovina* would be the essence of comfort and delight. He was at our command—and he bowed again. Thereupon he bowed once more and said that Slovenia— indeed, entire Yugoslavia—was honored and overjoyed by my homecoming.

All this I tried to take matter-of-factly and thanked the gentleman in as good Slovenian as, in my embarrassment, I could command after not having spoken it for sixteen years. Then I told Stella what it was all about.

Wide-eyed, she said after a moment: "But why? Because you're a writer?"

"I suppose so," I said.

"The boy who went into the big world and made good comes home!"

We laughed and the Slovene, who understood no English, politely joined in our laughter. Of course, I did not explain to him why the thing was funny to us. I did not tell him, for instance, that the two books I had published in the United States, while praised by the critics and reviewers throughout the country, had had tragically unsatisfactory sales; that in America I was a nobody—one of many young scribblers living in eternal dread of the rejection slip; that in America no writer draws much water; that for the government to officially honor an author was almost inconceivable in the United States.

Out of his briefcase the gentleman then produced a batch of Slovene and other Yugoslav newspapers of recent date. Here were long articles about my "wide fame" and "great achievements" in America, containing translated quotations from favorable reviews of my books. In addition, some of them carried brief editorials which ended: "To our distinguished countryman and visitor: WELCOME HOME!" —in capital letters.

"As you see, sir," said the man, "the whole country is agog. The newspaper men in Lublyana"—the capital of the *banovina*—"are extremely eager to interview you, but since the first thing you doubtless wish to do is rest after the trip and visit your people, I have warned them not to disturb you, say, until Monday or early next week, when and if it shall please you to talk to them."

"Oh, thank you very much! It was very nice of you." . . . Interview me! On what? I had never been interviewed in my life.

At first I could not understand how all this publicity had broken loose on the eve of my return. I recalled that I had sent copies of my books to my parents, but surely they had not engineered the ballyhoo. I recalled, too, that now and then my people had inclosed in their letters one or two little clippings about me from the Lublyana papers, but that could not be the genesis of all this.

Then it occurred to me that a week before we sailed a man had telephoned to me who said he was the American correspondent for several journals in Yugoslavia, and that he had read in New York papers about my getting a Guggenheim Fellowship and my forthcoming trip to Europe, which he hoped would include Yugoslavia. Would it? I said that it would. What ship was I going on?—and a few other such questions, which I had answered. Then he said that he had followed my "career in America for years" and, now that I was going home, he would write "a little article" about me. And these columns of stuff in a dozen papers printed in Lublyana, Zagreb, Belgrade, Split, Sarajevo and one or two other cities of Yugoslavia were the "little article."

But the real reason and significance of all this, which had little to do with me, I learned much later.

V

The short train ride from Trieste to Lublyana was a delightful experience, especially after we crossed the Italian border, when I was in my old country at last.

It was a perfect midspring afternoon, and most of my misgivings of the week before had vanished. Carniola, to all seeming, had not changed a whit. Here was the same river Sava with the same tributaries; the same little lakes and waterfalls; the same thickly wooded hills and mountains, with the snow-capped peaks above them; the same fields and meadows; the same villages and little churches, with crude frescoes of saints painted by peasant artists on the outer walls; and the same people, toiling in the same old way—slowly, patiently, somewhat inefficiently (to my American eyes) with semi-primitive tools and implements, on the same fertile black soil. The World War (although some of the worst battles were fought within hearing distance of Carniola) and the drastic political change, in 1918, from Austria to Yugoslavia had had no effect upon its essential aspects, its exquisite and wholesome beauty.

I do not mean to say that the regions of Carniola by themselves, with all their congestion of lovely valleys, lakes, rivers, hills, woods, and mountains, are more beautiful than other regions I have seen elsewhere in the world. I know of vastly grander places in the United States, but houses and towns in America, a new country, often spoil a natural scene. If not houses and towns, then outdoor advertisements and heaps of tin cans and discarded machinery. In Carniola, however, the simple peasant architecture of the small villages seems to enhance the beauty of the countryside. The houses and villages *belong*. They appear to have grown out of the soil. They belong exactly where they are, both æsthetically and economically. Most of them have been where they are for five, six, seven hundred years. They are harmonious with the woods, the fields, the lakes. They are in the pattern of the country as a whole, an elemental and sympathetic feature thereof.

The same goes for the people. The peasants driving the oxen on the dirt roads; the women, young and old, in their colorful working-clothes, weeding or hoeing in the fields and now pausing in their work to smile and wave to us in the train; the girls by the riverside, with their up-drawn petticoats, washing the heavy homespun linen by slapping it on big smooth rocks; the woodsmen floating freshly felled logs down the river; the barefoot, sturdy children playing before the houses—they all seemed to me inextricably and eternally an important, indigenous part of the scenery, the beauty-pattern, the deep harmony of Carniola.

I was glad to be back. My reaction to the beauty of Carniola, of course, was enhanced by the fact that it was my native land. I felt like shouting greetings to the peasants in the fields along the railroad.

There was another general impression that I got on the train. Carniola seemed so very, very small. I remembered, for instance, that in my boyhood a trip from Lublyana to Trieste was considered a long journey, an event in any-body's life to make it. And here Stella and I were coming from Trieste to Lublyana in a couple of hours by a slow train, humorously called an express, and we thought it was a short trip. The train stopped every few minutes in villages and small towns, which I suddenly recalled at least by names. With my consciousness of distances in the United States, and with the tens of thousands of miles that stretched behind me over the American continent and over two oceans, the distances in Carniola now seemed scarcely one-tenth of what I had thought them to be nineteen years before. Carniola had shrunk from an Austrian province to hardly more than a big Western ranch or a small national park in America.

When, toward evening, we arrived in Lublyana, which

{ 14 }

once upon a time I had considered a large city, it, too—with its 75,000 inhabitants—impressed me as a very small place; for I had behind me New York, Los Angeles, Kansas City, Chicago.

I had an impulse to go from Lublyana right on to my native village, not far from the city, but since I had written to my people that we would not come till Sunday afternoon, we let the *ban's* representative put us up for the night at one of the hotels.

After dinner, Stella went to bed, but I couldn't.

I went out and walked in the dimly-lit, quiet, almost deserted streets till past midnight, and discovered, to my great satisfaction, that, like the rest of Carniola, Lublyana, too, had not changed in its essentials; indeed, hardly even in its superficial aspects. The World War and the change from Austria to Yugoslavia did not touch it.

The old Roman wall seemed a little more crumbled than I remembered it, and in the middle of the city a twelve-story *nebotichnik* (skytoucher) was being built. But there were the same bridges over the River Lublyanica; the same nine-hundred-year-old fort and castle on the hill, now lit up at night; the same five-hundred-year-old City Hall, except that in place of the statue of the Emperor Francis Joseph in front of it there was now a new statue of the late King Peter of Serbia. There were the same old churches and monuments to writers, grammarians, musicians, orators, and poets; the same old stores, with the same old signs over the doors. Here, I remembered, I used to buy paper and pencils while attending the Gymnasium in my early teens. And here I used to buy rolls and apples for my midday lunch; here, my occasional piece of cake or chocolate; here, in this two-hundred-year-old bookshop, my books; and here my mother used to come shopping for drygoods once in a fortnight. ("She probably still does," I said to myself.) And here was the school I had gone to; here the house I had roomed in for two years; and here the theater where I had seen my first Shakespearean performance. Everything

{ 15 }

came back to me, and once more Lublyana was an important, vital part of my life.

Here were street-sweepers, old men with long birch brooms, sweeping the streets at night in the same old way. Here was a lamplighter with his tall pole, now, toward midnight, putting out some of the lights. Here I almost bumped into a black little fellow, a chimneysweep! and, amused at myself, I swiftly grabbed a button on my coat, for in my boyhood I had shared the folk superstition that to hold onto a button when meeting a chimneysweep meant good luck.

Here glowed the curtained windows of an old coffee-house. I entered and ordered a coffee, just to make sure its tables were occupied by the same types of men as nineteen years before, reading newspapers, playing chess and dominoes, talking, talking, talking in low tones so as not to disturb those who read or played chess. . . . Here was stability; or so it seemed.

I returned to the hotel tired, inwardly excited, deeply content.

VI

Tired as I was, I didn't fall asleep till after daylight. A tenseness, not unpleasant, from which I could not relax, held my body, and my mind throbbed with new impressions, newly stirred memories, thoughts of tomorrow. . . . My mother—how did she look? This, suddenly, was very important. When I had left, she was still on the sunny side of middle life, "rather tall," as I described her in my autobiographical narrative *Laughing in the Jungle*, "with a full bust and large hips; long arms and big, capable hands; a broad, sun-browned, wind-creased Slavic face; large, wide-spaced hazel eyes, mild and luminous with simple mirth; and wavy auburn hair which stuck in little gold-bleached wisps from under her colored kerchief, tied below her chin." That was how I remembered her. Now she was in her late

{ 16 }

fifties; she had borne thirteen children, raised ten, and worked hard without pause all her life. . . . My father? He was over eighty. . . . Our house? It was over six hundred years old, but with the possible exception of a new roof it probably was unchanged since I last saw it. . . .

On coming down the next morning, Stella and I saw two tall young men in the middle of the otherwise deserted hotel lobby. They did not see us immediately. One of them nervously paced up and down. The other was furiously smoking a cigarette.

"They must be your brothers!" breathed Stella. We stopped on the stairs. "They resemble you terribly," she added; "only they're handsome—Lord, they're handsome!"

Then the boys saw us, too. They recognized me, and their broad, bronzed faces split into big white-toothed grins. They rushed toward me, I rushed down, and we collided at the foot of the stairs. Shaking hands, we began to laugh, all three of us at once. Then Stella joined us, too. We didn't say a word for minutes; we just laughed.

They were Francé and Yozhé, my two kid brothers, Gymnasium students; only, unlike myself in my time, they did not room and board in Lublyana, but came in daily by train. Basically, however, beneath the thin crust of city polish they were young peasants, strong and healthy, exuding vitality, each with a pair of enormous hands. Looking at them, I had a weird-happy feeling. It was as if I looked in a magic mirror and saw myself at once twelve and sixteen years younger. Stella and I could not take our eyes off them. They spoke a little German and some French, and Stella could exchange a few words with them. But at first they could hardly talk at all, due to excitement only partly under control.

By and by they explained to me that mother had sent them to Lublyana on the early-morning train with orders to find us in the city and fetch us home on the first afternoon train without fail.

Francé said, "The whole village—the whole valley, in

fact—is excited as it never was before. For a week now nobody in the seventeen villages of our county has talked of anything but your homecoming, and the talk has already spread to other counties. In our valley the circulation of city newspapers has increased a hundredfold. Everybody has read about you. Everybody wants to see you. The girls and women want to know what sort of girl you married. You're the first from our valley to marry an *Amerikanka*. It's a sensation. . . . At home, in our house, of course, they are all beside themselves. None of us have had a decent night's sleep for a week. Mother, Paula, and Poldka—they sleep in the same room—scarcely closed their eyes for three or four nights, talking, speculating. Last night they spoke of killing our newest bull-calf to celebrate the return of the prodigal, but the calf, poor thing, is only two weeks old and as yet not particularly 'fatted'—so they decided to wait a week or two, till it gets a little closer to the scriptural weight."

We laughed for several minutes. I was unable to translate Francé's words to Stella till later.

I began to realize that during these nineteen years I, in America, had meant much more to my people than they, remaining in the old country, had meant to me. In the excitement of my life in America, I had lost nearly all feeling for them and for the old country in general. To them, on the other hand, I had been their own intrepid Marco Polo who had ventured from tiny Carniola into the big world at the age of fourteen. Now, after long years, I was coming home! And according to the newspapers, I had become a great man in the big world. I had become "famous," and thereby I had brought renown to their hitherto unknown, microscopic Carniola!

In the afternoon, going home in the train, Stella and I talked about this.

"It's very funny!" she said.

"Of a sudden," I said, "I'm a big frog in a tiny pond!"

At the little country railroad station, which is in the

village next to ours and which seemed ten times smaller than I recalled it, stood a crowd of people—elderly peasants, women, young men, girls, children, all in their Sunday best, some of the men in coat-sleeves, some of the girls in costumes of the region.

They stood in silence, save that some of the girls giggled. I didn't know any of them; only a few faces seemed faintly familiar.

It was a grand, sweet, painful moment.

Here and there, as we walked from the train, one of the young men stuck out his paw to me and said, "*Pozdravlyen!* (Greetings!) Remember me? I'm So-and-so."

I remembered him, then we laughed, and there was a loud murmur in the crowd.

Then two young men who looked very much alike and resembled Francé, Yozhé, and myself stepped out of the crowd. My two other brothers, a little older than Francé and Yozhé, and even a little taller. One of them was better-looking than all the other three put together. Stella let out a little shriek of delight. We shook hands.

"I am Stan," said the older one, grinning. He had a tremendous hand, but his grip and the look in his eyes with which he greeted me had the gentleness of a truly strong person.

"I am Anté," said the other, also grinning. He was the handsomest, but, like Stan, a young peasant without city education or polish.

Then all five of us brothers and Stella laughed for all we were worth, and the crowd joined in.

"Where are mother and father and the girls?" I asked.

"At home, all of them," said Stan.

And, I don't know why, but we all laughed again, and we walked home through the fields and meadows, with a mob of young boys and many dogs behind us. The valley seemed very, very small to me, and very beautiful. Spring was late and things were just beginning to grow. In the bright green of the meadows were big splashes of yellow buttercups and purple clover ahum with bees. Along the ditches grew forget-me-nots in great abundance, and in the shade of a row of hazel bushes I noticed more lilies-of-the-valley in one spot than I had seen during all my nineteen years in America.

For a minute everything threatened to go soft in me and I barely managed to hold back my tears.

In Blato, our village, was another, smaller crowd. I recognized a few faces. There were two or three uncles, and as many aunts and scores of cousins, some of whom had come from other villages, but no one said anything. With deep innate tact, they let me hurry on to our house.

VII

The sight of my mother, who waited for me (as I recalled in that instant) on the same spot in the courtyard of our home where I had said good-by to her in 1913, gave me a sharp sting. She had aged and her body had shrunk; her hair was gray and thin, her eyes and cheeks were sunken, but her hug told me she was still hale and strong.

Suddenly I was sorry that I hadn't written to her oftener. I wanted to say something, but what was there to say? What could anyone say in a moment like this? She herself said nothing. She smiled a little and, holding my hands stiffly in front of her, her body swayed a little, right and left, in sheer, unwordable happiness.

My father, also gray and shrunken, offered me a trembling, wrinkled hand, but on the whole, despite his age, was well and in full possession of his faculties. He smiled and said, "You have come at last. We greet you, son."

And there were the girls. Four of them stood against the wall of the house.

"I am Tonchka," said my oldest, married sister, who had come from Belgrade to be home when I arrived. She looked like a young matron.

"I am Paula,"—my next-to-the-oldest sister. Great coils

of brown hair were wound around her head. A tragic love-affair, of which I learned subsequently, had etched into her face, which was lovely before, a beauty that now causes a crisis in my vocabulary.

"I am Poldka,"—my third sister, a vivacious, open-faced human being in national costume. Two thick light-brown braids hung down her back. She was the only one who gave way to emotion and cried a little. "I'm *so* glad!"

"I am Anica,"—my youngest sister, the baby of the family, a reticent, shy young girl whom, like Yozhé, I had never seen before.

Finally, a nun appeared in the doorway above the stairs —my sister Mimi, now called Manuela. This was her first visit home since her ordination a year before. A victim of confused feelings, I ran up to her. She said nothing; she smiled; a young Madonna face, if a face was ever entitled to be called that. We shook hands. I had been told a moment before that because she was a nun I could not embrace or kiss her. I could shake hands with her only because I was her brother. I looked at her—at the oval, smooth, serene face, with its lively blue eyes and glowing red cheeks, under the broad starched white headgear of her order— and couldn't (and can't yet) understand why she became a nun.

After a while we all trooped into the house, in which all ten of us had been born, and before us our father and grandfather and our ancestors for I don't know how many generations back. But for some improvements here and there, the house had not changed; only, of course, with my consciousness of the Empire State Building and the interior of the Grand Central in New York City, it seemed much smaller to me than I had thought it was.

I noticed that mother and sisters used the same sort of utensils in the kitchen as were used in 1913. There were the same old tile stoves downstairs and upstairs; the same beds, tables, chairs, benches, and chests; the same pictures and ornaments on the walls. Upon the window-sills were flower-pots with flowers just beginning to bud. Throughout the house new curtains, bedspreads, and tablecovers had been spread and hung for my homecoming. They were my sisters' handwork—lace and embroidery, exquisite designs and color combinations. . . . (Later I learned that my sisters were members of the Yugoslav Peasant Handicraft Institute, which sold the products of their hands to Belgian lace merchants and English curio-dealers in Egypt, who then sold them to American importers and foreign tourists as Belgian or Egyptian native handwork. One of my sisters showed me lace she was making with Sphinx and Pyramid designs. She said, "Some American lady will probably buy this in Alexandria or Cairo next year!"—and we all laughed.)

In the large-room, the big table was set with a great bowl of forget-me-nots in the center. There was food and wine for all of us, and we sat down and tried to eat and drink, but, to mother's dismay, none of us was very successful. We were all too excited and happy, too full of emotions for which we had no expression.

In the middle of the meal, apropos of nothing in particular, my sister Paula, her sad face all in a big smile, silently pinned a few lilies-of-the-valley on Stella's jacket and a few on my coat lapel.

"They're lovely," said Stella, which I translated to Paula.

"Yes," said Paula; "there are so many of them this year that one could take a scythe and mow them like grass or clover." She smiled again, "I guess it's all in your honor, and your wife's."

Stella, understanding almost nothing of what was said, found herself in an awkward position. I translated some of the conversation to her. Everybody looked at her and tried to please her. I was discreetly questioned as to her family. Of course, unable to speak her language, it was as awkward for them as for her. But after a while she and they developed a system of hands-and-eyes language with which they managed to communicate some of their simpler thoughts to one another without my aid.

Essentially a simple, straightforward person, Stella won my people from the start. My sister Poldka said to me, "You have no idea, we were all so scared that you—a famous writer—would come home with some stiff, haughty foreign dame, and now, I guess, you can imagine how relieved we all are. How I wish I could talk with her!"

And Stella said to me, "It's almost unbelievable, this family of yours—the sort of family one could write a saga about. . . . I thought that, having let you go to America at fourteen, they were and would be indifferent to you. But now I see they love you without being possessive. I suppose that, peasant-like, they accepted your going to America the same way as they accept any other trick of fate, without changing their basic affection for you; when you didn't write for a long time, that was another trick of fate for them to accept; but it really made no difference so far as caring for you was concerned. I think it's wonderful to be that way. . . . Please tell them I love them all."

I told them.

"*Hvala lepa,*" said mother and Poldka. The others said nothing. They grinned and lowered their eyes. Poldka, who, as I say, is the most free-spoken in the family, said, "Tell her for us that we love her, too. We could just hug her, even though we have no practice in hugging."

I translated this to Stella. We all laughed again.

VIII

In the courtyard and in the apple orchard people began to gather—people of our own village and of near-by communities, neighbors, relatives, friends of the family's. "I guess they want to see you," said mother, "and since we can't ask them all into the house, you will have to go out."

So out we went, Stella, a few of my brothers and sisters,

and I. Then there was much sincere handshaking. *"Pozdravlyen! . . . Pozdravlyen!* Welcome home!" The men made some reticent remarks, asked a few hesitant questions. "I remember well when you went to America. . . . After all these years, how does the old village look to you, eh?" Some acted embarrassed, as they thought peasants should act in the presence of a man who was written up in the newspapers, but after a while this manner broke down, whereupon there was a lot of good, simple talk, punctuated by bursts of honest mirth.

I became acquainted with a young peasant, now married and the father of five children, who claimed that he had once whipped me in a fight over the possession of a whistle, and now that he mentioned it I seemed to recall the occasion.

Another young fellow, now also married and the father of several kids (one of whom was wrapped around his leg), admitted I had beaten him up several times and recalled to my mind the causes of our frequent battles.

One old peasant woman insisted I come to her house, a stone's-throw from ours, and there she showed me something I had scrawled on a wall about another boy in the village when I was ten or eleven years old.

I talked with Uncle Mikha, my favorite uncle, who is in his seventies, slightly bent and shrunken but still hale, with a hard peasant intelligence. Till lately, he had been mayor of our county. He and I had been good friends in my early boyhood. First we exchanged a few conventional remarks, then he drew me aside, cleared his throat, shifted the weight of his body from one leg onto the other, and said, "You may be a big man in the world, as the newspapers have it, but I am going to give you a piece of my mind anyhow. I think it wasn't at all nice not to write to your mother oftener than you did. She talked to me about you when you didn't write for a long time. She worried. At night she couldn't sleep, thinking maybe you were in trouble or dead. I am telling you this because I have liked you ever since you were knee-high and because your mother herself won't say anything about it to you—and when you go back to America I want you to write to her oftener."

"I will, Uncle Mikha," I said.

"But don't feel bad about what I said," said Mikha. "Now that you've come home, she's forgotten all about it."

Then there were the several *Amerikanci*—men who had been laborers in America for a few years and had returned home to stay. They each knew a few words of English and tried to parade their knowledge before their fellow villagers. They asked me about America. Was the *kriza* (the economic crisis) really as bad there as the papers said? Were there really so many people out of work? Was the depression hard on the Slovenian and other Yugoslav immigrants?

Other questions: Were the buildings in America really so tall? Was it true that there was a tree in California so thick that they had bored a tunnel through it for an automobile road? How did the American farmers till their soil? Was it true that most of the work on the land was done by machinery?—that New York had a population of seven million?—that there were ranches in the West bigger than entire Carniola?—that there were underground railroads in New York?—that there was a tunnel under a river in New York?—that Henry Ford was worth a billion dollars? —and how much was a billion dollars, anyhow, in Yugoslav dinars? And this man Seenclair Levees (Sinclair Lewis)— was he the biggest writer in America? Did I know him personally? Were these books *Arovsmeet* and *Babeet*, which have been translated into the Yugoslav, his best? . . .

Stella went walking with my brothers through the village, and the women, especially my cousins and aunts, commenced to ask me about her, at first discreetly, hesitantly, then more boldly: How old was she? How long were we married? Were her people well-to-do? How much dowry had she brought me? Had she sisters and brothers? Did she make

{ 25 }

her own clothes? . . . Which led to questions about American women in general: Did they all buy their clothes in stores? Did any of them bake their own bread, do their own wash, do fine needlework? Were houses in America very different from houses in Carniola? . . .

No end of questions, naïve, foolish, and sensible, which I found pleasure in answering, nevertheless. But I was glad, too, when, toward dusk, mother came and said I should come in to eat and drink something. "You must be starved and tired, talking all afternoon," she said. "And where is Styelah?" . . . I loved the way she pronounced her name. . . .

In the house mother said to me: "Yesterday I had a million questions to ask you, too, but now I forget them all. It doesn't matter. You are back and have a nice wife. Why ask questions? . . . Come now, eat something."

We sat down.

"Mother," I asked, "how do you all manage? I mean, what do you use for money?"

She laughed a little. "There's this *kriza*, of course, which does us no good, but now and then we sell a little of what we produce, so we can buy some of the things we need and can't produce at home. Ours is a big family, but Poldka and Paula make the clothes for all of us, and the clothes they make are better made than those one can buy in the city. Anté is handy with tools and he can make or repair almost anything. He can build a wall. Last year he and Stan put a cement bridge over the creek; you'll see it. The year before they dug the new water well, which you saw. Stan is a plowman second to none hereabouts. They are all healthy and capable, thank God. We don't need to employ help even at harvest time. . . . We manage, more or less."

That night, after a supper of home-cured ham and mildly spiced cooked wine which came from one of our relatives' vineyard in Bela Krayina, I slept, between sheets of rough homemade linen, in the bed I and all my brothers and sisters had let out our first wails.

IX

Stella and I wanted to stay in Blato a couple of weeks (and my people wanted us to stay forever), but that soon became impossible.

The Sunday papers had reported my arrival, and on Monday morning reporters from Lublyana and other cities came to the village. Would I tell them my impressions of the old country and about "the social, economic, political, and literary life in the United States." On Tuesday the newspapers carried columns reporting my impressions of Carniola, my views of America, and the fact that Stella, who was also delighted with Carniola, already knew a dozen Slovenian words.

The same day there began to come to Blato letters and telegrams by the handful. I was welcomed to my native land by literary and cultural clubs. One magazine writer requested "a comprehensive interview about America." There were invitations to house parties in Lublyana and elsewhere, to picnics and "evenings," to excursions into the mountains and the lake region of Upper Carniola.

To accept at least some of the invitations, we moved back to the hotel in Lublyana.

We no sooner re-registered than the gentleman who had met us in Trieste appeared, in semi-panic. Breathless and wiping his brow, he spoke about some hammering that was going on in the house next to the hotel and begged us to let him transfer us to another hotel where he was certain no noise would discomfit us. We laughed and told him that, used to the din and tumult of New York, we hadn't even noticed the hammering next door!

X

We were taken to Bled Lake by a group of young journalists, most of whom were also poets. All afternoon we drifted around the little island in the middle of the lake in a huge rowboat, which, besides us, contained several paper bags of sausages, loaves of black bread, containers of thick sour milk, flagons of red and white wine, an accordion, and two or three stringed instruments. By the end of the picnic my head whirled in consequence of our hosts' insatiable curiosity about America which, in my lame Slovenian, I tried to satisfy with such information as I had.

On Thursday was our first "evening," at the home of Slovenia's leading living novelist, who is also a Gymnasium professor, an editor and publisher, and a grand person. It was like two subsequent "evenings"—one at the home of Slovenia's foremost living poet and the other in the house of the editor of Slovenia's oldest literary review.

There gathered a dozen or more of Slovenia's literary and cultural lights and their wives. Fortunately some of them spoke or understood English and helped me with my Slovenian when I tried to answer a thousand and one questions about Upton Sinclair, Sinclair Lewis, Theodore Dreiser, Dos Passos, Edna St. Vincent Millay, Robert Frost, Countee Cullen, Langston Hughes, Hart Crane, Robinson Jeffers, James Stevens, Walter Winchell, and the new trends in American literature; about the depression, racketeering and Al Capone, the labor movement, the race problem, Henry Ford, the new woman in America, and the future of the United States.

Stella sat between a minor poet and a promising young novelist comprehending not a word, except my occasional bursts of English when I could not express myself in Slovenian. I answered questions from nine in the evening till three the next morning.

Then, according to custom, the host, the hostess, and all the other guests—some thirty people—walked Stella and me to the corner nearest to our hotel. Before we said good-night to all of them, dawn was breaking over the mountains.

There were ten days of this sort of thing, and opera, theatrical performances, and concerts, for all of which tickets were sent to us.

Gradually, I realized what I had dimly known in my boyhood, that, next to agriculture, Slovenia's leading industry was Culture. It was an intrinsic part of the place. In Lublyana were seven large bookshops (as large as most of the hardware, drygoods, and drug stores in town), two of them more than a hundred years old.

Every year, I learned, bookseller-publishers and the book clubs, of which there were eleven, published hundreds of books, few of which failed to pay for themselves. A "failure" was a book which sold less than 1,000 copies! Besides, each bookstore carried a selection of the latest German, French, Czech, Serbo-Croat, and a few English and Italian books. The publishers did almost no advertising, for in Slovenia nearly everybody—merchants, peasants, priests, teachers, students—bought books anyhow, or subscribed to book clubs. One book club had over 40,000 subscribers, another nearly 30,000, two over 20,000, and the rest had between 2,000 and 15,000. One juvenile book club distributed nearly 100,000 books every year among 23,000 children between the ages of ten and fourteen. And it must be remembered that there are only 1,100,000 Slovenians in Yugoslavia, with about 300,000 more in Italy and some 250,000 scattered as immigrants in the United States, various South American countries, and elsewhere; and over half of those in Slovenia live in villages with less than 500 population.

In two years, I was informed, there had been forty-eight performances of "Hamlet" in Lublyana. Most of the city's streets are named after poets, essayists, novelists, dramatists, grammarians. The largest monument in town is to a poet, Francé Presheren, who was at his height about a hundred years ago. When students take hikes into the country, their destinations usually are the graves and birthplaces of poets, dramatists, and other writers.

The year before I returned home there had been a hundredth-anniversary celebration of the birth of a writer, Francé Levstik, in the town of his birth, Velike Lasche, not far from Blato. It was the greatest event in Slovenia that year. Nearly 100,000 people attended the festival.

Shortly after I came back I happened to see a piece in a Lublyana newspaper that the village of X (the name now escapes me), somewhere in the mountains, twenty kilometers from the nearest railway, was about to unveil a modest monument to one of its sons, the late So-and-so, who a century ago had had a hand in the working out of certain rules of Slovenian grammar. The committee in charge of the occasion was frank in announcing that the village was very poor and the people would be unable to entertain the guests in suitable style; the peasants, however, would provide all visitors with such transportation from the railway to the village as they had, namely hay-wagons; and cherries, due to ripen by then, would be free to all comers.

In 1928, as I was told some time after my homecoming, Slovenia's foremost living poet—Oton Zupanchich—celebrated his fiftieth anniversary, and on that occasion, which was a special holiday for the entire province, nearly one hundred delegations from all parts of the country called on him. Most of them were peasant delegations, some from remote mountain villages and counties. All of them brought him gifts. Women came with exquisite national handwork. Some presented him with bags of potatoes, hams, sausages, and other peasant products. Nearly all of them brought him money which had been appropriated by their respective county or village councils. Singing societies came from country districts to sing under his window. Student quartettes from Lublyana schools sang his poems set to music.

Most larger villages and all towns have public libraries, reading-rooms, and little theater groups. My brother Anté and sister Poldka belong to one of the latter, in the town of Grosuplye, which is near Blato. Most homes, city and village alike, have bookshelves with books on them.

In the coffee-houses most of the talk I heard was about

plays, paintings, sculpture, architecture, books and music, and social and economic ideas. Most of the questions I was asked about America had to do with cultural and social problems, and among the people who asked them were a young priest, an army officer, the wife of a bookbinder, and a veterinary whom I met casually. Their interest, evidently, was not of a dilettante nature. It was definitely an intimate part of their lives, of Lublyana, of the country.

The fact that I had written a few things in America, and received some recognition there, impressed my native countrymen much more than if I had come back, say, a millionaire industrialist or a champion wrestler or pugilist. Hence all this publicity, this whirl of hospitality.

There were other reasons for the ballyhoo and excitement.

One was politicial. Slovenes, as I have stated, are a tiny nation; if I am not mistaken, the smallest in Europe; and for nearly a thousand years they have not had any sort of independent politicial or economic life. In recent centuries they have been a minority group under Bavaria, then under Austria, and now, inevitably, are a minority group in the new Yugoslav state. Economically, they are almost utterly dependent on Belgrade (as they formerly were on Vienna) and, as I discovered after a while, none too happy about it. All these centuries they have had but two things which they felt were completely their own and which gave them the status of a nationality—namely, their language (which is similar to the Serbo-Croat) and their culture. And of these two things, along with their lovely country, they are immeasurably proud. They are immensely patriotic, but not offensively so. Therefore, whenever one of "Slovenia's sons" achieves anything, either at home or in the outside world, they make a noise about it. If he achieves something in a cultural way, they are naturally impelled to make their noise even louder. They exert their utmost to make the Serbs and Croats take notice of him. This happened in my case.

Another reason was emotional—or perhaps I should say politico-emotional. Here I cannot begin to explain it in detail and in all its ramifications. The details, I think, will gradually appear in this book. Here I shall merely state that when I arrived in Yugoslavia, the country had been for over three years under the ruthless military dictatorship of King Alexander, which I knew but vaguely before I came there. I did not know what that really meant. I was not interested. I did not fully realize till months later that dictatorship meant that thousands of people were in prisons because they believed in such socio-political concepts as democracy, liberty, and economic justice, and dared to talk and act accordingly; that every city swarmed with secret agents; that newspaper, magazine, and book editors and publishers were under strict censorship; that public meetings, except those organized by henchmen of the dictatorial regime, were forbidden; and so on.

Anyhow, that, roughly, very roughly, was the political situation in Slovenia, in the whole of Yugoslavia, when I came there, although I did not see it at once. For three years and longer nearly everyone there had been living under an oppressive and suppressive government. I met people who whispered most of the time. Afraid to talk aloud in restaurants and coffee-houses or in the streets, they had been whispering ever since the dictatorship was established; now they whispered even when they asked me what kind of trip I had had or how I liked spring weather in Slovenia. At first I did not know what was the matter with them.

But to them, as it occurred to me later when I began to understand them, I was a rare and exceedingly welcome apparition. Here I came, by origin one of them, from distant America, from the great, free world across the sea, from beyond the horizon, where I lived a free man, a free citizen in a democracy; where I said what I pleased and no one put me in jail; where, in fact, I was paid money for writing what I wanted to write. And they clustered about me, scores and scores of them, full of "unemployed emotions," as George Bernard Shaw called them; full of eager questions about everything under the sun, semi-vicariously experiencing through me, by having contact with me, liberty, democracy, and everything else they were denied in Yugoslavia.

The papers were "playing" me up because the censor would not let them print anything else that was interesting. To make me interesting, they exaggerated my "success" and "importance" in America.

After I became better acquainted with some of my new friends in Lublyana, I tried to tell them that they had an exaggerated notion of me, but by then it was too late. Some of them accused me of modesty.

XII

Off and on, during the first ten days of glory, Stella and I managed to run to Blato for a few hours in the afternoon. We became better acquainted with my family, our relatives, and the other villagers. My brothers Francé and Yozhé taught Stella to say whole phrases and long sentences in Slovenian, which gave our family and the village much satisfaction and cause for merriment.

We were all very happy. We laughed a great deal. The spring was beautiful. Momentarily, somehow, it did not seem important whether Yugoslavia was under a dictatorship or not.

The young calf in our barn was gaining weight, and the family council at home decided that the feast of the fatted calf would occur on the second Sunday after the prodigal's return. My father sent for wine. My sisters and mother schemed for a week as to the sort of cakes they would bake. My brothers Stan and Anté took some lumber and improvised tables and benches under the apple trees, just then coming to full bloom. All our relatives and family friends were invited.

Then it occurred to me to invite all my new friends, the literati and their wives. The idea startled my whole family. But would they come? For a son of our family to invite to Blato the foremost living poet, the leading living novelist, the editor of the oldest literary review in Slovenia, and other writers potentially as great, was as though a farmer's son in Pennsylvania got the notion to invite to a Sunday dinner such people as Henry Ford, Will Rogers, Calvin Coolidge, Al Smith, John Barrymore, and Gene Tunney. It must be remembered that literati are the biggest people in Carniola, especially to peasant folk.

But I invited them, in my father's name, and they came with their wives—so many of them that Stan and Anté were required to hurriedly build another table.

It was a bright, warm Sunday afternoon, with a light mountain breeze blowing through the valley. The literati mixed with the villagers, praised the village, exclaimed over the beauty of the fields and the meadows, and raved about the prodigal's sisters and brothers.

The foremost poet was pleased to the verge of tears when a little peasant girl, urged by my sister Poldka, stepped before him and recited his most famous poem. Pleased, too, was the leading novelist when a peasant woman brought him a copy of one of his books and asked him to "write something in it with your own hand."

My sister Paula and mother were in the kitchen, both happy beyond utterance. Francé and Yozhé, coatless and beaproned, brought out the plates (borrowed from the whole village) and platters heaped with pieces of the fatted calf. ("Poor thing!" said Stella, who, three days before had seen it alive in the barn.) Stan and Anté poured the wine. Poldka pinned forget-me-nots and lilies-of-the-valley on the garments of the guests. My youngest sister, Anica, brought on the bread and the cakes. Tonchka and Manuela had had to return to Belgrade.

The feast lasted all afternoon. The mountain breeze shook the apple blossoms upon the tables and the heads of the guests. There was much light, irresponsible talk and laughter around the tables. No whispering. Dictatorship or no: it did not matter that Sunday afternoon. By and by, the villagers and the literati began to sing Slovenian national songs about love, wine, and beautiful regions.

Stella exclaimed: "I wish my mother were here! And my brother, and Seren and Meta"—the whole crew of her girl friends in America.

"And Ben and Kyle and Carey . . ." I began to enumerate my friends back in the United States.

During a lull in the singing, the poet rose, glass in hand, and everyone became silent to hear him. He spoke awhile of the fine afternoon, the breeze from the mountains, the apple blossoms, the fatted calf, the wine in his glass, into which the petal of an apple blossom had fluttered as he talked. He eulogized the village, its people, and especially my mother and father, and referred to the fields and meadows around the village in words of sheer poetry. Finally he came to "the prodigal" and spoke of his departure for America and his return. It is not possible for me to give his words. It was all I could do to hold back my tears.

The poet ended, "Let us drain our glasses!"

The glasses were drained and some one began another song.

CHAPTER II

My Cousin Toné Marries

THE SECOND OR THIRD DAY AFTER MY RETURN MY SISTER Poldka remarked to me, "There's talk Toné is liable to get married in a month or two."

Toné is one of our numerous cousins in Blato. He is a tall, blond, blue-eyed peasant of thirty-four, with a little mustache and tremendous hands; rawboned, simple, hardworking, soft-spoken, and good-humored as a rule, but capable of being otherwise. He is the oldest son of Uncle Mikha, whom I have mentioned in the preceding chapter.

"Whom is he going to take?" I asked.

Poldka smiled. "Even Toné doesn't know that for sure. He has his eyes on two or three"—mentioning the girls, all from adjacent villages,—"but right now, I guess, all he knows is that Mikha is going to give him the homestead in July—maybe."

"Why 'maybe'?"

She smiled again. "It depends on whom Toné will finally decide to marry. They say he's most inclined to take So-and-so, but Mikha is not exactly enthused about her."

A week later I spoke with Toné.

I said, "I hear you'll be getting married, now your father is going to give you the place."

"Ah, the devil!" he muttered. He was in a raw mood.

"Why, what's the matter?"

"Everybody in the damned village is trying to tell me what to do, whom to marry, when to marry——"

This, I presently realized, was a typical situation for a young Carniolan peasant to find himself in when he is about to come in possession of his father's property and is expected to wed. When a young man of my cousin Toné's standing in a village like ours, which is an average Carniolan village, is about to enter matrimony, the selection of his bride becomes the active concern of well-nigh the whole community—naturally, traditionally so.

II

In Carniola, as in most agrarian lands in Europe, getting married in the country is very unlike getting married in the city. In the city the young man meets the girl, they become engaged, and marry. Matrimony is almost exclusively their own affair. The relatives congratulate them, bring them gifts, and volunteer advice; at the same time the old family ties loosen up, a new family begins in some one- or two-room flat, and that is that.

In a village when a young peasant like my cousin approaches wedlock he is not only about to take a wife to himself, but to bring to the household, which often is centuries old and managed according to old traditions, a new mistress who, by virtue of her position, may strongly affect that household and the entire village.

To begin with, there are the old folks, who, although they are prepared to sign the property over to the son, are still interested in the place. In fact, more so than ever. On signing the deed they will reserve for themselves a corner of the old house—for they have no other place to go to—and certain other rights, which they expect the new mistress to respect with kindness and grace. Then there are other members of the family: the younger brothers and sisters who know the sister-in-law will inevitably influence their future; and the more distant relations: aunts, uncles, godmothers, godfathers, cousins, and so on, whose interests will be more or less affected by *ta mlada* (the young one). And, finally, all the other villagers (for the community is a compact socio-economic organism, within which everybody is everybody's neighbor) know that a good mistress on this

{ 37 }

homestead will improve the tone of village life, and a bad one damage it.

So, as a matter of course, almost, all these diversely interested people insist on having their say in the selection of the bride.

The young man usually is the only person concerned who is interested in the girl's looks. His father's chief heed is her dowry, health, and physical endurance—whether or not she is a good worker. The young man's mother desires a "good-hearted" daughter-in-law, one who is humble, pious, and can bear suffering without complaint; in fine, a model peasant woman. The relatives share the father's and mother's worries, doubts, misgivings, prejudices, and in addition hope she will not have an acrid tongue. The non-related women of the village fear she will be richer or nicer-looking than they were when they married, or a better housekeeper or worker in the fields than they are, so that their husbands will point to her as a rare example of womanhood.

All these relatives and neighbors are traditionally at liberty to come to the young man or his father or mother, or all three of them, with advice, suggestions, hints, and gossip. So-and-so, they say, has this and that virtue; she is rich and strong, a good milker, hoer, and reaper; if need be, she can plow and harrow a field; she is deft with the needle; *but*—they are full of "buts," big and little.

For weeks the young man hanging on the brink of matrimony is the focus of all eyes up and down Main Street. He knows that everybody is speculating about him: What is he going to do? Whom is he going to take? When is he going to decide? Has that hussy in the next village really bewitched him beyond rescue? . . .

This, of course, is anything but fun for the young man, who hitherto has been left pretty much alone. He is especially uncomfortable if, like my cousin Toné, he is still undecided about the girl. If he has made up his mind and tells who she is, some of the villagers—especially close relatives—do not hesitate to warn him that, while she has much in her favor, she is such-and-such, "just like her mother," and try to make him switch to their favorite.

But the old man has the deciding voice in the matter. He is still master of the place, has not yet signed it over, and controls the economic phase of the situation. If the young man fancies some fluffy chit the old man is apt to clearly state his position as follows:

"You be sensible, young man, and take the girl I want for a daughter-in-law—or, by God! nothing doing! Understand?"

In former years the young man sometimes broke with his father over a girl, told him to keep his old homestead or give it to the next oldest son, and went to America. Today, with America's "Welcome!" sign down, that is almost out of the question. The young man usually suppresses his romantic feelings and marries "sensibly."

III

In my cousin Toné's case the interest in his marriage was lively in all of the county's seventeen villages, for a number of reasons. Uncle Mikha's place, which Toné was getting, is one of the best in the region. It was expected that as an ex-mayor's son, after attaining the status of a property-owner, Toné eventually would himself be a candidate. But the most important reason, perhaps, was that in late years there have been almost no weddings thereabouts, owing to the *kriza* which has forced most peasants deep into debt; and when a Carniolan village home is in debt, only death or complete infirmity can make the old man yield it to his son and permit him to bring a new mistress under the mortgaged roof. The old man conceives it as one of his chief duties in life to pass the place on to his successor free of financial burden, which, in this day and age, however, is increasingly difficult.

At any rate, toward the end of spring, after most of the

relatives and other villagers had expressed themselves on the subject, Uncle Mikha and Toné finally agreed on a girl named Yulka, only daughter of old man Galé, a fairly well-off peasant in the village of Gatina, a short distance from Blato; and after it was discussed for a few days, everyone in the village was more or less satisfied. Some thought Toné probably could do better; on the other hand, Yulka was a worthy girl in any way one looked at her. It was no secret that Yulka and her whole family were delighted when a rumor of Mikha's and Toné's decision reached them. Toné was a fine catch, and everybody in the county knew they were as good as sealed.

Centuries-old peasant traditions and customs, however, which have their roots deep in the realities of the people's life, and are richly flavored with native humor and poetic spirit, required that before Yulka go to her new home she and Toné and her and his parents and relatives, in fact nearly all the people of their villages, go through a series of ceremonies and doings, which I—with my objective Americanized eyes and subjective native-Carniolan sense of appreciation—found extremely interesting, charming, and amusing.

After deciding on the girl the first step toward Toné's matrimony was that his father asked a friend of his, an elderly and substantial peasant in Blato, to act as his son's *stareshina* (bridegroom's elder) which, next to the groom and bride, is the most important rôle in the drama of a Carniolan wedding. At the same time, Toné, grinning a bit foolishly, asked me to be his first groomsman, or best man. The groomsman is usually a single man, but an exception was made in my case.

Then, late one Thursday afternoon, the *stareshina* and I went to Gatina. We had heard old man Galé was doing something or other in his wood near the village, and that was where we found him—a man in his mid-sixties, but younger-looking, with calm eyes, large-veined hands, a walrus mustache, and a deep voice.

For half an hour we sat on stumps in the woods, talking of this and that—of America, the depression, the colossal social experiment in Russia, the lateness of spring, the need of rain. Finally, the *stareshina* mentioned that a friend of his, none other than old man Mikha from Blato, the ex-mayor whom everyone respected and esteemed, was thinking of "going into the corner" and marrying off his eldest son, Toné, who had his eyes on Yulka.

Old man Galé expressed surprise and, as customary, would not hear of marriage for his daughter. It was absurd to think of it. Yulka, he averred, was still young, not quite twenty-two; he needed her at home; she was a good worker, too good to lose; besides, he hadn't yet begun to lay aside a dowry for her, and he knew that old codger, Mikha— "may he live to be a hundred!"—would demand an unreasonable dowry.

The whole interview was a game, a little act that had to be played, half serious and half in fun; and I had a hard time to keep a serious face while the *stareshina* argued with Yulka's father that this was her big chance, that Toné was a good boy, and his property the jewel of the region. They argued a long time. Yulka's father shook his head, "No, no! Why pick on my girl? There are lots of others, aren't there? I have only one."

"Well, if that's how you feel about it, Galé, we'll go elsewhere," and the *stareshina* rose.

I, whose traditional function was to echo the *stareshina*, also rose, saying that Toné unquestionably could get any girl he pleased.

We laughed, thus admitting to one another that all this was just a lot of fooling.

"Of course," peasant Galé then hastened to say, "to be fair all around, I'll ask mother and Yulka—see what they think."

Such a remark is equivalent to saying the daughter has the father's consent.

"Never mind," smiled the *stareshina*. "We'll come to

your house with Toné. We'll ask the women ourselves and see if they can resist our proposition."

All three of us laughed again, then parted. Each of us had acted his part as required by custom.

IV

Next Sunday afternoon, all eyes in Blato upon us, the *stareshina* and I went back to Gatina, Toné between us. He was in his Sunday best, with a fresh haircut, an extra twist to his mustache, and a red carnation behind his hatband.

Everything was quiet around Galé's house when we arrived. We knocked. We knocked again. Finally old man Galé appeared. He yawned and rubbed his eyes, pretending we had roused him from his Sunday-afternoon nap.

"Oh, *ya, ya!*" he said. "The devil! I forgot all about it. Now I remember. You two were over in my wood Thursday. *Ya, ya!* You said you were coming today. Good thing I stayed home. I wonder where my womenfolk are. They probably went visiting somewhere. As I say, I forgot all about your coming—forgot to tell them."

As a matter of fact, the entire household had been quietly excited with our impending visit for days, and Yulka and her mother were upstairs behind curtained windows, listening to us below.

Old man Galé invited us in, brought out a jug of wine, then we talked and talked of anything but matrimony.

The *stareshina* did most of the talking, which was the way it should be. He talked of the coming fair at the county seat; the latest rumor about King Alexander; the reports of corruption in the Belgrade government and virtual starvation of people in the industrial centers in Yugoslavia; the next war; the peasants' debt problem, and the fact that at the morning's church service the priest had announced a procession for rain and taken up an extra collection for it. He said: "I guess we'll have rain any day now. These priests—when they see the barometer jumping, they conduct a procession; then when rain falls they take credit for it, and the women believe them."

"Well, what can you do?" said Galé, philosophically. "Women will be women, and to pray and conduct processions is the priests' business. We must have religion."

At long last the *stareshina* brought his talk to Toné and commenced to praise him to the sky, while I, as previously coached, seconded everything he said, and Toné, a morbidly modest fellow, suffered agonies of embarrassment.

"And now, Galé," the *stareshina* said, after a while, "as I hinted to you last Thursday, the time has come for Toné to get himself a wife. His father and mother, like you and me, are getting on in years. Toné will be the new master of old Mikha's place. It's a big place, as you know, Galé, and he'll need a woman for the house. . . . Toné says he's taken a fancy to your Yulka. Am I right?" he turned to me.

"That's right, *stareshina*," said I.

"Well, now—" Old man Galé cleared his throat and paused to ponder—"I haven't anything against Toné or his father; we've always been friends; but as I said the other day, I'll have to ask mother and Yulka."

"Then call them!" cried the *stareshina*. "Let's get this business over with. Toné here is young and impatient to know whether it'll be Yulka or some one else."

Yulka's mother came down first. Then there was more talk, more misgivings and shaking of heads on the part of the old man and woman.

The girl's parents hesitated for about half an hour, whereupon, as instructed, I said, impatiently:

"Now let's call Yulka and see what she says. After all, she's the one to decide."

So Yulka's name was called out loud several times, and she came, dressed in a neat flower-printed cotton guimpe, tight-bodiced and full-skirted, with an embroidered white lawn blouse and apron; red-faced, with lowered eyes, as befits a Carniolan maiden when a young man comes with his *stareshina* and groomsman to woo her. This was the first time I had seen her. She was a comely, wholesome girl with a full figure, and sun-bleached hair twisted in thick braids round her head; no doubt just the wife for Toné.

She and Toné were anything but strangers; in fact, he had been with her the evening before; yet they did not look at each other. Toné stared at a spot on the tablecloth and Yulka stood a short distance from us, her eyes on the floor, her fingers busily twisting a corner of her apron, while the *stareshina* repeated all of Toné's virtues and I, ready to burst, put in a few words every time the *stareshina* demanded to know if what he was saying wasn't really so.

"Now, Yulka, what do you say?" was my next line. I was getting my cues—little kicks under the table—from the *stareshina*.

Growing redder and redder, the girl answered, "I'm in no hurry to get married. My parents need me. They raised me, and, now I'm grown up and can work, it wouldn't be right for me to leave them so soon. I want to help them in their old age."

It was exactly the speech she was expected to make. Her mother beamed as if to say, "See what a perfect pearl she is!"

"Don't be foolish, Yulka!" said the *stareshina*. "These two"—pointing at her parents—"will live to be a hundred. You can't wait that long to be married. By then you would be no good"—for child-bearing, that is.

By and by Yulka and her parents consented to her marrying Toné and said that some day next week they would come *na oglede*—to look over the place where Toné wanted to install her as mistress.

V

The Galé folks knew all about the condition and circumstances of old Mikha's homestead, but three or four days after our visit to Gatina they came to Blato, anyhow, to give it the customary official once-over. There were old man Galé, mother Galé, Yulka, and an elderly villager from Gatina whom Galé had appointed the bride's *stareshina*.

Uncle Mikha received them, then led them around the homestead, through the house, into the barns and over the fields, and Toné's *stareshina* and I went along to point out all the advantages. Everything was looked over and examined, and the value of the cattle in the barn, the pigs in the sty, and the tools and implements were estimated, as well as the productivity of the soil. But all this was only about half in earnest, largely a matter of form, to comply with custom, to keep unbroken the continuity of the drama of marriage in which the emphasis is frankly on economic matters.

Then all of us trooped into the big-room in Uncle Mikha's house and sat down at a table on which were platters of cold meat, bread, and cake, and a jug of wine. But it was an hour before we touched anything.

Toné appeared from somewhere and awkwardly, self-consciously, seated himself next to Yulka, who blushed. Neither of them said a word.

After the two *stareshinas* beat around the bush awhile, we came to the important question: how much dowry would old man Galé give Yulka? Uncle Mikha and Toné's *stareshina* demanded that, in view of the lucky break his daughter was getting, old man Galé should give her so much dowry (which was a goodly sum), while Galé and the bride's *stareshina* came back with loud declarations that that was preposterous. Where was a man to get so much money in these hard times? "Do you suppose I want to mortgage my place to give her a dowry?" said Yulka's father. "What kind of a *gospodar*" (master and manager) "should I be if I did that! It is true that we aren't as bad off yet as the peasants in Lika and the Dalmatian uplands, where they lack money with which to buy salt, petroleum and matches, but who hereabouts has that much ready cash to give to his daughter as dowry?"—and so on.

They argued and shouted back and forth. If one did not know the shouting was at least three-quarters in fun, one would imagine they were on the verge of breaking off the whole thing. But at the end they agreed on the sum which Yulka would bring to her new home, in addition to the usual hope-chest filled with linens and lace; then we drank numerous toasts and ate, and the conversation turned to less explosive topics.

The same day the bride and groom went to the parish-house to ask the priest to announce from the pulpit their intention to marry, and a few days afterward Uncle Mikha, Toné, and the two *stareshinas* rode to a notary public in the city to attend to the legal details.

VI

The wedding ceremony was set for the first Monday in July, when everyone was expected to be done with haying and there would be a lull in work.

Invitations were extended to almost everybody in the two villages and numerous persons elsewhere in the county, but, as usual, only the young people accepted; and those who, like myself, had not previously taken part in a Carniolan wedding were instructed how to act in the doings still to come.

Three days before the big event each of the guests sent to the bride's house a goose, a turkey, a duck, a ham, a lamb, two or three chickens, or several pigeons or rabbits, as his or her contribution to the feast, the preparation for which—baking, cooking—were in charge of a professional cook engaged for the occasion.

Late Sunday afternoon there appeared in Blato, mounted on a gayly decorated horse, a young peasant from Gatina, with flowers on his hat and jacket, and a box under his arm. With a great show of dash the "bride's messenger," as he was called, rode to Mikha's house and asked for Toné.

When the bridegroom came he said, "Toné, greetings from the bride! She sent me to you with this box, which contains flowers grown in pots on her window-sill, tended by her own hands."

Early next morning all of us "groom's people"—the *stareshina*, I, the several assistant groomsmen, four musicians, and all the wedding guests, male and female, from Blato—assembled in Mikha's house (for the old man was still master of the place until Toné brought home his bride).

Most of us were in national costumes of the region. The men wore tight-fitting trousers of heavy homespun cloth or soft leather, tucked into high boots; short snug waistcoats with large round gold, brass, or silver buttons; white shirts of rough homespun linen, handsomely bordered with needlework at the wrists and neck, with bright-colored silk neckerchiefs tied beneath the collars; and narrow-rimmed green felt hats adorned with wild-rooster feathers and flowers the bride had sent the day before.

The girls were in white cotton blouses with lace trimmings and immense flowing sleeves, silk scarfs, and voluminous dark skirts, some of them accordion-pleated, with dozens of multicolored ribbons flowing from narrow waists. Some of them wore a white headgear called *hauba*, embroidered with silver or gold; nearly all wore heavy old jewelry—necklaces, earrings, brooches, and elaborate girdles, most of it of tarnished silver and gold and silver filigree.

On setting out for Gatina with the groom, the *stareshina*, and me in the first of a string of diverse vehicles, those of the young men who, unlike the groom and myself, were not required to be dignified, began to whoop and sing, and the accordion-players to play. The buggies, wagons, and horses, and several bicycles were decorated with flowers, green twigs, festoons, and bunting.

As we reached Gatina our *stareshina* commanded everyone to be well-behaved: no more whooping, singing, and music.

Not a soul was visible anywhere near Galé's house. Our coming had been announced to them by the "watchman" they had stationed on the outskirts of the village; whereupon the house had been shut and everybody inside was supposed to be quiet, except the bride, for whom it is almost obligatory to sob on her mother's bosom.

Our *stareshina* knocked on the closed door. No answer. He knocked again, a little harder. Again no answer. Once more he knocked, this time with the crook of his cane. Still no answer. Then he shook the door by the knob, and all of us began to grumble, "What the devil! What kind of a house is this that they don't answer when people knock?"

Finally a voice inside, the voice of the bride's *stareshina*, called, "Who is it, and what do you want?"

"We are travelers from afar," answered our *stareshina* at the top of his lungs, so that everyone inside the house could hear him over the bride's sobbing. "We are tired and hungry. We ask to be let in, so we may rest and refresh ourselves."

"What kind of people are you?" the bride's *stareshina* asked through the closed door. "What can you say for yourselves?"

The groom's *stareshina* answered: "We don't like to boast, but since you demand to know, let me tell you we're God-fearing people. Prayer is our favorite pastime, charity our middle name. We never turn away a traveler when he knocks on our door, and we hope you, too, will turn the key and admit us."

The key turned, but the door opened only a few inches. The bride's *stareshina* looked us over, then said:

"You look to be decent people, true enough, and we believe you are pious, charitable, and hospitable; but can you say anything else for yourselves? Have you any *practical* virtues?"

Our *stareshina* said: "We don't lack practical virtues, either. We are hard-working people. Dawn never finds us in bed. We work in all kinds of weather and no form of toil frightens us. Look, our hands are calloused and chapped, and no matter how much we scrub them, we cannot make them look white, for the black soil of our fields has eaten itself into our skin. Only today, coming from afar, we are tired and hungry and appeal to your hospitality—the hospitality for which this country is famous."

The door opened, then ensued a further exchange of questions and answers between the two *stareshinas*. The rest of us outside pushed our *stareshina* from behind till we all got into the big-room and vestibule, which were full of "bride's people," most of them also in regional costumes.

The sobbing bride was in a little side-room with her mother and first bridesmaid.

The bride's *stareshina* pretended to be alarmed. "You people don't seem tired. I think this is only a trick. I trust you have no evil intentions?"

All of us "groom's people" laughed; the others looked puzzled, afraid, or indignant.

Said our *stareshina*, "No, we have no evil intentions, but you guessed right: we are neither tired nor hungry, and we did play a little trick on you folks—but with a good purpose. This young man here"—placing a hand on a shoulder of the wincing, awkward bridegroom—"is a gardener from our village. He has everything in abundance, but his heart is sad and forlorn, for he lacks a blossom which every young gardener must have. He has heard that a blossom grows in this home, and to keep him from moping around we, his fellow villagers, came with him to ask you to give him your blossom. We promise to pluck her gently and carefully plant her in his garden."

"Ah, so that's your idea!" chuckled the bride's *stare-*

shina, and all of the other "bride's people" laughed with him. "We have here not only one but many blossoms."

"Well, show us what you have!" said I.

The bride's *stareshina* went into an adjacent room and returned with a little eight-year-old girl dressed somewhat like a bride. "Now here's a sweet and tender blossom," he said.

"No, no!" I said. "Too tender. Transplanting would damage her. What else have you?"

Next he brought before us an elderly woman. (Custom requires that she be at least fifty, ugly, and in possession of a sense of humor and a ready tongue.) She was also rigged out like a bride, with too much finery, and tried to act coy before the bridegroom, who, panic-stricken, appealed to me to take her away, insisting she was not the blossom he had in mind, while the entire houseful of people laughed.

"Why all this laughter?" demanded the bride's *stareshina*. "Here we show you a blossom—a woman who is experienced, has most of her teeth, a nose in the middle of her face, and all the other organs and appurtenances in their proper places; a woman whose movements are as lively and graceful as one wants to see; a woman—" And as he praised her, the old woman showed her teeth and demonstrated her liveliness by dancing a jig.

But the groom's *stareshina* and I shook our heads and shoved the old woman aside. Finally, when they insisted on our taking this particular "blossom," we had to tell them why we did not want her—that she was old and cross-eyed, and looked like a half-empty sack of turnips. This, of course, provoked the "blossom" to tell us to go somewhere; she would not be transplanted to our garden, which probably was nothing but a dump, and so on, while everyone laughed, till she flicked her flouncy skirt and, pretending she was insulted, flew from the room.

"Now," I said, "we are in earnest. Show us the real blossom."

"You people are too choosy," said the bride's *stareshina*. "You all better go and leave us alone."

"Show us the blossom of blossoms," I insisted.

"We have shown you the best!"

"Well," said our *stareshina*, "if that's the case, we made a mistake. Come, people, let's go. We made a mistake." We all turned to leave.

"Wait a minute!" cried the bride's *stareshina*. "Maybe you mean this one. *Ya, ya,* I guess you do mean this one; she *is* a blossom of blossoms!"

And so Yulka came on her father's arm, crying, her face buried in a bouquet of white flowers. Attired like the other women, but more lavishly, she wore the same bridal outfit her mother had been married in thirty-eight years before. A garland of white roses, interspersed with green leaves, encircled her elaborate *hauba*.

"*Ya, ya,* this is the one we want!" declared the bridegroom's *stareshina* and I.

The bride's *stareshina* waxed philosophical for a bit: "Well, what can we do? Nature is nature, and nature demands that the blossom be transplanted in order to bear fruit. . . . Take her. We believe you will carefully plant her in good soil and guard her from evil."

Then we all went into the orchard behind the house, where tables were set, and ate the "pre-nuptial breakfast," which consisted of cold meats, cakes, wine. There was accordion music and old wedding songs.

The "breakfast" lasted two hours. The bride's *stareshina* made a speech. He talked long in a poetic-sentimental streak, and much of what he said would sound witless in translation, for Slovenian, especially as spoken by the peasants, is a poetic language and endows sentiment with more dignity than does English.

VIII

Shortly before noon we all started for the church, but down the road a little distance came upon a mob of young men from Gatina. They had stretched a chain of twisted willow shoots and field flowers across the road, and there was a table with a white tablecloth strewn with green leaves and red and yellow blossoms, and two jugs of wine and many glasses.

This was *shranga* (the "barrier").

The assistant groomsmen and I became indignant. "What the devil is this! What do you fellows mean by putting a rope across a public street?"

The leader of the Gatina boys, the biggest and handsomest of the lot, then said that Yulka was from their village and, by rights, *their* girl. "You folks come from Blato and take her. You don't expect us to like that, do you? If she wants to go to Blato, we don't mean to frustrate her wish, but we don't want the world to hear about this and say there are men in Gatina who let their girls go without saying boo. . . . Before you take her we demand you pay us *odskodnina* (recompense)."

Then our *stareshina* spoke. "We're not looking for trouble, fellows. If you think you have something coming to you, tell us your price."

"Fifty thousand dinars!"

Our side guffawed. "Your whole damn' village isn't worth that much."

For a few minutes there was a great hubbub, while I, as first groomsman, tried to console the bride, who laughed at the same time that she cried.

After a while the Gatina boys came down to five thousand.

"Don't be idiots!" said our *stareshina*. "For five thousand we can buy a good pair of oxen these days."

"Well, isn't she worth as much as a pair of oxen?"

The shouting and laughter continued. At the end the boys agreed to take five hundred ($7), which sum the *stareshina* paid them over the "barrier," to be spent by them as they saw fit; perhaps for wine or some improvement in the village's fire-fighting equipment.

Then wine was poured and the boys' leader made a speech telling Toné what a lucky dog he was, congratulating Blato on getting such a girl into one of its homes, wishing Yulka all the happiness in the world.

Whereupon the "barrier" was removed and we proceeded churchward.

IX

The ceremony in the church was brief. When it was over the party distributed itself among the three winehouses in Gatina, to dance, talk, sing, drink, and play practical jokes on one another till five o'clock, when the cook and the bride's *stareshina* had agreed we should return to the house for the feast.

The house, meantime, had been decorated by the bride's brothers and their friends. On the road leading to it stood two maypoles, holding a sign between them, "Greetings to the newlyweds!"

In good times wedding feasts last three or four days, never less than two, at the end of which period everybody is near exhaustion from drinking, eating, dancing, singing, and sleeplessness; now, however, because of the *kriza*, the feast was scheduled to last only till midnight of the first day.

The bride, the groom, their parents, the *stareshinas*, the groomsmen, and the bridesmaids went into the big-room and took places at a large table, in the center of which was a vast cake inscribed "Happy Life!" Under the ceiling, across the entire room, were stretched chains of flowers and green twigs.

In the orchard, tables were set for the rest of the guests. When it became dark, lamps hanging on boughs were lighted.

The feast lasted for hours, and the accordion-players and other musicians played almost without interruption, taking turns and time out to eat and drink.

The *stareshinas*, first one, then the other, delivered long orations on marriage, essentially alike, full of platitudes

and advice, charmingly presented. I give, in part, the words
of the bridegroom's *stareshina*:

"They are married now and only death can part them.
Today we eat and drink and sing. But this will all be over
soon. Tonight Yulka goes to her new home with her husband. It is a good home, but in the best of homes life is an
earnest business. The peasant's lot is not an easy one. We
pit our strength and wits against odds. Nature—the elements are not always on our side. Often we don't know
what, if anything, we'll reap on the spot where we have
sown. It's a fight—work from morning till night, from
day to day, year to year, summer and winter, spring and
autumn. There is no end to toil. That is our fate on this
earth. The peasant can never get far ahead and say, 'By
God, I win!' . . .

"Working on the soil, wresting a livelihood from the
fields, the lot of neither man nor woman is easy. Here is
Toné; he is young, at the height of his life, but before long
struggle, responsibility, and hardships of all sorts will chisel
lines into his face. He will have to toil in cold and heat,
and to complain will do him no good.

"And here is Yulka, our bride; her face is like a ripe
apple; but in her case, too, life will soon do its work. She
will have to toil; she will bear children. That is what she
was born for. . . .

"What can they do? Only one thing: stick together and
help each other. On his side, Toné will be harassed by one
thing and another; no peasant's life is easy; and as a wan-
derer trudging on a hot and dusty highway seeks the shade
of a tree, so will he, your Toné, come to you, Yulka, and
seek calm, rest, and courage for new effort. You will be
his refuge.

"And you, Toné, remember a woman is a tender thing;
she is the 'blossom' we came to seek this morning. You must
be to her what a wall is to the first flowers of spring. Protect her. You must be to her what a pole is to the vine.
Support her. Marriage is seldom a matter of pure joy.

Never for long. Storms come. When or if they come, calm them as soon as you can and close the doors and windows. Don't let those outside know of your differences. Straighten them out yourselves. Don't let anyone mix in your affairs. If you straighten out your own differences, your happiness will be so much the greater. In fact, only then will your marriage begin to gather character and depth, and the bond between you grow really strong. . . . Let us drink to the bride and the groom!"

There were other speeches by the *stareshinas*. The groom's eulogized the bride's parents, and the other way around. A toast was drunk to me because I had returned from America after nineteen years, become a writer in America, and had married an American girl, who was also a guest at the feast as companion of one of my brothers.

Thus until midnight.

X

At ten minutes to twelve the bridesmaids dimmed the lights in the big-room, and as many of the people outside as could came in.

The bride began to weep.

Then her *stareshina* rose and said, "We hear that in other lands *devishtvo* (purity, virginity) is a rare virtue. Among us, praise God, it still exists. Here is our bride, a jewel of this village, parish, and county. Her sun-browned brow shines under the flowers signifying *devishtvo* which entwine her head. . . . But life goes on and, like everything else, a virtue can be carried too far ——"

The clock began to strike twelve. Everybody was still, only the bride sobbed, with a few of the other women joining in with her.

"It is midnight," the *stareshina* continued. "The wedding feast is over. A new day begins and with it, Yulka, your new life. The flowers must now come off your head."

The bridesmaids removed the garland from Yulka's head and placed it before Toné.

"Toné"—the *stareshina* turned to the bridegroom—"the flowers lie before you. Your bride offers them—offers herself to you. . . . My friends, let's drink once more—to the future of our newlyweds!"

Outside, the assistant groomsmen were hitching a team of horses to a wagon on which were Yulka's hope-chest and other belongings and a small coop with a chicken and a rooster—for a bride must bring something alive to her new home.

Yulka then took leave of her mother and father, brothers, bridesmaids, and friends, and, amid much feminine weeping and masculine whooping, Toné helped her onto the wagon, and they drove off—man and wife—to their home in Blato.

The rest of the party broke up soon after, but all through the rest of the night there was much whooping in the valley, the young unmarried men of Blato and Gatina answering one another, their whoops echoing against the mountains.

CHAPTER III

Death Waits for My Uncle Yanez

ALMOST SIMULTANEOUSLY WITH HEARING THAT TONÉ was seeking a bride I learned that one of my uncles— Uncle Yanez, my mother's oldest brother, a fairly well-to-do peasant—was dying at his home in Brankovo, a village some distance from ours.

My mother told me there was virtually no hope for him.

"He is seventy-eight, you know," she said, "and his ailment"—with which he had become afflicted the previous winter—"can't easily be cured even in a much younger man. For a time, a few months back, we thought that, in spite of the great burden of his years, he might improve a bit when spring came again, and then maybe hang on awhile longer; but now May is more than half gone, the fruit trees are shaking off the white petals of their blossoms, June beetles already are about, and Yanez is no better yet. The illness is going deeper and deeper into him."

I was struck by my mother's simple way of telling me this. The slight inflection of her voice, when she pronounced his name, suggested to me that she liked her dying brother very much (and subsequently I learned that he was, in fact, her favorite relative) ; yet the main note of her whole manner, it occurred to me, was a profound fatalism, a calm acceptance of death.

At first this rankled me considerably, for, having lived in America for nineteen years, my own attitude toward the Great Reaper, if it can be said that I had one, was the typical "Western malady," as some one has called it, a mingling of dread and hate and false bravado.

After that my mother's manner when she talked to me

about Uncle Yanez continued to disconcert me a little, off and on, for nearly two weeks, until I fully realized what I had distantly suspected right along—namely, that her fatalism in the matter was not so much a personal characteristic as the sharing of a group attitude—the attitude toward death of most peasants in Yugoslavia. When I realized this, and began to understand this attitude of the peasants in relation to their environment, I commenced to think of it not as something disconcerting, but, on the contrary, rather fine and felicitous.

That it was not a personal but a group attitude I started to suspect almost immediately after mother first mentioned that Uncle Yanez was on his deathbed. My eighty-two-year-old father, who, while all gray and a bit trembly, appears to be good for many more years, heard her, and added that spring could not be expected to perform miracles on an old man whom winter had smitten with illness and who probably no longer felt the flesh on his bones. "Sooner or later we must all go to the long home, just like dew goes before the sun. . . . We are like everything else that has being in this world. Do you remember the big apple tree that grew in the middle of the meadow this side of the creek?" he asked me.

"Yes," I said.

"Well," said my father, "two years ago—or was it three? (of late my memory is beginning to fail me a little). . . . Anyhow, two or three years ago, when spring came, that apple tree did not bloom or leaf. It had not been hit by lightning, nor anything like that. It was just an old tree; my grandfather had planted it. It was mostly hollow inside, and it died; then Stan and Anté had to fell it and saw it up into firewood. People become hollow inside and go the same way." He shrugged his shoulders. "Yanez will go that way, then I ——"

Mother, I noticed, paid no heed to what father was saying; as I learned later, he often philosophized in that strain. We were in the kitchen; and while he spoke, mother was busy at the stove, asking Poldka if she had salted the potatoes, and wasn't it time to gather up the eggs?—for several hens were cackling outside. Then she sat down beside me again and, interrupting father, told me more about Uncle Yanez' condition:

"The week before you arrived, I went to Brankovo to visit him, and he said to me, 'Well, Ana, it won't be long now. I'll be gone before haying-time; surely by the time buckwheat will be ripe for reaping.' . . . I didn't say anything to him. What could I say? He was silent awhile, then went on to say: 'What can a man do? Seventy-eight is seventy-eight. True, some men at that age are still hale and hearty, and some live to be a hundred and over, but God did not will it to be so in my case. But, taking one thing with another, I am not complaining. We all come and go. This is the first time I've really been sick in my life. I've plowed my share of furrows; I've plowed them as deep and long as almost any man hereabouts. I've worn thin many a scythe, mowing hay. My wife bore me nine children; six of them are living, and four of the six have children in their turn.' . . ."

Quoting Uncle Yanez, mother did not realize that in a few short sentences, which bordered on poetry, she gave me the complete story of his life. She thought she was imparting to me only a bit of family news.

"The folks in Brankovo," she continued, "have been reading in the newspapers they get from Lublyana that you were coming home, and everybody in the village knows that you have been over half of the world, that you write English books and married a girl born in America who does not know our language, and that you yourself have difficulty in speaking Slovenian. Naturally, all that is strange to them"—as it palpably was to her—"and they are all very curious about you, Uncle Yanez perhaps more so than anyone else in the village."

I laughed, no doubt somewhat self-consciously. "There

probably is more excitement about me in Brankovo than about the fact that Uncle Yanez is about to die."

"*Menda ya!* (Of course!)" exclaimed mother. Then she smiled and, lowering her eyes, was silent a minute, and I knew that she, too, considered my homecoming vastly more extraordinary and exciting than the impending death of her beloved brother—and this not merely because I was her son whom she had not seen for nineteen years. In her mind, Uncle Yanez' final ordeal was a natural thing, simple, with countless precedents, hardly calling for any extensive comment or anything else, while—by her standards of experience—nearly everything about me was unusual.

"When I visited Yanez," she resumed, "he inquired when you were due to return. I told him, then he said I should urge you to come to Brankovo as soon as you can. He said: 'I'd like to see him before I go. I am sorry I can't come to greet him in Blato. He may be coming back from America just in time to go to my funeral.' Then he smiled a little and said he would not die till you visited him; he would wait."

And, telling me this, mother smiled herself.

II

Uncle Yanez was little more than a name to me.

For a decade or longer prior to my return home I probably had not thought of him once. I had no clear recollection of what he looked like. Nor had I any idea of the appearance of either the village of Brankovo or Uncle Yanez' homestead (my mother's birthplace), though I recalled, very vaguely, that I had made several visits there in my early boyhood.

Now, however, that I was home again, mother, eager that I should visit him before he died, mentioned something about Uncle Yanez every day. He had been very fond of me when I was a little boy. Did I remember when he had given me a gold coin as a namesday gift? He was not only my uncle, but my baptismal godfather. He was a very good man. . . . And so on, and so on.

But just then, as I relate in my first chapter, many pleasant things occupied me; but one day, perceiving how earnestly she wanted me to go to Brankovo, I said to mother that I would make the visit as soon as other engagements permitted me, perhaps during the coming week, and she promptly sent word to that effect to her brother's home.

A few days later some one brought me a message from Uncle Yanez that when I came to visit him I should come with my *ta mlada*, meaning my wife. He wanted to see her, too, before he died.

But Stella and I kept postponing our visit as long as possible. It was not only our engagements in Lublyana and elsewhere and my taking a part in finding Toné a wife that kept us on the go, but that the idea of visiting a dying man merely because he was my uncle and baptismal godfather did not appeal to us in the least. Still not comprehending the peasants' attitude toward death, I had a vague objection to dying and everything connected with it, on general principles. Stella's reluctance was based largely on the fact that the memory of the sudden and rather tragic death of her father in New York less than three years before was still fresh in her mind.

Our attitude toward death was in conflict with my mother's—the peasants'—attitude.

When we didn't go to Brankovo for several days after the week during which I had said we might go, mother reminded me several times of my promise.

"I hear Yanez is getting weaker and weaker," she said one day, "and he really does want to see you very much. You know how we all are in our family—sort of stubborn —and what we once take a notion to do or get we don't rest till we do it or get it. I know Yanez. Even before you came home he had gotten it into his head that he wanted to see you before he died, and now that is all there is to that! . . . The other day I saw Angela"—Uncle Yanez' oldest daughter—"and she thought he probably would have died a week ago if it wasn't for the fact that he is waiting for you and Styellah. Angela hinted he was a little hurt that you haven't come to see him yet. He requires that everything printed in the papers about you is read to him; to everybody who visits him he tells that you are his nephew and godson, and he can't get over the idea that you married an *Amerikanka*. It seems that now he is as anxious to see her as you, before he dies."

"Well," I said, "if that's the case, if waiting for us and being interested in Stella and what the newspapers write about me is what keeps him from dying, then maybe we should take our time about going to see him. We might thus do for him what spring has failed to do. . . . I know of a case in America where a man who was on his deathbed became well again and is alive today because he got angry at his son who did not come until nearly a week after a telegram had been sent to him informing him his father was dying and urging him to come home right away."

Mother smiled. "I am afraid nothing like that will work here. Angela said Yanez can't wait much longer. He is unable to move his legs and arms any more, and can barely move his fingers. They have to feed him like a baby. Only his eyes and brains are still alive. He doesn't suffer much, but even so, if his time has come to go, it isn't fair for anybody to keep him from going."

I told Stella what mother had said. "I guess we'd better go," I suggested. For a minute I felt vaguely guilty.

"Yes," agreed Stella.

And the next morning, nearly three weeks after my homecoming, my brother Anté hitched up the big buggy and drove us, mother, Stella, and me to Brankovo.

III

It was a fine late-spring day, cool-warm and bright, and for an hour and a half we rode through one of the most idyllic regions in Lower Carniola. The greater part of the way we talked of things which had nothing to do with Uncle Yanez.

Then Anté raised his whip and, pointing to a cluster of houses on the crest of a round little hill a few kilometers ahead, said that that was Brankovo.

I did not recall the place at once. From the distance it looked like any other small village in Lower Carniola. Fifteen or twenty minutes later, however, when we came to the edge of it, I recognized it. It had not changed at all in the twenty-odd years since I had been there the last time. There were the same ten or dozen peasant houses, most of them overlooking a narrow valley to the west and the others a small V-shaped ravine to the east. I recognized also the larger hills about the village, all thickly wooded and spring-green, here and there their slopes spotted with fields and glades. On the hill across the ravine was a tiny white church with a walled-in cemetery around it, the kind that one sees all over Slovenia.

Coming to the village, I suddenly remembered several little incidents of which I had been a part in my boyhood. There were the trees I had climbed, fences I had sat on. Several faces, as they appeared in the doorways or framed in windows along the little main street, seemed dimly familiar to me. I did not know who the people were, but I felt I had seen them before.

I recognized Uncle Yanez' house, which stands a little apart from the others, and recalled that twenty-odd years ago it had been thatch-roofed, while now, like a few other buildings in the community, it was covered with gray tile.

In front of the house was a crowd of people, mostly women and children. My mother helped me to recognize a few of them, including Aunt Olga, Uncle Yanez' wife—a shrunken little peasant woman in her early sixties, all gray and wrinkled and nearly toothless, with drawn lips, a pointed chin, and high cheek-bones that rose up almost to the lashless eyelids, which, due to sleeplessness during the last few days, she barely managed to keep open. As I learned later, Yanez had been hanging on less than a thread for more than a week, and, as his wife, or rather as his nearest kin, Aunt Olga had sat by his bedside night and day, waiting for him to die, for custom required that in his last moment she "close his eyes."

"You come just in time," she said, taking my hand. "He could not wait for you another day."

"Only the expectation of your coming today kept him alive," said my cousin Martin, Uncle Yanez' oldest son, a young man my own age, perhaps a little older, whom I suddenly remembered as a boy.

Cousin Angela said, "He's been asking every hour since daybreak if your carriage was yet in sight."

"We didn't know if you were coming in the morning or in the afternoon," said Aunt Olga.

"We were watching for you for the last two hours," said still another cousin, whom I did not know. "As soon as we saw you coming up from the valley, I ran in to tell him you were on the way."

Everybody was under a curious tension, a suppressed excitement, which I felt at once. Our handshakes were quick, jerky. The words of those who spoke to me came in little bursts.

Besides members of Uncle Yanez' immediate family, there were neighbors from the village, Aunt Olga's women friends, kinfolk from other villages. Some of the older men and women were faintly familiar to me, like figures in a fog. They had assembled to greet me and see my wife, and be near the house when the old man died; for, as I began to suspect, everybody believed Yanez would die shortly after he saw me. Two or three of the women already wore black mourning kerchiefs.

The tension and excitement, it occurred to me, were due not so much to Yanez' impending death as to the fact that he was still alive; that his determination to see me before he went had postponed his passing. For an instant I had a feeling that Aunt Olga looked at me reproachfully for not having come to Brankovo before. I tried to explain to her why we had not come earlier, but did not get very far with my alibi. Everyone seemed to want to talk to me simultaneously. I was not only Ana's son, who in his boyhood had visited Brankovo and now returned from the big world a grown-up man with a foreign wife, but was responsible for Ana's brother having stayed alive overtime.

I forgot all about introducing Stella, or explaining to her who all these people were. She stood near the carriage with Anté, not understanding what was being said, only sensing the drama into which we had been drawn, because the man inside the house was my uncle and godfather. The people, especially the women, were looking her over. A few of them whispered to one another, evidently about her. There were a few brief smiles.

Trying to postpone the confrontation with my uncle as long as possible, I hesitated going in. I went back to the carriage and explained to Stella that, to all seeming, I was —we both were—an important factor in the final crisis of a man's life; a sort of anticlimax in his life. "It seems he really will die as soon as he sees me, or soon after that."

"Pretty weird," said Stella.

I said, "Yes—and interesting."

We were the focus of all eyes.

"Well, come in, please," urged Aunt Olga. "He is asking why you don't come in."

IV

Inside, too, the house was essentially as I had last seen it. Over two hundred years old, it had been freshly whitewashed early that spring. In the kitchen, which was also the vestibule (that being the arrangement in most peasant houses in Carniola), a couple of small pigs grunted about, and a young hen, suddenly terrified, flew between my legs out of the door, but in spite of these animals everything was very clean.

From the kitchen Aunt Olga led us—Stella and me, with my mother behind us—through the big-room, heavy with the smell of rosemary, into a small side-room with a large bed, a chair, and two pictures on the walls, one of Virgin Mary and the other of John the Baptist, Uncle Yanez' patron-saint, for Yanez is Slovenian for John.

On the bed lay my uncle—a very old man with sunken eyes, as close to death as any living person I had ever seen before. Except for his head, he was covered with a clean, heavy linen sheet, under which his long bones were all too clearly outlined. His face was only faintly suggestive of the face I had glimpsed on an enlarged photograph in the big-room which had probably been taken about the time I had last seen him.

I greeted him rather nervously, I suppose, in a low tone of voice. I was terribly ill at ease. But when my mother and Aunt Olga exchanged a couple of short remarks, their voices seemed to me natural, normal; so then I repeated my greeting in a louder tone.

Uncle Yanez slowly turned his head on the pillow and looked at me, a curious glitter in his eyes. His lips twitched slightly, as though he wanted to say something. Then there was another twitch, which seemed like an attempt to smile.

Aunt Olga said, "You needn't talk, Yanez. Loyzé" (my first name in Slovenian) "knows that you're sick. . . . Just lie still, Yanez." She spoke to him as if he were a baby she was putting to bed.

"Of course," said I, "just take it easy, Uncle."

But my words sounded silly to me, while Aunt Olga's had sounded all right.

Yanez' eyes seemed to moisten a little, and his lips and one side of his face twitched for a minute or longer, till he succeeded in speaking, barely above a broken whisper:

"*Pozdravlyen*, Loyzé! Greetings! . . . I am sorry . . . going to die . . . can't talk much. . . . You don't see him

. . . but I see him . . . White Death . . . by the door
, . . with his scythe. . . ."

"Don't talk, Yanez!" Aunt Olga urged him.

"America," he began again. . . . "You are married
. . . *Amerikanka.* . . . Where is she?"

My mother said, "She is right here, Yanez—Styellah."

"Styellah," he whispered, then looked at Stella a long
time. . . . *"Na . . . pozdravlyena, ta mlada. . . ."*

Not being sure what the old man was saying, Stella felt
awkward.

"Uncle Yanez," I said, "she doesn't speak Slovenian, but
she greets you ———"

"—and wishes you a peaceful passing-on," added Aunt
Olga.

"Na . . ." Uncle Yanez looked back at me. *"Na . . .*
I hardly see you . . . your face, Loyzé . . . but you are
tall . . . your wife is small . . . *na . . ."* A long pause.
His face twitched, as he struggled to retain command of his
voice. "I always . . . knew you would . . . grow up tall,
Loyzé. . . . Your grandfather was tall . . . your mother's father. . . . Are you here, Ana?"

"Yes, I am here, Yanez," said my mother.

"Your grandfather, Loyzé . . . when he died . . . he
said . . . he said, 'Living is like licking honey . . . licking
honey off a thorn.' . . ." He was silent a long time, then
added, *"Na . . .* my father . . . your grandfather . . .
he died on this bed, too . . . he was ninety-six. . . . We
all die . . . go down into long silence. . . ."

He fell into silence and stared at me a long time.

"Maybe you better go out now, Loyzé," whispered Aunt
Olga, "you and Styellah; all of you, except you, Ana; and
call Nezha and Frantsa"—Olga's two sisters—"and light
a candle and bring it in."

"Yes," said my mother and went out to call them.

"Well, *adio,* Uncle Yanez," said I.

His lips moved again. *"Na . . . adio . . ."*

I whispered to Stella to say, *"Adio,"* and she said it.

"Na . . . adio . . ."

We withdrew. Aunt Olga stayed with him. My mother
returned with Nezha and Frantsa, one of them carrying a
lit candle, to kneel by the bed and pray.

They closed the door.

V

Stella and I sat down in the big-room and I told her in
English what Yanez had said. I noticed she looked pale.
"How do you feel?" I asked her.

"Not so hot, I must admit," she whispered, "but I think
that's my fault. That old boy in there seems all right to me.
The whole thing seems all right; only, I guess, I'm a little
too close to it. I'm not used to watching people die like that
or any other way. Death is not the same thing to me as to
these people. . . . You look pretty pale yourself! . . .
It's terribly stuffy in here—all the windows are shut."

I asked Cousin Angela if we could not open the windows.

"Not now," she said. She added that she knew it was
stuffy, and explained very simply that while one was dying
in the house all doors and windows were supposed to be
closed, to keep the soul in the house awhile after it left
the body.

Suddenly one of the older women jumped up, exclaiming
in a sharp whisper, "My heavens! You didn't turn the
mirror around."

I didn't know what to make of this. The mirror hung
on the wall opposite where we sat. The old woman (no
doubt some relation of mine) stepped over and turned it
to the wall. I looked at Anté, who smiled a little to Stella
and me, and remarked that it was an old custom when some
one was dying in the house. "I don't know just what it is
supposed to mean," he said; but subsequently I found out
that the mirror is turned so the soul can't look at itself, for
if it did and became interested in its looks, it might frequently return to the house to look at itself.

{ 68 }

Neither of us felt exactly comfortable. I told Stella that she looked paler every minute, and she said the same was true of me. So we went out.

VI

Outside, the day seemed even more beautiful than before we had visited the death-room. The sunshot spring air was sweet beyond words. Some swallows, whose nests were beneath the eaves, flew about the house in swift, vivid swoops.

We sat down on a bench at the table under the linden tree in front of the house.

"You and I, I guess, really should be ashamed of ourselves," said Stella.

I agreed with her, then listened to two women talking, one of whom, I learned later, was a half-aunt of mine. She was telling the other woman that Yanez had made his peace with everybody and the priest from the parish church, some distance away, had been up nearly a week before and given him the Last Sacrament. The other woman said, "May God give peace to his soul."

Cousin Angela came out of the house with a large elongated tub of water, which I had noticed in the vestibule a few minutes before, and placed it near the entrance.

"What's that for?" wondered Stella.

"I don't know," I said. I did not want to ask Angela; she appeared to be crying a little. A few minutes later, however, Anté came out and I asked him.

"That's for Death to wash his scythe when he leaves," he exclaimed.

"Do the people actually believe that?" I asked.

"Some do; most of them don't," he smiled; "but they all put the tub out. The idea is to be as accommodating to Death as possible," he smiled. "Some people believe that if they don't put the tub out and Death has to go down to the creek to wash his scythe, some one else will die in that house before the year is out."

{ 69 }

I was telling that to Stella, when one of the windows of the big-room flew open.

"He is gone now," said my brother.

Then the other windows opened, one after the other, and several people came out of the house. Two or three women wept a little, wiping their eyes with the corners of their aprons. My mother also came out; her eyes were dry.

Aunt Olga, having closed her husband's eyes, had wept a little, too, then lay down and fell asleep—she had been so tired from the long vigils at the bedside.

Through one of the windows I saw two women putting more candles onto candlesticks, lighting them. Some one stopped the large pendulum clock on the wall, so that the dead man would not "torment himself by counting the hours."

A half-hour later the bell in the tower of the tiny white church on the hill across the ravine began to toll slowly. It rang a long time and everybody in the vicinity learned that old Yanez was dead. After a while the bells of more distant churches, some of which were not visible from Brankovo, commenced to ring. They rang perhaps for an hour, and somehow, as it seemed to me for a while, enhanced the spring aliveness of the region visible from the hill.

The churches from which the bells were ringing were Catholic churches, for entire Slovenia is Catholic; but it struck me that what was going on here had very little to do with any particular organized religion, with doctrine of any sort. This was life; this was death—life . . . death . . . life ——

For the first time, while fully accepting and enjoying life, I thought and felt about death without any fear or hate or false bravado.

VII

The funeral was set for the mid-forenoon of the third day, and, to save ourselves the long ride to Blato and back again, my mother and brother and Stella and I stayed in Brankovo, along with numerous other relatives of Uncle Yanez' and his widow's who had been there before us or came shortly after the bells had started to ring. In a neighbor's house Cousin Angela found us lodgings, which, though lacking any suggestion of American comfort, were clean and restful.

And in the next two days, getting acquainted with most of the people of Brankovo and some of those who came to pray at the bier from near-by villages, listening to their talk and noting their beliefs and old customs in connection with the disposal of the body, I received, I think, a rather complete insight into the deep and, to me, downright poetic intimacy between life and death in rural Slovenia.

As already noted, right after Uncle Yanez had breathed his last, more candles were lighted, and Aunt Olga's closest female relatives washed his body from head to foot. They dressed him in fresh underclothes, his best Sunday suit, and a clean linen shirt, with a silk kerchief tied into a bow at his throat; put on his best boots and stuck a handkerchief, his favorite pipe and tobacco-pouch, his snuff-box and jack-knife, and a few coins into his pockets. Finally they clasped his hands around a small crucifix.

Meantime, Cousin Martin and one or two relatives of the family's had raised the bed on which Yanez had died by putting large wooden blocks under its legs; then the women spread the huge black bier-cloth—which, like the big candles and candlesticks, is communal property—over the bed and laid the body on it. They arranged some spring flowers about the head and darkened the two windows in the room.

Upon a small stand at the foot of the bier they put the candles, a prayer-book, and a small bowl of holy water, which some one fetched from the church across the ravine. In the bowl was a tiny olive twig—saved from Palm Sunday, two months before—with which everyone who came to say good-by to the dead man sprinkled a bit of water on him.

{ 71 }

Even before the bells ceased tolling the people—relatives, friends, fellow villagers—began to arrive. There was a sort of solemn excitement about it all. Men and women stopped in front of the house under the linden tree, to chat about how Yanez had died and about Stella and me. Everyone looked at us, but after a time, I think, we were generally forgiven for having delayed the old man's demise beyond the time when he would have died had we not come from America. Then they went inside and looked at the lifeless face, prayed a bit, sprinkled holy water on the body, and came out again, to remark what a good man Yanez had been and recall little incidents in his life which were to his credit.

Some came two and three times. They evidently liked it. During the two days that Uncle Yanez lay in state (if that phrase may be used in connection with a peasant) some two hundred persons came and went. It was a social occasion for the entire region. Women brought gifts to the widow. They, in turn, were given something to eat and drink either at Yanez' house or at one of the neighbors'. They exchanged views on the weather, gossiped about all sorts of things, and met the American author, who was old man Yanez' nephew and godson, and his American wife, who seemed very bright but knew only a few words of Slovenian.

In the evening the "watchers" gathered in the big-room to spend the night in the dead man's home. They were, for the most part, close relatives and friends, mostly men. I "watched" both nights, listening and talking with them, and had a thoroughly interesting time. Not comprehending the talk, Stella stayed a short time the first night, then went to sleep. All feelings of weirdness and uneasiness had left us.

One or two people were constantly in the death-room. They were the real watchers. They took care that the candles did not cause a fire and, still more important, that no cat came near, for, according to old belief, should a cat jump on the bier and cross the body, the soul of the dead person would become a werewolf.

We in the big-room had a regular all-night party. A few of the men played dominoes; not for money, of course, but for beans. To gamble for money was apt to have another (I forget what) evil effect on the soul of the deceased.

The rest of us sat about in groups, talking. There were pitchers and bottles of wine, cider, and prune brandy; loaves of bread, platters of home-cured ham and *klobasé* (smoked sausages), with raw horseradish, and bowls of dried fruit of the previous year.

I was asked about things in America; almost the same questions I had been asked when I first came to Blato. Was the economic crisis really so bad there? How was it affecting the farmers? The workers? Our immigrants? . . . Was all this they were reading in the papers about Lindbergh's baby really true? . . . I talked to them perhaps half of both the first and the second night, then turned the talk to what momentarily interested me more than America.

VIII

I learned that most Slovene, like other Yugoslav, peasants more or less, believe in the existence of the soul after death. The women's belief in the matter seems stronger than the men's. It is they who still insist on turning mirrors to the wall and keeping the windows closed.

The theory—with some variations in different localities —is that the soul leaves the body immediately or soon after death. In the case of one who lived a good, honest life it has a much easier time in parting from the flesh than when one has lived a bad life. I spoke with people who claimed they had seen souls leave the body. "Once," a woman told me, "when So-and-so died, I saw a little flutter right over the death-bed, like a bird flying. It fluttered around awhile, then out of the window."

The soul usually stays near the house for a couple of

hours, then visits all other scenes of the dead person's earthly life. In some cases, especially if one has been to America or lived in some other distant country, it takes the soul a couple of months to make the rounds of all the places, though most people say that forty days is the maximum. If the deceased had done some injustice or neglected to do some duty in the world, the soul attempts to right that.

Everywhere in Yugoslavia peasants believe that in the next world the soul leads much the same life the person led in this. It smokes, snuffs, blows its nose, whittles sticks, and needs money. That was why the women put all the things I have mentioned in Uncle Yanez' pockets, though in Slovenia—by and large, the most civilized section of Yugoslavia—this belief is only a kind of pretense-belief.

In the more primitive parts of the country people put into the coffin a few candles, so the soul in the next life may not grope around in darkness. If the dead man was a cripple, his crutches go with him. In some places they believe that in the next world the soul continues in the trade the man had worked at on earth, and so dead shoemakers often take with them awls and pliers; carpenters, planes, nails, and hammers; and peasants, little bags of seed for sowing.

Into the grave with the body go also food and bottles of wine; or else, for several nights after the funeral, the people leave food and drink on the table, so in the event the soul should return to the house it would feel welcome, seeing that the survivors think of it in a friendly spirit. . . . Later, when I traveled through the more primitive parts of Dalmatia, Bosnia, Macedonia, and other Yugoslav provinces, I saw people carrying bowls of food and bottles of wine in funeral processions. I saw them also bringing food and drink to the grave weeks after the funeral. . . .

In Slovenia very few people still believe that souls really eat, but the custom of placing food and drink on the table for them is widespread. On the night of All Souls' Day, in nearly every peasant house food and drink are on the table. In a great many villages, for several weeks after the funeral, the custom is to set an extra place at the table, whereby the people demonstrate as much to the soul of the deceased as to themselves how much they miss him or her.

IX

Having visited all the places where the dead person had once lived, and having righted as many wrongs as possible, the soul, if it is from the body of an old man or woman, goes to the next world; but it is different with some of the young souls, especially those of girls.

Young women, for instance, who die shortly before they are supposed to marry become *villé*, or nymphs, and as such live for years—in the belief of some people, forever— in the woods and fields, or by the streams, lakes, or water-falls near their villages. These nymphs, as a rule, are beautiful, benevolent spirits. Once upon a time, when the world was a much better place than it is today, they lived in close contact and friendship with human beings still in the flesh. In those days they regularly helped peasants at their work. At night people saw them in the fields, pulling out weeds and cockles; or in the meadows, dancing and chanting, urging grass to grow tall and thick, so the good peasants would have plenty of hay for their stock in the wintertime. When shepherds fell asleep, the *villé* watched their sheep and cattle.

Of late, however, since there have been so many wars and other evil things in the world, since men have departed from their old virtues and many peasants have taken to drinking and cursing, and shepherds have thrown away their fifes and drums and taken whips into their hands and commenced to crack them in the pastures so they sound like rifleshots—since then the good nymphs show themselves less frequently to human eyes. They are still around, for that is their fate; but they are doing fewer and fewer favors for people. Invisible, they hover about the old villages, sad young spirits donned in breeze and moonlight, and concern themselves chiefly with the souls of newly dead people and help them accustom themselves to being free souls; take them around and coöperate with them in fixing up the wrongs they had perpetrated while in the flesh.

One of Uncle Yanez' daughters had died some years before at the age of nineteen, shortly after her betrothal to a young peasant in a neighboring village. Now I found out that Aunt Olga and Cousin Angela, along with other women, firmly believed that the girl had become a *villa* and was taking care of her father's soul.

"What does she look like now?" I asked Aunt Olga.

The old woman answered, "Like when she was a girl in this house, only more beautiful—like an angel, but she is not really an angel. She'll be a *villa* maybe till all of us in this house die; then she'll go to heaven and probably become a real angel."

"Have you ever seen her?"

"No; but she's always near. Evenings, sometimes, when I pass through the orchard I hear her, I feel her. She'll be here when I die, just as she was yesterday when her father went."

Angela's ideas concerning her dead sister were approximately the same.

X

"In short," I said to Stella, after telling her what I had learned during the night watches, and after we had thought about and discussed the Slovene peasants' way of dying— "in short, to Olga and Angela the old man's death means simply that he is being transferred from their care to the care of the beautiful *villa*, who is a creature of their pagan imaginations, slightly overlaid with a dressing of Christian thought and practice. It is that to all the rest of them, more

{ 76 }

or less, depending on the degree of their power to accept such seemingly simple explanations, which, in fact, are really quite elaborate.

"These explanations and beliefs are the result of the people's long background, reaching back into the pagan era; and their background, in its essence, I suppose, has been a slow, painful process of adjustment on their part to their environment—of making peace with their environment. Slovenes have been living here for twelve centuries or longer, and that process now is more or less accomplished—so far, at least, as they who remain on the old soil and are not too poor are concerned. . . .

"This whole village appears to be in deep harmony with the region. It is an indigenous part of it. And these people belong here as much as these swallows flying about. They are intimate with their surroundings. They know what their function is without ever really thinking about it. Death is only a part, an inevitable incident, in that intimacy with their environment; and, like other incidents in their lives, they have glossed it over with poetry and semi-religious beliefs. . . .

"Christianity brought them the idea of hell, but it never took deep root in them. Essentially they are still pagans. Most of them, I guess, are too kind to believe in fire and brimstone."

Stella and I talked a long time and began to compare death in rural Yugoslavia with death as we—especially she —knew it in urban America. Her father, as I have mentioned, had suddenly died a few years before of heart failure, at the height of his career, as he sat down to dinner one Sunday afternoon. His death had been a great shock to the family and all their friends. After the funeral there had been much fretting about his business affairs, the insurance policy, and what not.

"There undoubtedly is a great difference," said Stella, "between your uncle's death and my father's. Here Death is a rather mild though inexorable fellow who comes and stands by the door with his scythe, waiting till his victim is through saying good-by to everybody, including his nephew who happens to return from America; then does his work because, somehow, it must be done. . . . In America, in the cities at least, Death is a gangster who puts one on the spot, then—*bang!* In America, he doesn't carry a scythe, but a sawed-off shotgun."

I said: "I imagine that's because in America most of us are gangsters, more or less—racketeers, in the broad sense of the word (I'll try to suggest how broad). When times are good, we all work furiously. We push and fight. We try to beat everybody; get the best of them; put them on the spot. We lead fast lives of one sort or another. We make no collective intelligent attempt to adjust our lives to the scene, to make peace with our environment. Few of us even make any individual attempt in that direction. In general the exact contrary actually is the truth. If we do make any such attempt, we usually fail.

"In America, even in the rural districts, few people really belong where they are, in the sense that these people belong here in Brankovo. Unlike here, there is no stability in America. Up and down, all the time. Just now"—in the middle of 1932—"we're as far down, perhaps, as we ever were. . . . Naturally, then, Death in America is a gangster, as you say. What else could he be? He will be a gangster, it seems to me, as long as the people of America fail to make peace with their environment; develop a sane and sound social order, which will give people the feeling that life has continuity. Or course, that'll take time: and, anyhow, America can't become another, vastly larger Slovenia. It's too late for that; and I'm not really in favor of believing in *villé* and such things; but there must be some other way for a great nation to make peace with its environment, and then work out of its circumstances a stout philosophy and attitude, which would enable them to die as well as these peasants die. . . ."

{ 78 }

As I say, it was the first time that I had really thought about death, and the same was true of Stella.

XI

The second day, Uncle Yanez' body was placed in a coffin of pinewood painted black. I learned that Yanez had had the lumber for it ready for several years. It was from a tree in his wood.

Into the coffin, under his head, was put a handful of dirt from one of his fields, so that he might "sleep on his own soil."

In the morning of the third day a priest came, then four men carried the coffin down the Brankovo hill, across the ravine, then up the opposite hill to the little cemetery, where his *villa*-daughter and his parents and grandparents already were buried. About a hundred of us followed the coffin, and the church bell rang from the time the procession started till after the burial.

It was a beautiful day.

The ceremony at the grave was brief. The coffin was lowered into it and Aunt Olga, Cousin Angela, and a few other women wept a little. Then each of us threw in a tiny spade of dirt, and that was all.

Returning from the cemetery, I tried to hear what the people were talking about. Some of them, of course, still spoke about Yanez—what a good man he had been; how much they would all miss him. But most of the talk—especially among women—concerned a pair of twins that had been born in a house in Brankovo during the night.

Even Aunt Olga was all excited about them. "I must go see them," she said. "I guess they are the first twins in Brankovo since ——"

CHAPTER IV

We Stay in Carniola

BOTH STELLA AND I, AS I HAVE SUGGESTED, FELL IN LOVE with Carniola at first sight; after that our affection for it—for most of its aspects, anyhow—swiftly deepened, and, instead of a few days as we had originally planned, we stayed in the tiny province about two months. We forgot all about our intention to spend most of the year in Italy or Austria.

During the first couple of weeks we spent in Blato only an occasional day or afternoon, never more than two days at a stretch. The reason for this was not only that we were invited and drawn to other places, but that my family, especially my mother and sisters, were so infinitely glad and thrilled to have us with them that, whenever Stella and I came to the village, all of us were under a great emotional and nervous tension from the moment we arrived till we departed.

On coming to Blato both of us were usually tired from the parties, long talks, and doings elsewhere, but there was no opportunity for relaxing and resting in my native house. The entire family and often several of our nearest relatives and neighbors gathered around us and gazed affectionately, but at the same time also very intently and scrutinizingly, taking in our every word, mood, gesture, and expression, noting every detail of our manner and attire. And naturally so. To them everything about us was interesting, significant. Studying me and my wife, they tried to figure out how I had lived my life since I had left Blato nineteen years before; for they still knew very little about me. It was too long a story for me to begin telling them. I noticed

that if I told them things I only increased the tension between us. Whatever I said I tried to make as casual, as
matter-of-fact, as possible, but it was no use.

When we sat around the table in the big-room, or in the
kitchen, a half-dozen or more persons always watched for
a chance to do something for Stella and me. They all tried
to anticipate our wishes and needs. If either of us reached
for a glass of water, at least three women jumped up in
unison and cried, "Oh, don't drink that; let me go to the
pump and bring you some fresh water." Then one of them
rushed out, and sometimes two of them, one to hold the
pitcher, the other to work the pump handle. Returning with
the fresh water, at least two of them asked us simultaneously, "But don't you want a little lemon in it? Or a little
raspberry juice? . . ."

My mother and sister insisted on cooking rich, elaborate
meals, to which—too excited by the experiences I have told
about—we could not do full justice. Then they would re-
proach us: "Lord! why don't you eat a little more? . . .
Isn't it good? . . . Don't you like it? . . . Tell us how
you like it prepared. . . . Styellah, you are like a sparrow,
you eat so little. . . ." They wanted me to make up in a
few weeks for all the meals I had not eaten home during
the nineteen years I lived in America. My mother, poor
soul, unable to think of anything else she could do for me
and my wife, ceaselessly urged us to eat something. Less
than an hour after dinner she would ask me if I did not
want a cup of nice linden-blossom tea with pure honey. It
would be so good for me, and no less good for Stella. Or,
"Do let me scramble for you a couple of eggs apiece. They
are fresh this afternoon, still warm from the hen." I told
her I was full. "Full!" she scoffed. "How can you be full?
Neither of you has eaten anything. No wonder you are
both getting thin, running around all over the country and
not eating!"

She reminded Stella of her own mother in New York.

"The old mother stuff!" we laughed. "The same all over the world."

After two or three weeks, however, it became rather a strain on Stella and me. There was for us no rest from affectionate gazes and my mother's food in Blato.

II

Off and on, especially during the time that Toné was getting married and I, as his groomsman, had to be a great deal in the village, I went to Uncle Mikha's house. It was one way to escape the endless ministrations of my good, eager mother and sisters; besides, I liked the old man and he interested me. We would sit for hours in the shade of an old pear tree in front of his beehives, and talk.

We talked of various things in the village, the death of Uncle Yanez, who had been a friend of Mikha's, my adventures since my return home, the weather, the condition of the soil, and other such basic matters, but most often about the world-wide economic crisis, which just then was beginning to be acutely felt by the Yugoslav peasant.

"It is pretty bad," said Uncle Mikha, "nobody can deny that. We find it harder and harder to sell our products. Last week, for instance, to make room in our barn, we took two calves to the stock-market in Lublyana, and sold one— at three dinars a kilo!" or slightly over two cents a pound. "It didn't pay to take the calf to the city. . . . Eggs we practically give away. . . . If we get fifteen dinars," twenty cents, "for a chicken, we are doing well these days. The city folk have no money to buy anything. Wages and salaries have been reduced all around this past year. I guess lots of people in Lublyana live merely on bread, beans, and lentils, and some of them eat very little of that. . . .

"We in the villages, at least most of us, I think, have plenty to eat; in fact, too much, since we can't sell our products; but, if this *kriza* keeps up much longer, pretty soon even those who once considered themselves well-off

won't have any money with which to buy clothes, salt, tobacco, and other things we don't produce ourselves." (Unlike in some of the other sections of Yugoslavia, which
Stella and I visited later, peasants in Slovenia no longer wear
homespun, except here and there; most of the clothes, even
national costumes, are factory-made.) "The prices of things
we have to buy in stores are higher than ever. And from
what I hear, we Slovene peasants are many times better off
than peasants elsewhere in Yugoslavia."

Uncle Mikha had been reading in the Lublyana newspapers that the economic conditions were even worse in
other countries: in Bulgaria, for instance, and in Rumania,
Hungary, Poland. Some of the articles he had perused
lately, he said, were full of evil forebodings. There was
great unrest the world over. What did I think? Was it
really as bad as all that? Did I, who had been over the
world, believe that things were on the verge of collapse?
Gold standard—what was that?—what did it mean? And
what did I think of all this that has been going on in Russia
these past fifteen years? And in Germany? Wasn't this man
Hitler a little mad or something? Would he ever get into
power? . . .

I told him at some length what I thought, but the gist of
my remarks was that, in my opinion, the whole world was
in the painful process of social and economic change.

Uncle Mikha then said, "Well, that may be so; in fact,
I don't doubt it, because lately everybody is saying the
same thing. For instance, I spoke with a lawyer in Lublyana
the other day; a sane and sensible man; and he told me
the whole of Europe was liable to 'blow up'—that's the
expression he used. He said all countries were liable to go
like Italy went or become bolshevik, like Russia. . . .

"Now, I am a peasant, not an educated man, and I don't
understand everything I read in the papers, and I have no
way of telling whether what I read is so or not. For all I
can say, it probably is true that there are thirty million
people with no work and little or nothing to eat and wear,

and it may be that these millions are liable to do something to bring about great changes. On the other hand, I have a feeling that in time, no matter what happens, so far as we here on the soil are concerned, things probably will straighten themselves out in one way or another, and in the end we tillers of the soil will be just where we are—here in the villages, on our little bits of land, doing the same thing we have been doing for a thousand years or more. The world has to eat, and it can eat only if the peasant—the farmer, as you call him in America—works his soil and produces things.

"As I say, I don't understand much of what is going on in the big world, far beyond our horizons, but I have a feeling that this sun above us is going to shine for a long time yet, rain is going to fall, and this deep, black soil hereabouts"—he swung his arms toward the fields around the village—"will yield as long as we know how to keep it fertile and have our tools and beasts and our hands and strength.

"Of course, it may be that in time we will improve our tools and we will work on the land as your peasants—I mean farmers—work in America, with tractors, motors, all kinds of machinery; we already have a few tractors in Carniola, which may or may not be a good thing; I don't know . . . but what I want to say is that these things together—the sun and rain, our hands and strength, our tools and implements, our beasts or motors, or whatever it will be—mean that we shall live here where we were born, continue the race, eat from the soil and feed the world."

In his own narrow way, I thought at the time, my uncle was largely right. No matter what happened in America, in Russia, and in the rest of Europe, nine chances out of ten the agriculturists in the village of Blato, as in Brankovo and other villages in Carniola, would stay where they were —for some time to come, at any rate. Agriculture in Carniola probably never would be industrialized, as it had been industrialized in great part in America and as they were trying to industrialize it in Russia, for Carniola, with its small valleys huddled amid the mountains and no great plains, was fit, perhaps, only for small-scale farming. Hence my uncle's sun-and-soil optimism, which, despite the hard times, was very close to smugness, and his sense of importance and stability, which are typical of the better-off peasants throughout Carniola. Hence my own mother's optimistic statement to me as to her economic problems which I have quoted in a preceding chapter; though it is possible, of course, that in her reply to my questions as to how they all managed she had exerted herself a little to appear more cheerful about their circumstances than she actually was, so as not to cause me to worry. . . . But the basic factor in the Slovene peasants' attitude toward their problems, which I have tried to suggest here, is their indigenousness, their instinctive feeling that they belong where they are— if for no other reason, because they have been there a long, long time, and they and their forbears have plowed endless furrows in their fields and sprinkled them with their sweat. . . .

III

I had work to do; and for a while shortly after we first came there I thought that Stella and I probably would establish ourselves in Blato and pay my mother for our board, which, however low the sum might be, would have helped her a lot. There was plenty of room in our house. There was, it is true, no regular tile bathroom, such as we were used to in New York, anywhere in Blato; but the creek was only a few minutes' walk from the house.

However, I soon gave up the idea. The emotional-nervous tension between my family and me continued and increased, and I decided I could not possibly write in Blato. I would be constantly conscious of my mother and the rest of the family, of their inner excitement concerning Stella and me. We could never get them to accept us calmly, matter-of-factly. Neither they nor Stella and I could ever relax near them.

So, after we had buried Uncle Yanez and Toné and Yulka were all set to be married, one of the Lublyana literati recommended to us a tiny *pension*-hotel at Lake Bohin, in the Alps of Upper Carniola, on the Italo-Yugoslav border (as established by the treaty of Rapallo), and in mid-June we put up there. Blato was within a few hours' train-ride.

We stayed in Bohin three weeks.

We had never breathed such air before, or enjoyed such peace—the first week, at any rate. For a while not many persons in Slovenia knew where we were, and the few other guests at the *pension* were, I think, Austrians from Salzburg or Wiener-Neustadt, who had no interest in us.

The *pension*, although *sans* many conveniences of American summer hotels, was fairly good and, if compared with prices in the United States, absurdly cheap. If I recall correctly, the rate for both of us was less than two dollars a day, and I had a separate workroom. But later we learned that that was one of the most expensive places in Upper Carniola. If we had put up in a peasant house in one of the villages near the lake, we could have lived almost as cheaply as at my mother's in Blato, say, on thirty cents each a day— and lived well.

Lake Bohin and its surroundings constitute one of the loveliest and most interesting spots we have ever seen. At first it reminded me a little of Lake Tahoe on the California-Nevada border, where I had made a trip a few years before from Los Angeles. Bohin, at times, has the same peculiar blue as Tahoe, only its surface is calmer, almost melancholy, reposed, nearly always smooth save for an occasional rippling here and there, where gusts of breeze suddenly sweep down from the mountains immediately around it. It is also much smaller than Tahoe, only some two miles long and about half a mile wide in the middle, where it attains a depth of over one hundred feet. It is ellipsoidal in shape, filling a great mountain basin, doubtless glacial by origin.

Next to Lake Bled, which I already have mentioned, Bohin is the best-known lake in Slovenia. I learned that in recent winters it had been the scene of several international skiing contests. Prince Paul, cousin of King Alexander of Yugoslavia, has there his summer home, a large mountain lodge. But most important of all, Lake Bohin is the source of the River Sava, which, gathering unto itself scores of lesser rivers and streams on the way, flows through the whole width of Slovenia, the entire length of Croatia, and part of Serbia, joining the Danube at Belgrade, thus tying together, symbolically as well as in vital economic interest, three of the most important sections of Yugoslavia, which for eleven years after its inception was known as the Kingdom of the Serbs, Croats, and Slovenes.

The window of my workroom was on the lake, and the first few weeks there I did very little work. Most of the time I leaned over my typewriter, watching the constantly changing moods of the place—lake and mountains. In fact, I did very little work while in Bohin altogether. Guggenheim Fellowship ("to do creative writing in Europe") or no Guggenheim Fellowship, the place was too nice, too fascinating to sit indoors and pull ideas out of one's cranium.

Except in the shallows, the lake was a bit too cold for swimming, but for fifteen cents an hour one could hire a boat and go rowing or fishing. There were also endless trails leading into the wooded mountains on which one could hike all day or for several days, if one did not mind sleeping in shepherds' huts or in the open; and, hiking, encounter young does and bucks, temporarily protected from hunters by the state game laws.

IV

Taking a walk one day, not far from our hotel, we discovered a charming, rather sizable mountain village called

Stara Fuzhina, which I subsequently learned was several hundred years old. It lies in the middle of a tiny, narrow valley, which is a prolongation of the lake basin, only a few feet above the water's surface. All around the village are (in the summertime, of course) green meadows, red-clover, corn, beet, potato, and bean fields. Across the valley and through the center of the village tumbles a mountain stream, which a short distance away flows into the Sava.

The village, one of the most picturesque we had seen till then, interested me at once, but especially after I learned that, like a good many other mountain villages thereabouts, it had a highly developed coöperative economy. In such communities in Lower Carniola as Blato and Brankovo, the peasants, while organized in loose *zadrugé* (economic coöperatives), are still rather thoroughly individualistic. Each *gospodar* owns his piece of land, house, barn and sheds, tools and beasts. In good times he uses the local coöperative only to sell things he cannot dispose of at a greater profit himself, or to buy his yearly supply of seeds and fertilizer.

In Stara Fuzhina the peasants also own their homes, tools and animals, and the fields and meadows in the valley immediately surrounding the village; most of the land within the economic system of the community, however, is owned collectively. This is the pasture land on the mountain slopes and tops, the so-called *planiné*, immediately above the village on both sides of the valley, where the cattle of all the peasants are grazed together from early June to mid-September, in charge of herders employed by the *zadruga*. The herders milk the cows and send the rich milk to the *zadruga's* cheese factory in the village, a thoroughly modern plant, where other employees of the coöperative convert it into *bohinski sir* (Bohin cheese), which, when properly aged, is held superior by many Central European restaurateurs to some Swiss cheeses. At the end of the season the profits from this business are divided among the peasants on the basis of the number of cows each of them has had on the collective grazing ground.

One of the highlights of life in Stara Fuzhina occurs in the spring when the cattle are driven into the mountains. I am sorry that Stella and I missed this event, for it doubtless has a high epic quality. It takes place the first or second Monday in June. The Sunday before is a day of general festivity in the village. The girls gaily decorate each cow, heifer, and bullock with garlands of field and mountain flowers. During the night the herders take charge of the animals, driving them up, and there is much blowing of horns, lowing, and ringing of cow-bells, whooping and singing up and down the valley and upon the slopes.

When Stella and I came to Bohin, the cow-bells could no longer be heard from the lake, for by mid-July the herds had already eaten their way high into the *planiné*, beyond the crests of the nearest mountains, out of sight and hearing. Only now and then, hiking on mountain trails, we came upon small herds in charge of boys in their late 'teens, or we met young men rushing the milk or cottage cheese to the village.

Toward the end of July, however, which was approximately mid-season so far as cattle-grazing in the mountains was concerned, we were suddenly roused late one night by a terrific racket (as it seemed the first instant) on the road that passed our hotel. We got up to see what was going on. There was a nearly full moon right over the lake, which enabled us to see quite clearly the scene beneath our window.

Hundreds of head of cattle, each with a bell and a garland of flowers around its neck, were being driven by herders from the mountains on one side of the valley to the mountains on the opposite side.

Feeling they were near home, the beasts lowed (especially, I suppose, the cows whose calves had been left in the village), and the herders, aided by most of the other villagers, shouted at them and beat them with light twigs, keeping them on the road, restraining them from starting a stampede for their barns. Now and then one of the young men let out a great whoop, which, like all the other sounds connected with this cattle movement, echoed clearly against the mountains on the opposite end of the silver lake.

V

By and by it became known around Lake Bohin, both among the peasants and Yugoslav summer vacationists from the cities, that I was the American writer about whom the newspapers wrote so much because I was a Slovene by birth, and I began once more to meet a great many people.

Of these, perhaps, the most interesting to me were the Slovenes who in recent years had either escaped or been exiled by the Fascists across the mountains from the Slovene territory that had come under Italy after the World War. Each of these persons was a personal tragedy. Most of them had once been well-to-do in their native villages and towns along the river Socha (or the Isonzo, as the Italians call it); now some of them make their living in Bohin as hotel servants, bus-drivers, lake boatmen, mountain guides, laborers, and the like. Several of them, after I became acquainted with them, told me stories of terror to which the 300,000 Slovenes and some 400,000 other Yugoslavs were subjected under the Fascist rule in Trieste and Gorizia, in the rural areas immediately to the north and northeast of those cities, and over the entire peninsula of Istria.

All these territories have been—and still are—predominantly Slavic for a thousand years. Until after the war they were part of Austria; but when that country was broken up, the Allies' statesmen, after considerable hesitation, handed them over to Italy, along with a section of the Tyrol. This was in payment for Italy's participation in the conflict against the Central Powers.

In 1923, shortly after Mussolini came into power in Italy, the Fascists began a reign of terror against the Slavs inhabiting these regions. Although they and their forbears had lived in the same villages for centuries before they came under Italy, Mussolini declared them "immigrants" and required them, under the provision of a special law which his government promulgated, to become Italians without delay. Hundreds of thousands of them had to change their names: as, for instance, from Adamic to Adami or Adamio or Adamicchi. In numerous localities people were forced even to Italianize the names upon the tombstones of their forbears. Slovene priests were—and still are—forbidden to preach in Slovene or Serbo-Croat, although those were the only languages that most of their parishioners understood. They had to preach in Italian, if they knew the language; if not, they were told not to deliver sermons at all.

Slovene teachers were deprived of their jobs, and in all the schools boys and girls were taught only in Italian by Italians. By 1927 or thereabouts children were forbidden to utter a single Slovenian or Serbo-Croatian word under any circumstances. They were told that their Slovene peasant parents were barbarians and they should be ashamed of the tongue their mothers had taught them. Teachers established spy systems among their pupils, and the children reported to them to have spoken a word of Slovenian were punished.

In this connection I want to tell what happened in 1929 at Vrhpolye (I forget just how the Fascists have Italianized this name), a Slovene village near the Slovene town of Vipava (now Vipacco). The teacher in this village was a young man, I think, from southern Italy, Sottosanti by name. He was tubercular and a passionate fascist. When his little spies reported to him a Slovene pupil whom they had heard utter words in his native speech, he would fly into a rage, call the offender before him, order him to open his mouth wide, then spit on his tongue.

This, of course, enraged the entire Slovene population in the vicinity of Vipava, and particularly in the village of Vrhpolye itself. When Sottosanti had spat into about a dozen children's mouths, a group of Slovene peasants—

{ 91 }

probably fathers of those boys and girls—waited for him one dark night and killed him after which dozens of Slovenes were arrested and tried, and several of them are now serving life sentences on Signor Mussolini's prison islands north of Sicily, while the Fascist organization in the Vipava district erected a monument to Sottosanti in the village where he had taught, glorifying him as a Black Shirt martyr, a victim of Slovene barbarism.

The monument stands there today.

The story of Sottosanti was told to me by one of the peasants who had had a hand in his murder, following which he had escaped over the mountains to Bohin. Later I authenticated it in every detail.

During my stay in Bohin I heard other stories, almost as horrible. Here I give only one more, because most of the others circumstances have not permitted me to verify, and because it has a certain relation to the customs I have described in connection with the death of my uncle Yanez.

For several evenings at about the same time—in 1929—that the peasants near Vipava killed Sottosanti thousands of Slovene homes in Italy had four empty chairs at their supper tables. They had unseen guests—four young Slovenes whom a company of Italian Fascist militiamen had shot in the backs that week. The young men had been accused (and possibly were guilty) of acts of violence and propaganda against the Italian state, and the Fascist court, as approved by *il Duce* himself, had ordered them executed as traitors. Whereupon the Slovene peasants—these "immigrants," as Mussolini again called them in his recent conversations with Emil Ludwig—spontaneously and secretly observed this strange ceremony throughout the occupied territory, entertaining the souls of the dead boys, unconsciously exploiting their ancient customs and beliefs concerning the dead for political propaganda purposes.

CHAPTER V

Mr. Guggenheim and I Become a Legend

TALKING WITH A COUPLE OF LUBLYANA NEWSPAPER
men who came to Bohin one week-end, I told them, in
reply to their questions, that I was more and more impressed
by my native country; that I had written an article about
my return home, which a New York monthly, *Harper's
Magazine,* would publish, and was thinking of writing more
about Slovenia and, perhaps, the rest of Yugoslavia—
maybe a book, a full-length portrait of the land and people
as seen by my Americanized eyes. Would I deal also with
the political, social, and economic conditions in Yugoslavia?
I said I didn't know; the idea for the book had only just
occurred to me.

I mentioned, too, that my wife and I were planning to
leave Bohin and Slovenia for some other part of Yugoslavia, probably Dalmatia. Later we would also visit Montenegro, Bosnia, Herzegovina, Croatia, Serbia, Macedonia.
We would stop here a few weeks, there a month or two,
and thus gradually take in the whole state. Our plans were
vague, indefinite; possibly we would spend the entire year in
Yugoslavia.

The following Monday the Lublyana papers printed
long articles about my projected book, and before the week
passed those articles were translated into Serbo-Croatian
and reprinted in journals all over the country. Most of the
newspapers—having difficulty, as I have said, in finding
anything else to write about that would pass the dictatorship's censor—went at considerable length again into my

"great success" in America, and for the tenth or fifteenth time informed their readers that my trip was being paid for by the Guggenheim Foundation (*Gugnhaimova Fondacia*), an organization established by a liberal American industrialist who owned no end of mines in western United States, where tens of thousands of Yugoslav immigrants have worked during the past decades.

Immediately after that Stella and I began to receive invitations from people and organizations we had never heard of before to visit their various towns and villages in Dalmatia, Croatia, and other provinces. Which was all very flattering, exciting, and strange.

But the strangest thing in this connection—as I found out shortly before we left Bohin—was that Slovene peasants in different sections of the country began to make the founder of the Guggenheim Foundation and me into a kind of legend, which, when I fully realized what it meant, struck me as extremely interesting and significant.

Like most legends, this legend apparently was a simple thing; behind its origin, however, was a vast array of facts concerning the Slovene people's circumstances in their country which I think is necessary for me to touch upon before I relate the legend itself.

II

To a foreigner casually passing through Slovenia, or staying there only a short time, it would never occur that anything was troubling the tiny country. In fact, it seems to me at this point that, in the preceding chapters, I have insufficiently stressed the brightness, picturesqueness, and gayety, not only of the land itself in its spring and summer loveliness, but also of the Slovene character, which, as I have tried to suggest, is closely indigenous to the country. Going about, on weekdays or Sundays, one hears singing and laughter; this especially in villages and small towns, in the fields and meadows, on mountain pastures and trails, in wine-houses and beer-gardens. I am now referring to the two-thirds of Slovenia that forms the northwestern corner of Yugoslavia, but I was told that the Slovenes under Italy, at least a good many of them, despite the Fascist terror, often are as gay and jolly as those in Yugoslavia, where, as I gradually discovered, everything was not light and sweetness, either, for vast numbers of people.

There is much that is troubling Slovenia; and its troubles are part of the problems and difficulties, economic, social, and political, of nearly the whole Western World.

For one thing, the Italian Fascist imperialists are not satisfied with having one-third of Slovenia; they seem to want the rest. The other two-thirds is even nicer than the third they already have. The largest Slovene forests and rivers and the best Slovene soil are still in Yugoslavia. Also, in the Yugoslav part of Slovenia are rich coal and ore deposits, of which Italy has practically none. It does not matter to Fascist imperialists that Slovenia is more than 98 per cent Slovene and that the other 2 per cent probably does not include a half-dozen Italians. They say that eighteen hundred years ago the territory now inhabited by these singing, laughing Slavic barbarians was a valued possession of the noble Roman Cæsars; hence it still belongs to Rome, to Fascist Italy. The fact that the Slovenes, then a branch of the Old Slavs, peacefully settled there when no one else occupied that area and the Roman Empire, without any fault on their part, had long been in a state of collapse, does not interest the Fascists.

While I was in Yugoslavia, a war between that country and Italy appeared imminent and certain. Since then the situation has slightly improved, but the danger continues and is one of the worst enemies of Slovenia's—and, in fact, entire Yugoslavia's—happiness and well-being.

There are two other great enemies of Slovenia's happiness. One is Yugoslavia's complicated and extremely unfortunate internal situation, to which I shall come later in this book; and the other, over-population—a problem that besets not only Slovenia, but also some other sections of Yugoslavia and, indeed, entire Europe—a problem that may be said is one of the general causes of the various upheavals on the old continent during the last two decades and in no remote future, I think, promises to produce even greater upheavals.

Taken as a whole, Slovenia is not the most densely populated section of Europe. Per square mile its population is only about 120, as against, say, Denmark's 150. But if one considers the facts that nearly two-thirds of the 1,100,000 Slovenes in Yugoslavia are peasant people, for the reason that, unlike Denmark, Slovenia has no big industries or large cities, and that over half of its geographic surface is either hilly or mountainous, suitable only for forestry or vineyards, so that the average peasant owns only about seven acres of arable soil—if one considers this, one probably can realize what the peasant is compelled to face on the economic plane of his existence.

My own family in Blato, with whose circumstances the reader by now is more or less familiar, and several other peasants there, as I have stated, are relatively well off, for the village is situated in a comparatively large and rich valley, and I believe that even some of the poor peasants in that community have more than the average share of plowable soil. If my father and mother were in Russia, the Communists there probably would call them *kulaks,* members of the peasant upper class; but even so, as I have tried to show, they have nothing too much and, in fact, barely manage to get along. Their entire tillable soil, I think, is only fifteen or twenty acres, every inch of which is carefully cultivated within the limits of their semi-primitive methods; and now, knowing this, you probably can imagine on how narrow an economic margin rests the existence of the overwhelming majority of the 145,000 peasant families in Slovenia who own only from one to four acres of land fit for cultivation.

A Slovene village has all the charms I have described,

but there is also an underside of harsh economic realities which one perceives only if one looks for them. Two of these realities are the scarcity of soil and the lack of large and profitable industries capable of absorbing the population surplus in rural districts and paying them decent wages. What industry there is in Slovenia—as in the rest of Yugoslavia—is mainly foreign-owned, and industrial workers are compelled to work under unhealthy conditions for incredibly low wages; as low, in fact, as eight, ten, twelve cents for ten, twelve, fourteen hours a day!

Song and laughter conceal many difficulties and grievances which spring from these conditions, but every once in a while the seemingly perfect village life is shaken by fierce quarrels among peasants over the possession of a few feet of ground or a tool or beast, or some such fact as that one's pig or chicken crossed the road to another's vegetable patch. Off and on such petty affairs prompt a peasant to set afire another's shed or barn, or even kill him out of revenge. The reason for such occurrences is to be sought mainly in the meager economic margin on which the peasant must function as a procreative human being, and which—what with these world-wide business panics and ever-increasing taxes —is growing smaller every year.

Once upon a time the hard-put peasant could emigrate to America for a few years, or let his son go there to earn some money in a hurry; now for more than a decade that is no longer advisable. In some respects America, with her unemployed millions, is even worse off than Slovenia.

I must emphasize, however, that, all factors considered, such crimes over petty property rights as I suggest above are remarkably few. Most of the troubles are laughed off, sung away, or drowned in wine, which Slovenia produces in abundance.

This temporary drowning of troubles is highly successful in Slovenia. When the average Slovene gets a few liters of *cvitchek* or *lutomerec* into him, he is jollier, he laughs and sings more than when sober.

His laughter is variable; sometimes mirthful and humorous, clear and outright, but often, too, mirthless and unhumorous, pain-born and pain-transcending. Of late there is more of the latter than the former. . . .

A small nation inhabiting a small country, the Slovenes' national life is perennially affected, now more, then less, by forces not of their own making and over which they have no control. Now comes a war, then a depression; now they are under the tyrannical rule of Austria, then they are "liberated" and become a part of a new country in which a small group of selfish go-getters (of whom more later) achieve complete control of the government and tell them what they may or may not write and read. Slovenia is full of fine, physically sturdy men and women, but, individually and collectively, they are impotent against the diverse wrongs and world-stupidities which they must endure; so they laugh and sing and drink, occasionally murder one another and burn down one another's barns, and, like other small nations in equal circumstances since the beginning of history make up legends about messiahs who will come to straighten things out for them.

III

The favorite and most ancient legendary messiah in the Slovene popular imagination is a peasant king called Matyazh, who, long, long ago, reigned over Slovenia wisely and justly. A friend of the people's, he always strove to be at peace with all the neighbor nations, so that the peasants in his domain were able to work their fields and raise their families in calm and contentment. But just as everything was beginning to run smoothly in Slovenia, powerful forces of evil, which originated in distant lands, suddenly swooped down on the little country and King Matyazh and his small army were overwhelmed.

But the good king did not die. Defeated, he collected the scattered remnants of his troop and marched them into the cavern of a great mountain. There are dozens of mountains all over Slovenia in which King Matyazh and his soldiers are said to have taken refuge. One of these mountains, called Krim, is about an hour's walk from Blato, and I remember that I was told about King Matyazh in my earliest boyhood and heard of him till the time I emigrated to America.

The legend has many versions. The one I remember hearing as a child has it that the cavern into which the old king and his men escaped is a vast one, ample to hold a small army. In the center of it is a marble table, where sits King Matyazh, his gray beard winding itself around the table legs. He is old and weary from the long reign and the terrible war against evil, and sleeps most of the time. Off and on he stirs a little, looks at the faithful warriors who guard him, smiles at them, then dozes off again. . . .

Some day, however, King Matyazh will rouse himself, rise from the marble table, order his army to re-form, come out of the hollow mountain, vanquish evil that now still dominates the world and Slovenia, and resume his reign of peace and good-will, under which the peasant will once more have the opportunity to quietly work at his ancient and necessary business with the soil and raise children.

How that day will come is variously prophesied in the different versions of the legend. One version maintains that the old boy will awaken after his beard has wound itself around the legs of the marble table nine times. How he will disentangle himself from the table is not stated.

Another version says that he will emerge from the cavern when the Antichrist comes and starts sowing money in the fields instead of corn, rye, and wheat.

A third rendering tells about an immense sword which hangs on the wall of King Matyazh's cavern and a powerful young hero—sometimes a native Slovene and sometimes a foreigner—who some day will find the entrance to the cave, go in, and pull the sword out of its sheath, which somehow will cause the sleeping king to bestir himself and, with the aid of the young man, lead his army against the forces of evil.

I have heard a fourth version, which is the most elaborate of the lot. It seems that on a Christmas night, with snow all around, a tall, green linden tree will suddenly spring out of the ground in front of the entrance to King Matyazh's cave. It will bloom for an hour, from midnight till one, its sweet scent filling the air all over Slovenia and beyond the borders of Slovenia, causing winter to pass and give way to spring. At one o'clock the tree will begin to shed its blossoms, whereupon the King will come out with his army, vanquish evil and bring back peace, justice, and good times. . . . "But that day," the narrator of the legend usually adds, "probably still is far off." . . .

The legend, in these various versions, has been told in Slovenia, with increasing pretense at naïveté, for four centuries or longer. The legendary King Matyazh is built around a historic character, a Hungarian ruler who once did the Slovenes a good turn, but really was no paragon of regal virtues.

Now and then, however, the plain people of the Slovene villages, smiling and singing the while groaning under their various troubles, take contemporaneous figures and facts and, with the same pretense at naïveté, half amusedly and half sadly, put them into messianic fables.

That was the case with Mr. Guggenheim and me after the newspapers had reported my decision to spend my whole year in Yugoslavia, go all over the country, and then write about what I saw.

IV

When I first heard the legend, it also had several versions. A composite version of it, as I noted it down while still in Slovenia, went something like this:

"I suppose you have all heard of this young fellow Loyzé Adamich"—as my full name is pronounced in Yugoslavia.

"He is a very bright young fellow. He was a peasant boy in Blato, then went to America, where he was a worker, a soldier, then a worker again, and finally became a writer in the English language, which is spoken in America.

"For several years Loyzé wrote and became very famous in the big world beyond the mountains and the seas. He wrote a pile of fat books, some with pictures, others without; but they say that those without are almost as good as those with. He wrote all kinds of things, but mostly about our immigrants in America who work there in the mines and factories, and became the best known Slovene in America.

"One day Loyzé received a letter. He opened it, and— what do you suppose? The letter was from a man named Gugnhaim, who is a terribly rich man in America, one of the richest in the world. His property is greater than entire Slovenia, and it is no ordinary property; it is mining land, which for miles and miles down into the earth—in fact, they say, halfway to hell—is all stiff with silver and gold, iron and copper, metals of all sorts. He is richer and more powerful than a king, this man Gugnhaim. He could buy Yugoslavia and still have money left in the bank. In some ways, in fact, he is a bigger man than any king anywhere; bigger even than the President of the United States, whom the people elect only for a few years, while Gugnhaim is Gugnhaim all the time.

"Imagine Loyzé's surprise when he saw who was writing to him! And when he read that this big man was asking him to come to see him! . . .

"Loyzé went to see him, and Gugnhaim said, 'I'm very glad you came; sit down, won't you?—there's something I want to talk to you about that probably will interest you.'

"So Loyzé, this boy from Blato, sat down, of course. Then the rich and powerful American, who is not like other rich and powerful men, offered him a cigar, and the two of them, Loyzé and Gugnhaim, smoked together for an hour or more, talking.

" 'Well, young man,' the big American then said to Loyzé, 'as you may have heard, I'm a very rich man. I have more wealth than I need. And how did I get it all? As you know, I have lots of mining land; but that isn't the answer to the question how I became so rich. Mining land is good only when the mines are opened up and worked. Well, we opened up the mines and worked them; and when I say "worked them," I mean that our workers, our miners worked them.

" 'And who were these workers, these miners? All sorts of men; but lots of them were immigrants, and some of the immigrants were your fellow countrymen from Slovenia, Croats from Croatia, Lika, Bosnia and Dalmatia, and Serbs from Serbia, Banat, and Montenegro. As a matter of fact, I shouldn't say "were," because they still are. They are the best miners I know of. They are tough and hard; they can work longer and better than anyone else. And the wealth that I now have I owe as much to them as to anyone or anything else. . . .

" 'I like your people, the Slovenes, the Croats, and the Serbs, very much. I am interested in those who are here in America and those who remain in the old country. I'd like to know all about them and about Yugoslavia from one end to the other.

" 'If I am not mistaken, you came to America,' the big man went on to say to Loyzé, 'when you were still a boy, and I don't suppose you know much about what has been going on over there since then. But you are a smart young man; you have a head on the top of your neck; and I want to make you a proposition. Go back to Slovenia, to Yugoslavia, and look over the country for me. I'd like to know everything that is going on over there—politics, books, pictures, industry, how the plain live: everything—but especially about politics and this *kriza* that I hear is bad there, too, as it is in America.

" 'I hear they have a king in Yugoslavia who may or may not be the best man for the country; also, that Mussolini is giving the Yugoslav people no end of worry these last few years. . . . Now, as I say, I don't know much about anything over there, because my mines and money keep me busy most of the time; but I'd like to know; then maybe we—you and I and other people here—can figure out if there is anything that can be done about it all.

" 'My idea is this: that you let me pay for your and your wife's trip there and back, and all your expenses while you are over there. Stay there a year, then come back and tell me all you have seen and heard—tell me honestly, just as things are—and after that, if you like, write a book about your trip so that other people in America will learn about your country also. . . .'

"Loyzé, of course, could hardly believe his ears; so he ran home to tell his wife, who is an *Amerikanka*, and then he and she immediately packed up and took a ship for Yugoslavia. Now they are here—for the time being up in Bohin somewhere, as the papers have it—and after a while they will go to other parts of Yugoslavia.

"After they have been here a year, Loyzé and his wife will return to America, and he will tell this rich and powerful man what is going on here. He will tell him about our king in Belgrade and the dictatorship—about everything, everything—and also about Mussolini and the Fascists; that they are aiming to start a war with us.

"The big man will listen to Loyzé; and some people say that after Loyzé will tell him everything and the man will know what's what and who's who in Yugoslavia, he will probably come to Europe himself. First he will go to Italy and tell Mussolini to stop annoying and worrying the people of Yugoslavia. Then he will come here and look over Slovenia, Dalmatia, Bosnia, Herzegovina, Montenegro, Croatia, and Serbia, to see what a nice and rich country we really have. Finally he will go to Belgrade and tell a few things to King Alexander and his ministers and generals.

"No one ever spoke to King Alexander and his men as forthrightly as this great American will speak to them. He will ask them all to get together in the king's palace or some other large place in Belgrade, and then he'll tell them that Loyzé Adamich has given him an earful, that he believed Loyzé—and, to his mind, they would better do away with this dictatorship, this terror—there is no need for it, no excuse for it—and give the people their rights, because the people are a good, hard-working people who deserve a good, honest government which governs in their interest—gives them a chance to live their lives in peace and contentment, to work their soil and raise their children.

"He will talk to them a long time, and at the end he will say, 'Now you fellows better do what I say—straighten out the country the way it ought to have been straightened out years ago, or get out—I say get out of the government and I'll see to it that the plain folk—the people of the villages and the working people, who I know are the finest in the world because I saw them work in my mines and Loyzé Adamich told me so—will do with their country what they have a mind to do. I don't care, they can elect a new king or a president, or try something like the Russians are trying. . . .'"

V

The fable, as I say, started in Slovenia. It was built around the few facts the people gathered about me and the founder of the Guggenheim Foundation from the newspapers. Its form was the result of the plain peasants' natural creativeness. The impulse behind it came out of their profound discontent with things as they were. In it, too, although it was told with tongue in cheek, was a dash of the European peasant's old, still living faith in America as a source of good things, a land of promise.

Later, when Stella and I traveled in Dalmatia, Bosnia,

Croatia, and the other provinces, I heard of similar fables being told there—or rather, it was the same fable with variations. I met returned immigrants who came to tell me that once upon a time they had worked in Guggenheim mines.

PART TWO

The Coast and Mountain Regions

AN ASIDE TO THE READER

Slovenia, or Carniola, to which I devote the foregoing chapters, is my old country in the narrow, intimate sense. Yugoslavia, within which Slovenia is but one-twelfth part, is my old country (since 1918) in a broader, less intimate way: for the other eleven-twelfths are rather unlike my native province.

As a matter of fact, Yugoslavia, with its 14,000,000 population, is made up of several tiny countries: Slovenia, Croatia-Slavonia, Voyvodina, Serbia, South Serbia (sometimes called Macedonia or Old Serbia), Montenegro, Bosnia, Herzegovina, and Dalmatia, each of them dissimilar from all the others in many characteristics. Because it is my native place, and I had known something about it prior to my return from America, Slovenia, naturally, interested me most, in a closely subjective and personal way. Objectively, however, Slovenia, while, one of the loveliest, perhaps is the least interesting of the several provinces. It is, as I have suggested, the most civilized.

But all the provinces have also a great deal in common. Indeed, their similarities are more fundamental than their divergencies. The people inhabiting them are all South Slavs (Yugoslavs, yugo meaning "south"). The language of Slovenia, for example, is very similar to the Serbo-Croatian, used through the rest of Yugoslavia. Slovenia is the northernmost part of the state, but many folk-sayings of the cultured Slovenes are the same as those of the primitive Serb peasants in the southernmost villages of South Serbia. Natural, spontaneous kindness and hospitality are general among the common people. Marriage and death customs in certain parts of Dalmatia and Croatia are much the same as I describe them to be in Slovenia. My mother I consider in her own way an extraordinary woman, but mothers as mothers, of course, are essentially about the same throughout the country. Had I returned from America to a village in Croatia, where culture is almost as deep as in Slovenia, my homecoming might not have differed greatly from my return to Blato.

I ask the reader to bear this in mind: for in most of the ensuing chapters I deal largely with parts of Yugoslavia, where things, customs, and situations differ from those in Slovenia.

L. A.

CHAPTER VI

Southbound

E ARLY IN JULY, LEAVING SLOVENIA, STELLA AND I TOOK
a train for Sushak, the new harbor in northern
Adriatic.

Sushak is next door to Fiume, only a narrow channel
separating the two towns. In fact, they are one city, just as
Brooklyn and New York are one. But Sushak is in Yugoslavia, while—due mainly to the Allies' secret diplomacy
during the World War and D'Annunzio's nationalistic-
imperialistic adventurism immediately after the war—
Fiume is in Italy. Sushak, although in the grip of a serious
shipping slump as a result of the world depression, seemed
a lively, almost booming port town; rather ugly in spots,
with new steel-and-concrete docks and warehouses, and
ships moored here and there. Fiume, on the other hand,
while much grander-looking, with its palaces and spacious
squares dating back to the Austro-Hungarian days, is virtually a "dead city," as Count Sforza, an ex-Minister of Foreign Affairs of Italy, describes it in one of his books.

The port of Fiume, what there is left of it, receives only
an occasional passenger-vessel from Istria, across the bay,
or tramp-steamer from Trieste or Venice. Dingy, rust-
streaked ships ride at anchor, near by. Where the Fiume
wharves touch Sushak there is a high iron fence, erected by
the Italians—a symbol, it seemed to me, of all the stupidity
and injustice of the Allied and Italo-Yugoslav diplomacy
during and since the war.

Fiume's Slavic name is Riyeka (literally "River"), after
the rivulet, called Rechina by the Croats and Fiumara by
the Italians, that flows into the sea east of the town. When

the Romans took possession of the place in the second century A.D., its name was Tarsatica, indicating that its founders and original masters were Illyrians or Celts. In the fourth century, when the Roman Empire had begun to disintegrate, the Croats came down from the Carpathians, peacefully settling in the hinterland of Fiume, and before long quietly absorbed the old inhabitants. For over a thousand years thereafter the town was predominantly Croat. In the nineteenth century, however, the Magyars, having come in control of Croatia, forcibly Magyarized and Italianized most of the population, driving the Croats who refused to become Magyars or Italians across the channel, into what eventually became Sushak.

In 1919, D'Annunzio, in search of new sensations, and his military-nationalistic coadventurers, who later developed into Mussolini's Fascists, seized the Magyar-Italian city, taking *"Italia o morte!* (Italy or death!)" as their slogan. Two years following the stupid Treaty of Rapallo, the town was made a part of Italy, along with Trieste, the whole of Istria, the city of Zara in central Dalmatia, several islands in eastern Adriatic, and parts of Slovenia (whose plight under the Fascists I have already mentioned). This separated Fiume from its *raison d'être*, its hinterland; and the hinterland was compelled to hastily develop a new harbor at Sushak, while on the other side of the iron fence the Italian and Italianized people, shouting *"Viva il Duce!"* in public, whisper among themselves that now they have both "*Italia e morte* (Italy *and* death)."

Eventually, I suppose, if the post-war imperialist-nationalist madness in European politics subsides somewhat, or gives way to some semblance of sanity and true statesmanship, Fiume will be returned to its hinterland, which for hundreds of kilometers to the east and northeast is 99 per cent Slavic. In time, perhaps, Italy will abandon the wholly unsound idea of conquering and dominating the Balkans and simultaneously tire of pumping, as she does now, lifeblood into Fiume in the form of financial subsidies which yield no return. And this goes also for Trieste and Zara, two other cities that likewise constitute a strain on the Italian people's financial energies.

II

In Sushak and Fiume we spent only a few hours altogether.

We boarded a small steamer under the Yugoslav flag whose run that summer was Venice-Trieste-Sushak, then south along the coast of Dalmatia.

Our plan—which a number of people who knew Dalmatia had helped us to work out in Slovenia—was to stop at Split, in central Dalmatia; stay there two or three weeks, perhaps a month, and visit the near-by towns of Trogir and Shibenik, the islands of Brach and Hvar; then go on down to the island of Korchula, which some claim is the birthplace of Marco Polo; from Korchula to Dubrovnik, spend at least two months there and during that time make short trips to Montenegro, Bosnia, and Herzegovina; and so on—but we weren't yet halfway to Split when we changed our minds.

Almost immediately after leaving Sushak we became acquainted with a couple of Serb immigrants from the United States, returning to Galichnik. When they told me they were from Galichnik, they seemed to expect me to know what and where Galichnik was. They acted as if Galichnik was as well known as, say, Paris or Hollywood. But I had never heard of it before, and after a while told them so. Whereupon one of them, who said he had once seen my name on a magazine cover in New York, proceeded to tell me about the place, which, it seemed, was in the mountains of Old Serbia, near the Albanian border. He talked to me about it for an hour or two, and what he told me was so interesting that, when, about halfway between Sushak and Split, both of them—they were brothers—invited Stella and me to come with them to Galichnik as their guests, we accepted their invitation.

{ 111 }

Instead of getting off at Split, we continued south on the same ship to Kotor, the ancient port in Boka Kotorska (the Bay of Kotor, or Bocche di Cattaro), where we got off with the two men from Galichnik—in our hiking clothes, for part of the trip to Galichnik, we were told, could be made only afoot or on horseback.

For reasons which will appear in the next chapter, our hosts were in a great hurry to get home; and, although we reached Kotor toward nightfall, Stella and I barely had time to check our baggage in the steamship company's office before we found ourselves in a huge Buick taxi they had hastily engaged for the trip across Montenegro, which begins immediately above Kotor, and then along the Albanian border to within about thirty-five kilometers of their destination.

It was the most breath-taking automobile ride either Stella or I had ever had. Luckily, as we learned on the way, our driver probably was one of the best in Europe. During the war he had been the personal chauffeur of the late Emperor Charles of Austria-Hungary.

In the semi-darkness, as we roared out of Kotor, we barely glimpsed some of its old Venetian architecture. "You'll see it when you come back," said one of the Serbs.

Less than an hour after we had left the ship we were climbing the serpentine highway that winds up the steep side of Mount Lovchen; one of the most perilous automobile roads in Europe, offering a view that once seen is never forgotten. Only, as the darkness rapidly thickened, we saw nothing save some lights below, in what seemed a pit, and the headlights ahead flooding the next turn, which invariably was sharper than the preceding one.

Reaching the top of Lovchen, one of the Serbs remarked, "Now we're in *Tserna Gora* (Black Mountain: Montenegro)." But we continued to see nothing but the road some thirty feet ahead and the rocks on both sides of it. It was a great relief to be off the serpentine, and the mixture of the high-mountain and sea air felt marvelously pleasant in the nostrils and the lungs.

Now and then we passed through what appeared to be a village. A dog barked. We caught sight of a human figure in the headlight's glare by the roadside. Once a man who seemed tall as a tree shouted to us a greeting, "*Sretan put!* (Happy going!)," though, of course, he had no notion who we were or where we were going.

"*Hvala liepa, Tsernogorché! Laku noch!*" shouted back our two Serbs ("Thank you, Montenegrin! Good night!").

There were no lights in the villages. We did not know, as we learned later, that most of the Montenegrin villagers were too poor to be able to afford petroleum for their lamps —if they had lamps.

The road was narrow, but fairly smooth and firm; all rock. Toward midnight we passed through what seemed a little Main Street town. Some one said, "Cetinyé"—the capital of the former kingdom of Montenegro, now the seat of the provincial government within Yugoslavia which includes Montenegro, parts of Herzegovina, and the littoral of southern Dalmatia. We did not stop.

We drove all night, perhaps at no time faster than thirty miles an hour, but it seemed twice that speed. We covered the entire width of Montenegro. On the running-boards the driver had two cans of gasoline for the return trip. We had supped aboard the ship and had with us a bag of sandwiches, two bags of fruit, a bottle of prune brandy, a canteen of water.

We talked very little. Our two Serb hosts were in a mellow mood and sang for us their national songs, whose strange mingling of melancholy and vital exultation no writer has yet been able to describe. One has to hear them.

At two o'clock one of our tires went flat, but a half-hour later we were on the way again. At four, when it suddenly began to dawn, we came to a tiny, primitive, half Albanian, half Serb hamlet in the mountains that form the boundary between Yugoslavia and Albania, and the chauffeur, as he stopped in the middle of the main and only street, said to us, "Well, this is as far as I can take you." He told me that only a few days before he had brought thus far a group of men bound for Galichnik. "They are a peculiar bunch, these Galichnikers," he whispered. "Have you been to Galichnik before?"

"No."

"Interesting!" he said, making a meaningful face. "Very strange."

We finished our sandwiches, procured some goat milk and cheese at a peasant house, and that was our breakfast. Somehow, none of us was the least sleepy. Stella and I ascribed it to the bracing mountain air and the drive which had kept us tense all night.

I looked at a tiny map of Yugoslavia I had bought on the ship. I said to Stella, "It looks like now we're pretty deep—also pretty high in the Balkans—and almost as far from Slovenia as we can be without leaving Yugoslavia."

By and by a half-dozen or so other men appeared from somewhere. They wore the same kind of clothes as our hosts: tight waistcoats, tighter trousers, and tiny caps, all of the same material, which was thick, rough, brown wool, obviously homespun and homesewn. They were also homebound Galichnikers. They had come thus far from the coast the evening before, some of them by bus, some on foot.

We still had thirty-five kilometers to go. We found a horse for Stella, whose shoes were not tough enough to cope with the sharp rocks on the mountain trails we had to cover; and the rest of us, after buying some simple food from the villagers, proceeded afoot.

We started off at seven o'clock. By mid-afternoon, after some of the toughest hiking I had ever done, we were in Galichnik.

CHAPTER VII

A Village of Lonely Women

THE VILLAGE OF GALICHNIK—NEARLY THREE THOU-
sand feet above sea-level in the barren and not easily
accessible mountains into which we headed—probably is
one of the most extraordinary civilizations in the world. It
is a village of grass widows. For approximately eleven
months out of the year, no men—aside from a priest or
two and a few octo- and nono-genarians—live in the hun-
dred-odd homes. The majority of adults in the community
are women, young, old, and middle-aged, most of them
meagerly schooled but startlingly intelligent, and not a few
possessed of unusual beauty.

Their husbands and oldest sons (if more than fifteen
years of age) are scattered over Central and Western
Europe, Greece, Rumania, and Yugoslavia, the north coast
of Africa, parts of Asia Minor, Russia, and the United
States, where, during the building seasons, they work at
highly specialized trades of masonry, stonecutting, wood-
carving, cabinet-making, and the like, earning a living for
themselves and their families *kod kuché* (back home).

II

The story of Galichnik—which, incidentally, is but one of
several such villages amid the lofty, jagged peaks and crags
on the boundary between Albania and Yugoslavia—is a
dramatic one. It goes back to the time when, more than
five hundred years ago, the Turks conquered the mediæval
Serbian Empire and, in consequence, it suddenly became
urgent for many Serbs to take their families, especially their

wives, daughters and young sons, and their movable property either into some foreign country or into the high Balkan Mountains, out of the lustful reach of the Sultan's officers and soldiers.

When the Turks seized Serbia, the subsequent founders of Galichnik were all skilled artisans, living and working in the cities and towns in the lowlands. They were organized in trade guilds and extremely proud of their skill.

The guild headmen, it seems, figured the Turks would not stay long and urged their members who had families to seek safety in the mountains, and several hundred of them took the advice. The families moved as high as they were able to go, taking with them everything they could, including sheep, the tools of their trades, and the coats-of-arms or insignia of their guilds.

Contrary to the guild headmen's expectations, however, the Turkish occupation of Serbia lasted nearly five centuries, in which period, like all the other settlements thereabouts, Galichnik became a firmly established community in spite of the terrific disadvantages of its location, and is today essentially what it was hundreds of years ago.

After it became apparent, back in the fifteenth century, that the Turks probably would stay a long time, the original settlers of Galichnik began to build their houses, and built them so well that most of them still stand today and some are inhabited by descendants of the initial families. They are stone houses, of course, most of them done in the rather clumsy, primitive style of mediæval home architecture in Balkan cities and towns. Not a few, however, are fairly spacious, comfortable, and well ventilated; and, although not anywhere near so handsome as some modern homes in the suburbs of American and European cities, all of them together form as harmonious-looking a community as perhaps any town elsewhere in Europe or in America.

Galichnik is intimately a part of the mountain scene where it stands, or rather hangs onto the side of a mountain. Its walls and roofs, made of stone and slate found on the spot, are as gray as the mountain-side. When Stella and I came there, we did not see the village till almost the minute before we were in it.

Those mountains, as I have said, are practically all stone. Only here and there one sees a clump of twisted scrub trees or a stretch of land covered with short coarse grass. What soil there is is unfit for producing anything else. And so, unable to make their living on the spot, the men of Galichnik, as of all similar villages in those mountains, commenced to go into the world (*"trbuhom za kruhom,* with stomachs seeking bread"*) centuries ago; in fact, almost immediately after they had settled there. In the course of time they became known in many parts of the world as excellent craftsmen with a strong tradition of pride in good workmanship, and until recent years, when the whole world began to groan under the worst depression in history, never had difficulty in finding employment wherever they went.

They call themselves *pechalbari* (toilers of the world). Many of them practice the same trades that their great-great-great-(etc.)-grandfathers practiced four or five hundred years ago. Struck in stone and built in over their doorways are the insignia or coats-of-arms of their ancient and honored trade guilds.

When their oldest sons become fourteen or fifteen, the fathers, according to custom which is as old as the village, take them along to Germany, France, Greece, Italy, Denmark, Egypt, Russia, or the United States. There they teach them the family trade and gradually instil in them the pride in workmanship, in the Galichnik tradition, in the accomplishments of the men of Galichnik which are strewn over the globe.

Galichnik masons and stonecutters have worked on the palaces of Versailles, the bridges of Budapest, the Cathedral of St. Stephen in Vienna, the great hotels facing the Bay of Naples, the royal palaces in Belgrade and Bucharest, the Mormon Temple in Utah, the colossal Dnieperstroi in Russia, the Empire State Building in Manhattan.

And while the men are away, the women—these grass widows—of Galichnik take care of the homes, the children, the village. They spin thread with their fingers from distaffs holding balls of wool shorn from the backs of sheep they raise on the coarse grass growing here and there about the village. The thread they then weave into woolen fabrics on hand-looms in their homes, and out of these fabrics sew their picturesque costumes, just as their great-great-great-(etc.)-grandmothers made them centuries ago.

Galichnik is, in Balkan terms, a well-to-do village (or was until the depression smote it) and the men could well afford to bring or send their women from the great cities of Europe and America the best factory-made materials for clothes, or ready-made garments, but that would be contrary to the old traditions of their community. The women of Galichnik are required to make their own clothes, and most of them like it. "Besides," one of them said to me, "if we did not weave and sew the clothes for ourselves and our families, how would we occupy our hands most of the time?" Also, to my mind, the costumes they make, while somewhat cumbersome, are as charming as and more becoming than any dress or gown their men could send or bring them from the great world of machines and mass production.

Another traditional duty the women of Galichnik have is to keep themselves lovely as long as possible. That is necessary, for, to quote an elderly woman with whom I discussed the matter, "the surest way to bring a man back from the big world, which is full of lures, is for a woman to be so sweet and attractive when he leaves her that he will, from that moment on, look forward to seeing her on his next return—and when he comes again, she must not disappoint him."

For a woman to keep herself beautiful is comparatively easy in Galichnik. The air and the sun rays in those mountains are very healthful. The food they eat is simple in the extreme. From their earliest childhood they walk a great deal up and down the steep trails about their village and leading to other villages. Their work, unlike that of most women elsewhere in the Balkans, is seldom arduous. And the result is that many of them, as already suggested, naturally are beautiful, some of them even after they pass middle age. Their features are cut into clear lines by the sharp chisel of hereditary hardship and historical experience, of which they are perennially conscious, and withal softened in expression by the deep healthiness of simple fare, good air, mountain sun, and the moderately slow but distinct and flowing, wisely routinized movement of their lives.

Most of them are of medium height, graceful in their movements, almost swanky in a restrained way. Watching them for days, while we were there, it occurred to me that their beauty was less individual or personal than a part or characteristic of the harmonious whole called the village of Galichnik and the mountains about it. Both Stella and me they impressed as something perfect; but perfect, we thought, only as long as they stayed where they were.

Resting, or even while working at their looms, they sing old, rather melancholy songs, full of longing, about their loneliness and their husbands' and sons' labors in far countries. But actually they are not what one could call unhappy women. Certainly not miserable. The loveliness of their faces, like their songs, has a touch of sadness, which, however, is not individual or acute on a personal plane. It is a communal, traditional, almost formal sadness—a matter of centuries and of a common lot, which the women understand and accept.

When they don't sing, they as likely as not narrate to their children the endless stories of Galichnik from its inception to the present day. These tales, simple in themselves, are a vast unwritten saga whose scope in time and space, as well as in sheer heart interest, perhaps surpasses that of any saga between book covers.

Some of the stories, dealing with the village and the men's adventures in the world, the women retail in vivid poetic language. Not a few of the stories are tragic, almost Greek in quality. They tell of men who left Galichnik and never returned because they were killed in accidents while at work in France, Spain, Egypt, or the United States, or —worse yet—succumbed to some powerful lure of the big world which caused them to forget the village.

These, briefly, are the chief factors in the continued existence of the curious village even now when Old Serbia has been liberated from the Turk—first, the whole rich and dramatic history of Galichnik which the women keep alive in the heart and mind of one generation after the other; second, the old Galichnik tradition of pride in excellent workmanship and the resultant world fame of the Galichnik *pechalbari* among builders and contractors the world over; third, the deep beauty of Galichnik women, which helps to bring back the men; and fourth (which links together the other three), the essential tragedy inherent in the origin and centuries-old circumstances of the place.

Many Galichnik songs and tales, as I say, are sad, even tragic, but their power lies just in that fact. Nothing has a stronger appeal for the Serb—and generally for the Slavic —mind and soul than tragedy: and there is nothing morbid in that. Serbs, both men and women, thrive on it. They exult in it. It makes them strong. Out of the defeat at the hands of the Turks in the fifteenth century they—not professional bards or poets, but the nation as a whole—produced an endless, epic song-poem which they sang, hummed, and declaimed for five hundred years, till Serbia was liberated and the present Yugoslavia came into existence. The Galichnik folk are a chip of this strangely vital and spirited Serb nation (of which more later in this book) and the story of their village, as I briefly suggest it here, is a fragment of the saga of the tragic defeat and triumph of the Serb and other Yugoslav peoples.

IV

Once a year, between the 1st and 15th of July, most of the men return from the big world. Those working in Europe, in Asia Minor, or in North Africa get home yearly; those in America and the distant parts of Russia return but every two or three years.

When Stella and I arrived in Galichnik, the men had begun to return. The women, of course, were at their best, and ditto their houses. There was much restrained excitement, rejoicing.

There is a post-office in the village which also handles the mail for other communities in the region, and on mail days, which come twice weekly, the tight little square in front of it was thronged by eager, gorgeously attired women and their children, waiting for messages from their home-bound husbands and fathers. It was an intensely human scene. However, only a few of the men write ahead; most of them just come; but the women gather in front of the post-office, anyhow.

Two routes lead to Galichnik. The distance from Skoplyé (or Uskub), in South Serbia, is thirty-odd miles as the crow flies, and a little more from Cetinyé; but, either way, the trip takes nearly two days, unless one travels by car, as we did, which few *pechalbari* can afford. They usually return in small groups, for most of them carry on their persons their year's earnings and the mountains along the way are not altogether innocent of Albanian bandits; though in recent years, Stella and I were told, few attacks on the returning men have occurred.

In America, in Greece, in Germany, wherever they go, they wear the clothes of those countries; when they return to Galichnik, however, they always arrive dressed in home-spun village costumes handmade by their wives or mothers.

The trip was a strenuous one, but once we got there we never regretted making it. As in Slovenia, the people are hospitable to a fault. When they learned that I was by birth a Yugoslav who became an American writer, and that my wife was an *Amerikanka* born in New York, we became virtually guests of the whole community. A few of them had read about me in the papers. Nothing within their means was too good for us. In the course of the two weeks we stayed there we had to visit practically every home and in each take at least a sip of wine or brandy.

I could talk Serbian, but Stella, to whom that language is as distant as Siamese, was not left out of all conversation. Not a few Galichnikers, though their formal schooling is slight, know two, three, and even four languages, including English. In fact, during the few weeks in the summer when the *pechalbari* are back, Galichnik is, perhaps, one of the most cosmopolitan communities in the world. Talking with the men, as they continued to arrive till the majority of women ceased to be grass widows, I learned of things in Greece, Italy, Turkey, Egypt, Austria, Germany, Spain, and Russia. Several accounts of social, economic, and political conditions in the various countries seemed to me as intelligent as anything one could find in the average European newspaper or magazine.

Since their well-being and prosperity depend to a great extent upon the state of world economy, their interest in the general economic crisis and the possibilities of recovery was intense. They assumed that as an American writer I had some valid views on the subject, and daily for hours at a stretch I had anywhere from ten to twenty men around me. They were especially eager to know about things in the United States, both those who had and those who had never been in America. They sensed that world recovery, so important to Galichnik, depended a lot upon the ability of the United States to raise itself from the slump.

I was asked again about the Lindbergh baby. Was it really true? Could such a thing really happen "under God's sun?" . . . (I had been asked about this case at every turn in Slovenia and, later, everywhere else I went in Yugoslavia. I tried to tell what I knew about it, explain it, but few could understand. Peasant women shook their heads slowly in speechless horror.) . . .

I learned that at least two men from Galichnik were working on the Radio City buildings in New York, then under construction. We met their wives, two of about a dozen women whose husbands had not returned home that summer.

While we were there another grass widow learned that she had become a real widow. In an accident on a job in Innsbruck, Austria, her man had been killed only a few days before he planned to lay off and return home.

But, as far as I could discern, this was the only dark note in Galichnik during our stay. There was much feasting and gayety. On the tables were fine Dalmatian wines and (for Galichnik) rare foods bought at the local store, which had had them shipped up for the occasion from Skoplyé.

The feasting and gayety, however, were nicely balanced. In fact, one of the keynotes of life in Galichnik is balance, self-control. There are no extremes in manner or speech, no excesses in eating, drinking, or anything else.

I had a feeling that this virtue was due more to the women than to the men. They *must* be well-balanced and self-controlled. Their lives depend on that. As they walk the rocky, precipitous trails around their village, a slight misstep may mean death; and those trails are symbolical of their lives in general.

In this connection I might mention that the morals in Galichnik are of the highest and strictest. One of the local sayings is, "When a man comes home after a long absence, he expects to find everything in order." And the men, in their turn, generally are as faithful to their wives as the women are to them.

{ 123 }

V

The men's return is the climax of a year's life in Galichnik. But there is a climax within the climax—the communal wedding day, when all the couples married that year are wedded simultaneously. This occurs on the same day every year: July 12th.

When we were there, sixteen couples entered matrimony. All the bridegrooms were from Galichnik. All but two were regular *pechalbari* who had just come home to be married. The other two were sheepmen whose flocks' grazing-ground was several hours distant from the village, and so were hardly ever home, either. Half of the brides were from Galichnik, the other half from near-by villages. One was a young widow with two children; her husband had been killed in an accident in Alexandria, Egypt, two years before. One of his friends married her.

The wedding ceremony, performed by a priest of the Eastern Orthodox Church, was picturesque but brief; the ensuing communal feast, however, lasted three days and included much singing, the like of which Stella and I had never heard; much beating of drums and playing of fifes, and dancing of *kolo*, the Yugoslav folk dance. It was what one of the men from America called the year's "grand whoopee."

On the last day of the wedding festivities I talked with an octogenarian who in his younger days had worked on buildings and bridges in eleven different countries. He said, "In two weeks nearly all of these men, including, I suppose, most of the bridegrooms, will be gone again—to Egypt, to Italy, to Constantinople, Prague, Barcelona, New York, Philadelphia. The women, including these brides, will once more be alone. And"—he chuckled—"nine months hence anywhere from fifty to eighty babies will be born in the village in the same week; from five to ten new-born babies a day; and their fathers will not see them till four months later, next summer, when they come home again. . . . That is how life goes on here in Galichnik."

CHAPTER VIII

Montenegro in the Daytime

NOW AND THEN, DURING OUR TWO WEEKS IN GALICHNIK, we thought of going down toward Skoplyé, to see some other parts of South Serbia, which we had been told in Slovenia probably was the most primitive and picturesque part of Yugoslavia; but the fact that we had our baggage in Kotor (along with other personal reasons) made us decide to return to Dalmatia by the same route we had come up, and visit the lowlands of South Serbia later.

From Galichnik we departed early one morning in late July. Perhaps half the population was on the main street to bid us *"Sretan put!"* and eventual return. Women gave Stella gifts, mostly pieces of handwork, which we strapped to her saddle. Then about twenty people walked with us down the trail for several kilometers, a young man leading Stella's horse, lest the animal stumble on the sharp stones.

Our Galichnik hosts, who were immediately returning to America, and two other *pechalbari*—one going back to his job in Trieste and the other I forget where—accompanied us the whole way to the Albano-Serb hamlet on the highway, where we arrived just in time, late in the forenoon, to catch the bus running from points in South Serbia to Cetinyé. Of course, no cars driven by ex-imperial chauffeurs were available there.

The bus was two-thirds full. With the exception of Stella and me, all the passengers were *pechalbari*. Of these, four were Galichnikers; the other five or six came from other villages in those mountains—Serbs, Albanians, and men who were mixtures of both. Nearly all the Galichnik *pechalbari*, as I have said, are highly skilled artisans with rich traditions in their various trades; most of those who come from villages nearer the Albano-Yugoslav border, however, are common laborers, railway porters, hodcarriers, muckers, and the like, many of them too poor to be able to afford a bus ride or transportation of any sort whatever. Once a year, or every other year, they walk home from Italy, Greece, Dalmatia, Austria, or wherever they work, then back again: hundreds of kilometers each way. Our bus passed scores of them on the road—tall, lean, sinewy men, possibly not a coin in their tight-fitting, homespun breeches. Most of them had been home but a few days, to see their wives and insure the continuation of their virile race and their grotesque economic problem, which kills many individuals who attempt to solve it, but somehow keeps the race tough and triumphant.

II

The rugged, rocky mountain scenery was weirdly beautiful, as we rode Cetinyé-ward that afternoon, and our fellow passengers sang their vital, melancholy songs, as weird and beautiful as the mountains. Had it not been for this beauty, the bus trip would have been a dreary experience indeed. The machine was a prehistoric affair, roomy enough, but held together by all sorts of ropes, chains, wires, and braces, a squeal or groan at every joint of its frame. Unlike the elegant taxi that had brought us up, it had no snubbers; its springs were weak, and the driver, a young Montenegrin, had a rare talent for hitting every rut in the road and missing the precipices by little more than a hair. Behind a boiling radiator we bumped, jugged, swayed along, now up, then down, at probably less than eight miles an hour. The heat from the motor added to the heat of the day. The exhaust fumes somehow found their way into the bus. Luckily, we got a flat tire approximately every two hours, and, while the Montenegrin was busy fixing it our bones enjoyed a welcome rest from being bounced in our seats. Of course, what was close to torture to us was hardly mild discomfort to the *pechalbari*, even to the Galichnik "aristocrats" who were more or less used to the comforts of Western civilization.

After the second puncture, I asked the driver when he expected to get us to Cetinyé. He said, *"Ako Bogu drago sutra.* (If it pleases God, tomorrow.)"

"What time tomorrow?"

He shrugged his shoulders, "Tomorrow."

Late in the afternoon we stopped in a large village. Stella and I were hungry, tired to death, and half sick from gasoline fumes; although I, trying not to disgrace myself before my fellow Yugoslavs, pretended otherwise. Stella made no attempt to disguise the fact that she was nearly "all in."

For a few dinars we bought some cheese, cornbread, and goat milk, and as we ate by the roadside, lo! there came down the road a noisy, topless old Ford roadster, headed in the same direction as we. A chunk of bread in one hand, a ball of cheese in the other, I jumped up, swung my arms, and yelled to the driver to stop.

He stopped.

Excusing myself for stopping him, I inquired where he was going.

"Podgorica," he answered, curtly. Podgorica is a town on the way to Cetinyé.

He was a young man with sun- and wind-burnt face. His accent on "Podgorica" indicated that he was not a Serb, and it occurred to me he probably was a Slovene. I asked him if I was right. He nodded, rather impatiently. I introduced myself, then his face lit up a bit; he probably had been reading the newspapers; and when I asked him, he said he would be glad to give us a lift.

So, although our bus fare was paid to Cetinyé, we hastily took leave of our Galichnik hosts and friends, wished them all, including the driver, *"Sretan put!"* and drove off with the Slovene.

In point of comfort, the ancient Ford wasn't much better than the bus, but it went at least three times faster; fast enough, at any rate, to leave behind its exhaust fumes. Unlike most Slovenes, the driver was a taciturn young fellow. Although tired as I hadn't been for years, I made some attempts at conversation, but about all I got out of him was that he was a sanitary engineer in the government health service—the Ford was a government car. He obviously did not want to talk, but, on closer study, did not look to be normally the quiet kind. It occurred to me that he probably was in some trouble—a girl or something—or on an urgent official errand. Tensed over the wheel, he drove as fast as he could within the limits of comparative safety. Whatever the reason for his hurry, however, we were grateful for it. I never found out who he was, exactly.

Toward midnight, seven hours after he had picked us up, we came to an ill-lighted town. "Podgorica," said the young sanitary engineer, then stopped in front of a building. "This is the only hotel here that deserves to be called a hotel." He blew his horn several times, more impatiently each time.

Weary and half sick, we barely managed to get out of the machine. The fellow helped me get our bundle of Galichnik gifts from the back of the car.

Finally a tall old man bearing a lamp appeared in the hotel's dark doorway, asked who we were and what we wanted, and learned from the man in the Ford that we were two very famous people from America and he should put us up as well as he could.

I thanked the young man for his kindness—very inadequately, no doubt, for I was all but falling asleep on my feet. Saying he was glad he had been of service to us, he quickly drove off. We never saw him again. . . . Later it occurred to me to write to the director of the provincial health service and, by describing how and where I had met him, find out the young man's name and address, then thank him for the lift more adequately; but on second thought I decided not to. For all I knew, such an inquiry from me might get him into some difficulty. . . .

About noon the next day we awoke in a dingy little room, hungry and stiff all over, but at the same time gloriously refreshed.

That afternoon we stayed in Podgorica, then took a car to Cetinyé, and spent several more days in Montenegro, visiting villages between Mount Lovchen and Lake Scutari.

III

For many decades now Montenegro has been more or less a joke in the minds of ill-informed people living in large, so-called civilized countries. Comic operas and motion pictures have been produced dealing with life—especially the court life—in Tsernagora. Even nowadays foreigners incline to be amused when they come up from Dalmatia in comfortable autos for a day's visit.

Really, however, the Black Mountain—so called because of the dark-leafed shrubs which here and there cover the stony peaks and ridges—is anything but comic. On the contrary, basically and essentially, it is a tragic country—but not in any morbid or maudlin sense. When one really tries to understand the tragedy of Montenegro, one is not moved to tears, but to deep respect, for the people caught in it. Tennyson, I think, caught some of the quality of Montenegro in the following little-known lines:

They rose to where their sovereign eagle sails,
    They kept their faith, their freedom, on the height,
    Chaste, frugal, savage, armed by day and night
Against the Turk, whose inroad nowhere scales
Their headlong passes, but his footstep fails,
    And red with blood the Crescent reels from fight
By thousands down the crags and through the vales.
O smallest among peoples! rough rock-throne
    Of Freedom! warriors beating back the swarm
    Of Turkish Islam for five hundred years.

Great Tsernagora, never since thine own
Black ridges drew the cloud and broke the storm
Has breathed a race of mightier mountaineers.

And Gladstone, in 1895, said that, in his opinion, Montenegro exceeded in glory both Marathon and Thermopylæ and all the military traditions in the world, for, although one of the tiniest countries in existence, it successfully fought a war of defense against a great empire for hundreds of years.

Montenegro is an extension of Galichnik. Settlements of Serb clans existed there—in the few and tiny fertile sections—already in the twelfth century, when the region was called first Duklya and later Zeta; but Tsernagora, as its inhabitants commenced to name it in the fifteenth century, really began to come into existence late in the fourteenth century, after the battle of Kossovo, which resulted in the fall of the Serbian Empire and forced great bands of Serbs —men, women, and children—to seek refuge in the mountains northwest of Galichnik, close to the Albanian border. But unlike the Galichnikers, these refugees were soon discovered by Turks operating from Albania and the Adriatic. Compelled to fight almost unceasingly in order to preserve their freedom from the time they reached the Black Mountain to nearly the present day, they could not become *pechalbari*. They had to be constantly in Tsernagora.

Back in Old Serbia they had had a comparatively high civilization: good houses, art, literature, silk garments, delicious foods, and at that time one of the then most advanced forms of government. Now, hurled by fate on top of barren mountains and forced to make war their main occupation, they swiftly reverted to primitive conditions of existence on the material plane, but preserved—so far as possible amid ceaseless warfare and with meager resources—their culture, especially their "heart culture," which included hospitality and a profound sense of values based upon virtues in nature.

The highest of these values was freedom. Aided by the

rocky mountains, they never completely lost their independence, till after the World War, when Montenegro became a part of Yugoslavia. But in consequence of their endless warring, the little country—except the larger towns, such as Podgorica and Cetinyé—today is almost as innocent of civilization as it was centuries ago.

However, no citizen of the United States, even if he lives in the best imaginable circumstances, loves his rich and powerful country more than the average Montenegrin loves his poor, tiny, rocky Montenegro. Foreigners, with their different sets of values (if any), find it hard to understand this patriotism and incline to consider the Black Mountaineer more or less a fool and a semi-wild man. They smile or laugh at him and crack jokes about him. As a matter of fact, he is neither a fool nor a semi-wild man. He is, to use a slang phrase, a tough guy, agile and hardy, fearless, impatient of restraint; and, moreover, a poet and philosopher despising life when it is separated from freedom.

When Bernard Shaw, visiting Tsernagora in 1929, was asked by a native what he thought of their stony mountains, he replied: "I don't think anything of them. If you people do, you must all be philosophers."

"But," added the Montenegrin who told me this Shavian wisecrack, "if we are philosophical about our rocks and mountains, there is a reason. For centuries they have been a factor in our struggle for freedom; except for them we could not have beaten back the Turk time after time; and they are precious to us also because we have spilled much blood over them."

As poets the Montenegrin has added vastly to the wealth of Yugoslav national poetry (of which more later in this book). Indeed, it would be hard to say in which field he excels more—fighting, philosophizing, or versifying. It probably would not be inaccurate to say that these three fields are to him but one field.

The Montenegrin character was excellently summarized

in the lives and works of two outstanding sons of the Black Mountain, Peter Petrovitch Nyegosh and King Nicholas, or "Nikita."

IV

Nyegosh, who lived in the first half of the nineteenth century, was Montenegro's one great poet; although not generally known, perhaps one of the world's greatest poets. For twenty years (1830 to 1850) he was the Bishop and Ruler of Montenegro; in those days the head of the Orthodox Church was also the head of the state. The Montenegrins had just defeated the Turk in a great battle, and in the ensuing period of peace Nyegosh, a true son of Tsernagora, devoted much of his time to philosophy and verse, only, unlike his illiterate countrymen, who composed their poetry as they recited or sang it in public, he wrote his pieces on paper.

He was one of the few educated men in the country. He had been to Russia, Austria, and Germany; knew several foreign languages, and had read Shakespeare, Byron, Goethe, Milton, Lamartine, Dante and Petrarch. A foreign visitor described him as "tall, of good stature, magnificent appearance, kind and courteous," which can be said of most Montenegrins to this day.

The greater part of his work is in the blank verse of Yugoslav folk-poetry, mainly in the trochaic pentameter. His principal poems, each a full-length book, are "The Light of the Microcosm" and "The Mountain Wreath." In both of them—the latter recently translated into English by James W. Wiles and published in England—Nyegosh simultaneously portrays and expresses the Montenegrin character, mind, and soul. They are a superb record of the great, awesome tragedy of the Serb race and of Montenegro; and, symbolically, of human existence in general.

In the "Microcosm" poem, which reminds one of Milton's "Paradise Lost," Nyegosh conceives of life, at least as lived in Montenegro, as a nightmare:

Man has been thrown into a heavy sleep,
And terrible visions come to him,
And he can scarce discern
Whether he is of them or apart.

"The Mountain Wreath," a long dramatic poem of vast conception and suggestive of Shakespeare, is his masterpiece. It contains a passage worth quoting (in Mr. Wiles' English version) in this connection. . . . Toward the end of the seventeenth century, several Montenegrin chieftains are conversing on top of Mount Lovchen. One of them, Voivoda Drashko, has just returned from Venice, where he had gone on an official mission to the Doge, to procure a supply of powder. The others question him about his trip, and his replies are a powerful criticism, from the Montenegrin viewpoint, of civilization outside of Tsernagora and an indirect, humorous statement of the Montenegrin values and keen sense of superiority to so-called civilized people. The passage follows, in part:

KNEZ ROGAN

Tell us something, Drashko, of what you've seen in
    Venice!
What sort of people found you over there?

VOIVODA DRASHKO

Brother, many a handsome man I saw,
But ten times more of ugly folk;
Too ugly much to look upon!
Many a rich man was there too,
Whose wealth indeed had made him mad,
Made him like a silly child.
On every hand the poor did stand,
Toiling hard with sweat of brow,

Simply to earn a crust of bread.
Two men I saw between them bearing
Some kind of female on their shoulders.
Seated in chair so round and lazy,—
She weighed close on three hundred pounds!
All through the streets they carried her,
In daylight broad now here, now there,—
Regardless of all manly honor,
Simply to earn a crust of bread.

KNEZ YANKO

What sort of houses have they, Drashko?

VOIVODA DRASHKO

No finer houses in the world!
But with it all is pain and need;
All closely pack'd are they together,
'Mid odors bad and noisome air;
Pale and bloodless, too, their faces. . . .

.   .   .   .

SERDAR RADOGNA

On everything we've questioned thee;—
But the Doge, Drashko, didst thou see?

VOIVODA DRASHKO

Him saw I, brother, as I do see thee now.

RADOGNA

And was he . . . What was he really like?

VOIVODA DRASHKO

Why! just a man of middle size!
If his position weren't so high,
Sure he need fear no jealousy!

.   .   .   .

{ 134 }

What kind of food gave they to thee?
Didst thou get good dishes, Drashko?

VOIVODA DRASHKO

'Mong them I saw no food save bread;
Though true they serve some sort of sweets;
Three hours tasting they think makes a meal.
Two out of three of all their men,
Though still quite young, are lacking teeth,
For they eat sweetmeats all day long!

. . . .

They like better egg or chicken
Than sheep's flesh or ball of cheese;
Untold the quantity of chickens
That they eat up within a year!
From this lordly life they die,
With bellies big and no moustaches,
Their craniums dusted o'er with powder
And, like ladies, dangling rings at ear!
When they reach their thirtieth year,
They get a face like some old hag,
Too ugly are they to be seen;
And even should they climb a stair,
All pale they grow and linen-white,
And something rattles in their throat,
As if had come their dying night!

The poet now is buried on top of Mount Lovchen in a tomb he had built for himself shortly before his death, in 1850. It is the principal monument in Montenegro, visited yearly by thousands from all over Yugoslavia. Stella and I went up with a small group of "pilgrims," and, looking down, saw to the west the Adriatic Sea, to the east the whole of Montenegro.

Like Nyegosh, Nikita, too, was representative of some of the good qualities of the Montenegrin people, but also of some of the worst.

He was the Black Mountain's first lay ruler, initially calling himself Prince, then King. He ruled for fifty-seven years and in that period, although lacking any broad education in statecraft, organized the country into a semblance of modern state. He made the hamlet of Cetinyé into a tidy little town and built himself a "palace," which still stands today and looks like a neglected town hall in a small American community. Every Sunday afternoon he dispensed patriarchal justice under an elm tree near the palace. All his life he wore the national costume and seldom left his country.

His subjects called him *gospodar* (boss) and he greeted them by their first names. He was not only their supreme judge and ruler, but their physician and horse doctor, principal poet and orator, commander-in-chief, one and only postmaster, theater director, and minister of finance, war, foreign affairs, the interior, and education. He combined in his person practically all the activities of state, and Tsernagora was the most intimate country in the world.

Nikita, though primitive in many respects, was a man of rare gifts. His memory was astounding. By the middle of his reign he knew by sight, first name, and surname, every man over thirty years of age in his country. A tireless worker, he personally kept track of everything. If you, a foreigner, came to Cetinyé and registered at the Grand Hotel, which he owned, he knew your name and business ten minutes later. If you wanted to send a registered letter, the clerk at the post-office, who was an ex-warrior with a wooden leg and blind in one eye, sent you over to the "palace," for the king kept all stamps of higher denomination in his private safe. And when he sold you a stamp, as likely as not he asked you to sit down with him and have a drink and some food. If you had any claim to distinction at all, in whatever field, he bestowed an order on you.

He was handsome even in his old age—tall, strongly built, dark-eyed, as a rule kindly-expressioned, embodying in his own person all the poetic tradition of courtesy and courage of his people. Once he said, "My country is a wilderness of stone; it is arid, it is poor, but I adore it. If I were offered the whole of the Balkan Peninsula or even entire Europe in exchange, I should not say one word more than, 'Leave me Tsernagora.'" And in saying this he doubtless was wholly sincere—at least at the moment.

His wife, the queen, kept house in the "palace." Mornings, with her basket and petroleum-can, she went shopping in the market place. She bore him ten daughters and three sons. The boys never amounted to anything; the girls, however, were famous beauties. One married the present King of Italy; another Prince Peter Karageorgevitch, who later became King of Serbia and whose son Alexander now is King of Yugoslavia; a third a wealthy Russian archduke; a fourth an Austrian aristocrat.

Nikita was the owner-editor of his country's only newspaper and composed two patriotic metrical dramas and the national hymn, in which he expressed the mountain shepherds' longing for the green meadows of the lowlands. Before becoming a ruler at eighteen, he had been a shepherd.

Politically, the old man was interesting. (I describe Nikita here at some length because, although dead, he still lives in his grandson, the present King of Yugoslavia, who has inherited important phases of his political character, and whom I portray later in this book.) To an English visitor he once declared that he was a liberal. "There is no objection," he said, "to personal rulers and potentates being liberals, but all good subjects in a well-run state should be conservative, and I intend that mine shall, at all events. . . . Should any subject of mine agitate for anything at all, I would very soon show him who was master here." He was an absolute autocrat, a tyrant, with the charming, democratic manner common to most tyrants.

One of the central points of his domestic policy was that no man in his country, with the assumed exception of himself, should become prosperous. Opulence might mean power, and he wanted no competition. As for the people in general, his aim was to keep them in a state of "wholesome poverty"; then they were easiest to govern. Of course, to carry out this policy in Montenegro was no difficult problem. The productiveness of the entire country, with its 200,000 population, is not equal to that of a good-sized Texas ranch.

A "wholesome poverty" of the people was desirable to Nikita for other reasons. He derived more bountiful secret subsidies paid him by intriguing governments—Russia, Italy, and Austria—than he could have procured by scientific taxation and highest industrial development possible in Montenegro, and these foreign bounties would have ceased if he could not exhibit visible evidences of national destitution. Also, if he attempted taxation, he would lose much of his popularity with the people.

In times of peace thousands of Montenegrins emigrated to America; Nikita afforded them no opportunity to prosper at home. He discouraged initiative on the part of anybody. In fact, he and the traditions of Montenegro were against men doing any work at home. Traditionally, the Black Mountain was a country of *yunaki* (professional "heroes") warriors, poets, and philosophers; and in Nikita's and the "heroes'" own eyes sordid labor tended to spoil and degrade a *yunak*. . . . Even to this day few Montenegrins deign to work in Montenegro; all hard toil is done by women. Once they come down from their mountains, however, even if they go only to some other part of Yugoslavia, many of them become veritable demons at work. In America, for instance, some of the best, certainly the toughest, coal miners and steel workers are Montenegrins. . . .

To keep his state going according to his ideas, Nikita

constantly begged the big powers for subsidies. He probably was the greatest "chiseler" that ever lived. This made him and his country a joke in the chancelleries and editorial-rooms of entire Europe. A thousand fictitious beggar tricks were attributed to him by international gossip, but that was hardly necessary. Nikita invented enough genuine schemes to fill a chapter. He made himself and his country ideal comic-opera and film-play material, and as a result to this day the world at large knows mainly the funny, ridiculous side of Tsernagora.

The Tsar of Russia, for years his main stand-by, sent him money and shiploads of grain for his subjects. Nikita disbursed the money as he saw fit. Much of it went into his personal funds, with which he educated his children in foreign countries. In fact, he usually treated the public treasury as his private purse. The grain he occasionally distributed free of charge, but often, too, sold it to his subjects for money earned by their kin in the copper mines of Montana and iron foundries in Pennsylvania. Much of his loot he deposited in foreign banks and probably saw nothing wrong in such a procedure. After all, he was king! In this he was typical of ruling politicians throughout the Balkans (and, of course, elsewhere). Although they are of the people and genuinely love their various countries, their tendency is to plunder and trick their own flesh and blood as soon as they attain to power.

His end came with the World War. During that conflict, trying to save himself and continue the independence of his country, he tried to play into the hands of both the Allies (especially Russia) and the Central Powers (especially Austria), and finally betrayed both and got in trouble with a good many of his followers. When, after the conclusion of hostilities, Yugoslavia was created, the Black Mountain was logically absorbed into the new state. In 1921, Nikita, a bitter, disgraced octogenarian, surrounded only by a handful of his loyal fellow scoundrels and patriots, died an exile in Paris.

At first sight, Tsernagora is the same today as it was twenty or even a hundred years ago. It is as poor as ever. Rocks, rocks, rocks. Sheep, goats, and scrawny cattle snatch up every blade of coarse mountain grass as soon as it sticks its point above the stony bleakness, meantime nibbling at the leaves of scrub trees and bushes. In little gullies and ravines we came upon "fields," tiny patches of more or less fertile soil, few larger than a city lot and most considerably smaller, hidden away among cliffs, as if they were something very precious, and therefore to be concealed. On such "fields," growing corn, tobacco, cabbage, and potatoes, and often communally owned, subsist anywhere from one to ten families.

"But how can they?" wondered Stella.

The cruel and simple answer is that their wants, restricted by centuries of lack and struggle, are extremely small. Thousands of families do not see the equivalent of five dollars in cash throughout the year. In many homes there are no matches or (as already mentioned) petroleum. Salt and sugar are luxuries. Tens of thousands of persons, especially women, live on a meager piece of crudely baked cornbread and a little sheep or goat cheese a day. Both men and women, if necessary, can go foodless from two days to a week without thinking they are starving. They get hungry, to be sure, but their proud bearing is unchanged, their energy unimpaired. In wartime Montenegrin soldiers frequently went without a substantial meal for months, and endured hardships as soldiers of no other country could endure.

Here, as in some of the other sections of Yugoslavia, child mortality is very high. Practically no infant gets anywhere near what well-to-do American mothers consider proper nourishment for a baby. The result is that every fourth or fifth child dies in its first year and every third or fourth between the ages of one and five (though of late this condition is slightly improving). The surviving children, however, having in them the blood, nerves, and sinews of their parents, become tough as nails almost before they emerge from the cradle—if they ever have a cradle! After that the continuous hard life keeps them tough, unless, as is frequent, they develop tuberculosis and die in their twenties. Many of them, especially the males, grow up incredibly tall, graceful, and handsome in a somber way. Stella and I came upon giants measuring from six-feet-six to nearly seven feet. Not a few live to be a hundred. In Montenegro there is as yet little interference with the law of the survival of the fittest.

The woman's position in Tsernagora is not much better than it was fifty years ago. Living in a patriarchal society which till lately was in constant state of war, they are treated by men as their mental and physical inferiors. They certainly do not compare favorably with the men either in looks or stature. As already said, they do all the hard work, just as they had been doing it through all the centuries of warfare, and about the only recognition they get for this comes in the form of contempt. Their men really respect them only as "mothers of Montenegrins"—that is, mothers of *male* Montenegrins. For a woman to give birth to a girl is not one-tenth the creditable achievement that it is to bear a boy. If she bears only daughters, she is a disgrace to her husband and treated accordingly. When I asked a man how many children he had, he said four, but I found later that he had six—he did not count his two daughters! When a son is born, the old-time, conventional Montenegrin father fires six shots in the air, whereupon all men who hear the shots exclaim, "May he be a hero! Luck to him!" When a girl is born, no shots are fired.

Men wear gorgeous costumes, which frequently represent the major part of their wealth. They are made (by their women, of course) to last them through most of their adulthood. They consist of dark-green or blue, gold-embroidered woolen coats reaching to the knees which in recent years sometimes are abbreviated to short jackets, blue breeches with enormous baggy seats, knee-high boots, and tiny black-and-red caps, also embroidered with gold on top. The red in the caps symbolizes the blood that has been spilled in Montenegro; the black, the fatal battle of Kossovo; and the five gold bands, the five centuries of struggle for freedom.

The women's costumes are not half so showy as the men's. Working, they usually wear the drabbest garb imaginable, most often black or dark blue. Their holiday outfits, which almost invariably last them from marriage till death, include long sleeveless woolen coats of the most delicate shades, with heavy gold embroidery of exquisite design and finish all over it. Under the coats they wear cotton, silk, or satin waists and skirts. Their caps, of the same design and coloring as the men's, are somewhat smaller, covering only the tops of their heads.

The Montenegrin houses are extremely primitive, inside and out, perhaps no better than they were a hundred years ago. Only a few families in such towns as Cetinyé and Podgorica, who in late years have raised themselves to what they consider prosperity, enjoy a suggestion of modern comfort and refinement.

In their everyday life the Montenegrins are a sober people. To get drunk is a disgrace. But the men smoke a great deal; one of their chief products, especially around Podgorica, is tobacco. Among the general run of people there is no crime such as we know it in America. People take things when they are hungry, but that is not stealing, only "taking" (*uzimati*). Unlike in Albania or Macedonia, there are no highwaymen. Nowhere in Europe is it safer for a stranger to travel than in Montenegro. Everybody is hospitable. To a total stranger they give their last piece of bread, their only bed for the night. Stella and I received some sort of gift wherever we came; if nothing else, a ball of goat cheese or a piece of dried goat meat and a little bread.

There is a story about a Montenegrin sentenced to death whom the king asked, just before he was to be shot, "Have you ever been in a worse predicament than this?"—"Yes," answered the condemned man.—"And when was that?"—"Well, one day a man came to see me from afar and I was so poor that I had nothing in the house to offer him." . . .

Another story about Montenegrin hospitality concerns George Bernard Shaw. When he visited Cetinyé they made him a guest of the town and before he departed presented him with a gold-embroidered Montenegrin costume worth several thousand dinars; and later, when some one asked him how he liked the people of Tsernagora, he said: "Oh, I like them fine! In fact, I have just written to all my friends in England that the Montenegrins are a very marvelous people, extremely wealthy, but so generous and hospitable that they will soon all be poor. They paid my transportation and hotel bills and gave me a suit of clothes so splendid that it is beyond description. So, writing to my friends in England, I urge them all to hurry and come to Montenegro before its people's hospitality bankrupts the country."

An interesting phenomenon we witnessed in Tsernagora was the peasants' and goatherds' ability to communicate with one another at great distances without any instruments. When we first saw a man yelling, with no one else anywhere in sight, we thought he was crazy, but the explanation was that he was talking with some one we could not hear or see several miles away. This is a kind of national wireless telephony, a natural gift which, I was told, no stranger can acquire.

Like most of the other Serbs, the Black Mountaineers are Eastern Orthodox Christians, but religion with them is a very loose matter. They have few churches and priests. In most cases their homes are their churches. Their conversation is full of such phrases as *"Hvala Bogu!"* and *"Boga ti!"* ("Thank God!" and "By God!") but they are rather meaningless.

On close scrutiny, however, it immediately appears that Tsernagora has undergone a profound change. Fundamentally, the Montenegro of Nyegosh and Nikita is vanishing.

The Montenegrins described above are most in evidence; or I should say that by reason of their picturesqueness one notices them first. They are the old-timers, with a few younger men who have taken on the old traditions of the Black Mountain. They are, as I say, grand-looking, courteous, at ease with anyone. As your auto passes them on the highway, they wave to you with an inimitable aristocratic gesture and shout greetings of welcome. If you know Serbian, you discover that the poorest and most illiterate peasants speak a language that in ordinary conversation often rises to the level of poetry. They boast of the fact that their blood, unlike that of some Serbs in Serbia, is pure—*i.e.,* unmixed with Turkish blood. They impress you exceedingly and you exclaim, "What a breed!"

Then, if you stay in Montenegro for a few days, as Stella and I did, you begin to see them in a somewhat different light. Now that the Turk is no longer a menace and their fighting against him is over, they strike you as at once ridiculous and pathetic. They are the last of their kind. To be a Montenegrin now is no longer to perform a tough historic function. It is a rather vacuous profession; in America we would call it a "racket," and a thin one at that. Some of them, as former soldiers, are on the government pension lists, receiving the equivalent of six or seven dollars monthly. Looking at them, you feel that, were it possible, a dozen of them should be pickled clad in their costumes and posed in characteristic attitudes, and put in a museum. And the next moment, when you see their women carrying huge burdens on their heads and backs, scratching for food among the rocks, spinning thread while watching their sheep and goats, and weaving and sewing for their families, your impulse is to step up to the first elegantly attired six- or seven-footer and address him, "Say, big boy, don't you know the war is over? Why in hell don't you cut out this hero stuff, take off that elegant coat of yours, and give your wife a hand, why don't you?"

And awhile later, if you talk with some other people besides the professional Montenegrins, you discover that not a few natives of Tsernagora think as you do. They are the young people, the post-war generation—students, workers, intellectuals, male and female, who in late years have been going to school or to seek work in Belgrade and other parts of Yugoslavia, and, having picked up many advanced ideas, now constitute perhaps the most determined section of the progressive and radical-revolutionary element in the Balkans. They are against everything that was and is, and in favor of "liquidating Montenegrism." Many of them are Communists or close to it, and as such, along with the fact that they are Slavs, look for their future to Russia. They have only contempt for the memory of Nikita and intense hate for Nikita's grandson, King Alexander, who now rules over them with an iron hand from Belgrade.

These new Montenegrins are utterly unlike the Slovenes. The latter, as I have told, secretly invent messianic legends and complain in whispers. The Montenegrins, whose traditional urge to freedom is stronger than perhaps in any other people, openly state their ideas and convictions, and stubbornly hang onto them, even at the cost of their lives. Since Alexander made himself dictator, dozens of them have been tortured to death and hundreds beaten unconscious in the royal prisons. In other cases, the government sadists, stupidly trying to convert Montenegrins from their anti-regimist attitude or force them to tell the names of other anti-regimists, have put live coals under their armpits and tied their arms close to their bodies, stuck needles under their finger- and toe-nails, driven awls into their heels, and inflicted upon them other tortures too awful to be described in print. You meet young men who, if you insist, take off their shirts and show you their burned-out armpits and other marks of torture. You meet young women who calmly tell you how they have been tortured for their ideas. They are the daughters of the hard-working, drab-looking women you see everywhere. Their radicalism is partly a reaction to the age-long slavery of their mothers, who along with a few practical business men in Tsernagora and Cetinyé are the only people in Tsernagora who live in the present. The girls' fathers live in the past, in the time of Nikita and even farther back. The girls and their brothers have hooked their stars to the future, which probably is still far off, but for which, Montenegrin-like, they are willing to suffer to hasten its coming.

VIII

One afternoon, in front of our hotel in Cetinyé, we came upon the former chauffeur of the last Emperor of Austria, who, three weeks earlier, had driven us across Montenegro toward Galichnik. In the morning he had brought up in his taxi from Kotor a Scandinavian honeymoon couple who were touring Yugoslavia. They were going back that afternoon. There was room for us in the car, so we returned down with them.

At Kotor, picking up our baggage, we took a steamer for Dubrovnik.

CHAPTER IX

Dalmatia—A Peasant Riviera

O F THE SEVERAL REGIONS COMPRISING YUGOSLAVIA, WE
stayed longest in Dalmatia—nearly five and a half
months, from early August, when we returned from Montenegro, till late December, when we left for Bosnia. We
remained so long for the simple reason that we liked it very
much and became more attached to it from day to day.

Shaw, when he was there in '29, enthused about Dalmatia
in this fashion:

> Englishmen, Irishmen, Americans, and holiday-makers
> of all nations come here in your millions! You will
> be treated like kings: the government will provide
> you with a perfect climate and the finest scenery of
> every kind for nothing. The people are everything you
> imagine yourselves to be and are not. They are hos-
> pitable, good-humoured, and very good-looking. Every
> town is a picture and every girl a movie star. . . .

But this blurb is only partly, superficially true. Dalmatia
is no "paradise," but a real, very real country, in its daily,
yearly, continual existence; more interesting, if less perfect,
than Shaw's words suggest.

II

Geographically or physically, Dalmatia is a narrow strip
of land, in some places only a few miles wide but nearly
300 miles long, forming part of the northern half of the
Balkan Peninsula's shore on the Adriatic, with several
hundred islands, large and small, strung close to the main-

land. Part of the weird Karst limestone region, which starts in the section of Slovenia now under Italy and thence stretches along the coast into Albania, it is largely mountainous, barren, arid, with only here and there a bit of level, fertile ground. In central and southern Dalmatia the steep, rocky mountains crowd straight into the Adriatic. Elsewhere they stand slightly back from the shore, or slope gently, allowing room for bright little towns and villages, tiny fields and gardens, vineyards, and fig, orange, and olive groves.

A land of almost perpetual sunshine, Dalmatia's climate resembles that of Southern California's coast line, except that the occasional *bora* (north wind) makes the Dalmatian air clearer, more bracing. Such colors, sunrises and sunsets one sees nowhere else on earth. No matter where one puts up for the night, on waking early in the morning and looking out of the window one sees the ultramarine or amethyst of the sea all mixed up with the perfect purple of after-dawn, the bright gray of olive groves and clumps of aloes and agaves growing from the rocks, the red brown of the terraced fields, the deep green of the vineyards, the darker green of the tall, slender cypresses, and the dull gray of the high mountains. All day the short, broad-topped olive trees shimmer in the sun, tremble in the breeze, as do also the prouder, gayer-looking oleanders, myrtles, verbenas, and semi-tropical palms. At any time of the day fishing-smacks and tiny cargo-ships with wind-filled orange-colored sails are visible on the gently rippled water. Then, toward evening, the sea gradually changes, sometimes to milky gold, to coral red, and sometimes even nigh to scarlet; stays that way for an hour, whereupon the gray olive trees, like the huge aloes and agaves, become delicately purple or mauve and sad, and the tall cypresses stand somber, majestic against the gray stones.

Dalmatia is heavy with history, smothered in it. Once upon the time it was known as Illyria; Shakespeare referred to it by that name. The powerful imperialistic urges and ambitions of ancient Greece, Rome, and Byzantium, of mediæval Turkey, Venice, and Russia, of Napoleon and England and Austria-Hungary, touched it and left their marks. For two thousand years Dalmatia was a factor in the struggle between East and West. For seven hundred years its numerous islands and mainland fjords were the haunts of pirates preying on both Christian and Moslem shipping in the Adriatic and Mediterranean seas. . . . And this past now hangs on heavily. Every stone is a reminder of something. The twentieth century has a hard time getting started.

Ninety-five per cent of Dalmatia's 700,000 population, mainland and island together, is Croat, the rest largely Italian. But the Dalmatian Croats are rather different from the Croats of Croatia proper. The latter (whom I describe more fully in a following chapter) are for the most part a mild-eyed, blond, or brown-haired people, patient, subdued, ponderous, truly peasant, not easily articulate, whereas most of the Dalmatians along the Adriatic are dark and spirited. It takes a lot of abuse and injustice to stir an inland Croat to indignation or fight; the Dalmatian, on the other hand, is apt to flare up the moment he suspects some one is trying to hand him the dirty end of the stick. His fists tauten, his eyes flash, and from his lips comes a torrent of words. There is a story about St. Jerome, a learned and holy man in the fifth century, who was a native of Dalmatia. One day he hauled off and laid out a man who had provoked him with a remark, then clasped his hands in prayer, looked skyward, and said *"Parce mihi, Domine, quia Dalmata sum!"* (Forgive me, O Lord; I am a Dalmatian!)

The explanation for this difference lies in history. The present-day Dalmatians, at least those living close to shore and on the larger islands, are partly descendants of the ancient Illyrians, a bold race of sea-rovers, whom the Croats, with their amazing racial vitality, quickly but peacefully absorbed. These Slavicized Illyrians and Slavs with

{ 149 }

the admixture of Illyrian blood became in a few centuries the most enterprising and adventurous mariners and pirates, rivaling the vikings of Scandinavia (who, by the way, frequently came in their ships to the Adriatic, with the result that even now one comes upon blond, viking-like Dalmatians). The Croats who settled in Dalmatia mixed also with the Romans and, later, the Venetians, but never surrendered their language and "heart culture"; developed a folklore closely akin to that of the Croats of Croatia and the Serbs of Serbia, always considering themselves Slavs— Yugoslavs, Croats. The population of Croatia, on the other hand, came largely under the Byzantine, Turkish, and Austro-Hungarian influences, and, living on plains or in valleys shut in by mountains, developed into a mild, plodding, patient peasant people—though their patience is more defensive than real.

For a hundred years immediately before the World War, Dalmatia was a valued part of Austria. When Austria broke up, there ensued a diplomatic struggle between Italy and the new state of Yugoslavia for possession of the province, which ended in Yugoslavia getting most of it. Italy obtained the cities of Fiume and Zara and a half-dozen of the lesser islands.

Most Italians admit that Dalmatia is preponderantly Slavic, but insist, none the less, that it rightfully belongs to Italy because it once was part of the Roman Empire and, later, a large section of it was dominated by Venice. They argue that Dalmatia is "a Slav body with a Latin soul," which is entirely wrong, the exact opposite being a sort of half-truth. The "body" of Dalmatia is part Latin, but its "soul" is almost totally Slavic.

III

Of the five and a half months in Dalmatia, we spent nearly three in Dubrovnik. We succeeded in finding board and lodgings in a small, quiet *pension* upon a cliff overlooking the Adriatic, some distance outside the town proper, and I managed to do a little work. Nearly a month passed before anyone discovered we were there; meanwhile we had a chance to look over more closely by ourselves the ancient little city which had so pleasantly impressed us when we landed there the previous May from the Trieste-bound liner.

Our initial impression of the town, as I describe it in my first chapter, was of course as superficial and incomplete as is Shaw's blurb on Dalmatia as a whole. Dubrovnik, or Ragusa, is vastly more interesting than we could possibly have guessed on that brief visit in May.

It is a bit of mediævalism scarcely touched by modernity. Perched upon a great rock that juts into the sea at the foot of a high, gray mountain called Srgj (pronounced *Serge*), the old town proper is scarcely a quarter of a mile in diameter and is completely walled in, with a tiny harbor just outside the southern wall and immense defense towers all around. Viewed from some near-by point, under the changing light of day, or in the bright moonlight, its variable beauty is *ein herrlicher Ausblick*—a treat for any eye, a startling close-up of the distant past.

In its deeper inner realities, as well as in its outer aspects, Dubrovnik is largely of the past, a museum piece which looks as if it should be placed under a glass case, but, none the less, is the scene of a dramatic human or social situation.

Its history, as already said, reaches back to the fifth century. During its first seven hundred years it was an unimportant seaport, destroyed by barbarians and rebuilt several times. In the twelfth century, however, its inhabitants—Ragusans, as they called themselves, a mixture of several Slavic, the Greek and Latin, but chiefly Slavic strains—bestirred themselves in a big way and swiftly made their tiny community into a commercial center of world importance. An independent city-republic for over five hundred years, Ragusa dominated a territory never inhabited by more than 40,000 people, yet in its day was a greater

{ 151 }

sea power than Britain. In fact, for nearly a century and a half all Levantine goods were brought to English markets in *ragusies*, vessels from Ragusa, and "ragusie" eventually became the lovely English word "argosy."

For hundreds of years Ragusan ships and seamen were among the most famous in the world. Ragusan shipmasters and sailors served not only under the Ragusan ensign, but under the flags of various Italian states, Greece, Spain, and other foreign countries. It is almost certain that Ragusans were on Columbus' ships when he sailed to India and bumped into America. In fact, it is probable that Ragusan ships touched the American continent before Columbus. Certain it is that a number of them reached Mexico, Central and South America, in the few years immediately after Columbus' adventure. Ragusans went around the Horn early in the seventeenth century; they were old-timers in California when the first Yankee got there.

For many decades Ragusa was Venice's chief rival in the Adriatic; then, for a time, the southern republic was forced to acknowledge the supremacy of the northern. There were times, too, when Ragusa, to keep its political independence, was compelled to pay tribute to Hungary and Turkey; none the less, the tiny state enjoyed great prestige throughout Europe during the Middle Ages.

Unlike some other Dalmatians, the Ragusans were not fighters and, despite the formidable aspect of their city walls, never engaged in a war. They were primarily diplomats, schemers, bribers, intrigants; and in dealing with their commercial rivals and political enemies used their talents to the full. In all the great struggles in the Adriatic and the Balkans they strove to be neutral. They paid bribes to pirates that they might not attack but, instead, protect their ships.

Theirs was a commercial, a Babbitt civilization. Greatness was measured by business success. The citizen who owned the largest number of ships was generally the greatest man in Ragusa. Shipowners were the ruling class, the social aristocracy. They called themselves nobles and were recognized as such throughout Europe. Most of them were educated at the Universities of Siena and Bologna, and, besides Slavic, all of them spoke and wrote Latin and Italian, a few Turkish, English, and Spanish. Their women were ladies of charm and accomplishments. In snobbery they surpassed the dames of Milan and Venice.

In the city the patricians had their palaces and business offices, the latter usually in charge of Jewish secretaries. Their ships sailed every known sea. They had branch offices and banks in Brindisi, Naples, Palermo, in Spanish, English, and North African ports. In the valleys and on the terraced mountain slopes, north and south of the city, they had their farms and vineyards, worked by tenant-peasants whom they treated well. Like themselves, their peasants were Slavs, Croats, calling themselves Ragusans. According to a contemporary writer, "every Ragusan peasant lived in a small house, but clean and well furnished, in many cases with things bought in distant lands. . . . This tiny country was most wonderfully cultivated, not an inch of soil was neglected."

The Ragusan government, headed by the Rector, who was elected by the Senate, was a kind of glorified Rotary Club, in which the Babbitt nobles decided among themselves what was good for business. Already in the thirteenth century they strongly and officially believed in honesty, dignity, formal honor, and "service" as the best policy in commercial dealings. Early in the fifteenth century they forbade their captains to transport or trade in slaves. In the seventeenth century they passed up enormous profits, refusing to ship negroes to the American Colonies. Later Cromwell adopted their code of business ethics for England.

Successful and esteemed everywhere, they developed great pride, patriotism, and magnificence. At their height they encouraged the arts, especially architecture (as is the case of big business men in present-day America), and for a long period their city was among the half-dozen loveliest, most advanced towns in Europe, "the Slavic Athens," renowned also for its dignified manners, orderliness, good government, "contentment of the lower classes," and general social atmosphere. The Rector's palace was built in the style of the Doge's palace in Venice. Ragusan architects were the foremost of their time. The government, as well as individuals, sent for and gave commissions to such giants of the Renaissance as Titian and Tintoretto. The Ragusan churches and monasteries owned the bones of great saints, pieces of the Cross and the diaper of Nazareth, and other precious relics which in those days were a part of a well-run commercial republic's power and prestige, for the saints whose bones the Ragusans honored were expected to protect Ragusan ships.

Rich Ragusans spent vast sums for public purposes. They encouraged science and the drama. The great physicist, Boscovich, who influenced and became friendly with Benjamin Franklin (they met in London), was a Ragusan. Through a good part of the Middle Ages performances of plays written in Ragusan Slavic by native dramatists were given in front of the Rector's palace. Most of these plays, of course, glorified Ragusa and its far-flung commercial enterprises.

In 1667 the town was destroyed by earthquake. Hardly a building remained. But after a month of panic and chaos Ragusa regained its spirit and orderliness, and reconstruction began. The churches, the Rector's palace, and other public buildings were restored, rich families erected four- and five-story palaces, and the result was Ragusa, or Dubrovnik, as it stands today—a city not nearly so grand as, say, Venice or Florence, but of their limited category; a compendium of the Renaissance, a testament of early Slavic culture in the Balkans, a statement-in-stone of the enterprising, artistic, and orderly phases of the South-Slavic national character; and a testimonial that culture and beauty once had (and still have) a place in the Balkans along with wars, terrorism, regicides, and intrigue.

But the earthquake and reconstruction, together with the paying of tributes to great powers and pirates, proved too much for the financial energies of the tiny state. Gradual economic decline ensued. Late in the eighteenth century there was another upswing in Ragusan commerce and culture, but then Napoleon came and forced Ragusa into his "Illyrian state," which proved unsuccessful, and the republic was finished.

Napoleon was followed by Austria, which occupied Dalmatia early in the nineteenth century. When, in 1814, the Emperor Francis the First visited Ragusa, the nobles, dressed in their finest silk costumes, received him coolly, almost haughtily, for, after all, they had been Ragusan nobles, recognized and honored as such everywhere, when 'the Hapsburgs were not yet even robber barons! The Emperor, resenting their reception of him, remarked that, while *they* might act insolently, their sons and grandsons would grow up to be loyal subjects of the Austrian Crown. Whereupon the Ragusans' spokesman bowed a whit and declared His Majesty was mistaken—*they* would have no sons so long as Ragusa was not politically free! They had entered into a pact of honor among themselves not to marry or, if they already were married, to have no more children while under Austria.

Ragusa remained under the Hapsburgs over a hundred years, and as a result of the "no sons" pact most of the old families, some of which could trace their lineage to the seventh century, have disappeared. The patricians as a class deliberately committed a slow suicide. The remaining members of erstwhile noble houses obviously are in a swift process of all-around degeneration and decline.

Stella and I met a few doddering old fellows, Conté de So-and-so and Conté de This-and-that, most of them extreme eccentrics. One lives in a palace full of cats, another in a house full of dogs; a third collects all manner of nonsensical objects. Their palaces, while seemingly all right from the outside, are dreadful within. All gayety, dash, and character have gone out of them. Their corridors and rooms virtually smell of tragedy and death. Most of their occupants seldom appear in the streets. That is all for the best, for most of them are horrible caricatures, mere ghosts of their illustrious ancestors. Many of them are badly off financially. Nearly all are bachelors or old maids, carrying out the pact. A few haunt the coffee-houses, saunter about (chiefly at night), collect rents, and play low, reactionary politics with corrupt politicians in Belgrade.

We became acquainted with some of them through a young Yugoslav painter of great power, originality, and social understanding, Peter Dobrovich, who is well known in most European countries and was one of the few people we met in Dubrovnik proper with whom we became friendly. He was there for the summer and fall, painting the portraits of these remaining nobles. His plan, more than half executed when we last saw him, was to do thirty or forty of them and call the whole series, "Decadence." Posing for him, his subjects did not realize what he was about; they were flattered that a real artist should desire to paint them, and liked his pictures, although each of them clearly showed their dark, twisted inner make-ups as well as their wholly uncharming exteriors.

But, as I have suggested, these unpleasant people are little in evidence. Indeed, unless one knows of them, one never notices them. Dubrovnik is very much alive with people utterly unlike the declining *gospari*.

These are the peasants who daily come to town from near-by villages, and the porters, laborers, would-be laborers, bums and vagabonds, young and old, who descend on Dubrovnik during the tourist season from Herzegovina, Bosnia, Montenegro, and various parts of Dalmatia. These are, especially, the peasant girls and women from the Konavle Valley, an hour distant from the town, who more or less monopolize the business on the market place, which, so far as I know, is the grandest, most picturesque market place in existence.

Here they bring their baskets of eggs, figs, grapes, oranges, lemons, and vegetables; jugs of hand-pressed olive oil, balls of homemade goat cheese, bundles of kindling-wood, and their glorious smiles and laughter—such as one sees and hears, I suppose, nowhere else in the world. Mounted on donkeys, they arrive early in the morning to realize their thirty or forty cents; then, toward noon, re-mount and, talking and laughing, ride out of Dubrovnik, back to Chilipi, Gruda, Cavtat, Mlini, or one of the other villages in Konavle. Evenings the younger ones return to town to parade about in their exquisite Konavle costumes and flirt with the boys.

The porters, laborers and would-be laborers, bums and vagabonds of all ages are mostly huge fellows in vast, baggy breeches, tight jackets, with tiny caps on top of their heads. All day long they loiter about, watching for a chance to make a few pennies. They gather about the fountain on the main street, munch bread, talk, laugh, drink from the fountain. The circumstances of most of them are nothing to joke and laugh about, but they joke and laugh none the less; then suddenly quarrel and fight, perhaps over the pos-session of a few cigarettes.

Stella and I were interested in the Rector's palace, the fantastic baroque cathedral, the skull and thigh-bone of St. Blasius in the bishop's reliquary, the really beautiful court-yards in the several mediæval monasteries, Ivan Mestrovic's bas-relief of the late King Peter over the Pilé Gate, the second-oldest apothecary in the world which is part of one of the monasteries, and other places and objects of historic interest, but not half so much as in the people—these men, women, boys, and girls, some direct descendants of peasants in the old Republic of Ragusa, who, with their laughter and talk, their healthy, beautiful faces, save Dubrovnik from being really a mere museum piece. They are for the most part poor people, but there is no decadence among them; on the contrary, they give the old town an expression of contentment and happiness.

I wondered what could be the basis for the happy appearance of these people. They lived simple lives. Was this simplicity itself an explanation? Was it inherent in the sunniness of Dalmatia? . . . Then, after we had been in Dubrovnik about a month, we became acquainted with a gentleman, not a native Dubrovniker, but deeply in love with the town and its environs, who had numerous friends among families in the Konavle villages; and one Sunday he took us there.

The people of Dubrovnik proper are not hospitable as a general run. Commercial tourism, coupled with ancient social complexes, have spoiled them in this respect. Social life among old-time Dubrovnikers is almost at a standstill—another definite sign of decadence in the city. In the villages, however, the old Slavic sport of hospitality continues in full flower. Everywhere the people received us with open arms—and such *nice* people! I thought that if I had the great talent of Peter Dobrovich I would much rather paint these peasants than the decayed nobility.

We met girls we had, and some we had not, seen in Dubrovnik, tall, full-bodied, strong and beautiful, their beauty being not the artificial, self-conscious business of the average Hollywood movie star or American magazine-cover "sweetie," but a wholesome, indigenous product of their region and circumstances. The girls' mothers are the girls grown or growing old and more gracious; their fathers and brothers, tall, straight men, hard as the rocks around them, but usually charming, jolly, at ease with anyone, able to converse on many subjects.

Most of the families have been living in these villages for centuries; some, they say, for nearly a thousand years. Several houses are much older than my native home in Slovenia.

In 400 B.C., the site of the present Slavic village of Cavtat was the site of the famous Greek colony of Epidaurus, the birthplace of Æsculapius, Homer's "blameless physician," who became a god and whose cult of snake worship spread throughout the ancient world. Of course, no trace is left of Epidaurus, which was destroyed by earthquake before the Slavs came there, but in the faces of people, especially the women, one finds a happy mingling of the classic Greek and Slavic features.

The houses in Konavle are typical Dalmatian stone affairs, simple, solidly built, sparsely furnished, for Dalmatians spend little of their time indoors. Like the Italians, they go in only when it rains and to sleep; in the summertime many even sleep outdoors.

Nearly every third person in these villages knows some English; here and there we came upon old copies of American magazines. The explanation is that every other Konavle family has some one in America. Konavleans are officers and seamen on American ships, fishermen along the coasts of Florida, Louisiana, and California, restaurant-keepers in San Francisco, fruit-growers in the Santa Cruz and Santa Clara counties in California. Konavleans, in fact, were the Ragusans who came to California before the Americans. They were pioneers in California's modern fruit-growing industry. Jack London described them in *The Valley of the Moon*. The town of Watsonville, near Salinas, for instance, is almost entirely Konavlean.

In the village of Gruda a girl asked me if I knew the American movie actor, John Miljan. I said I had seen him on the screen. She said, "He is a Konavlean born in the Valley of the Moon, in America. His parents' name was Marinovitch; they came from this village." Other people asked me did I know So-and-so in San Francisco? I did not. "He is a big banker there." Or So-and-so in Santa Clara? I said no. "He has a big fruit-cannery there." . . . Both in Konavle and in Dubrovnik I was asked about Henry Suzzallo, the great American educator (who died during the writing of this book). Had I ever met him in New York, where he was president of the Carnegie Foundation

{ 159 }

for the Advancement of Teaching? I had thought Suzzallo was of Italian parentage, but now, here in Dalmatia, I learned that he was born in California of Yugoslav parents who had emigrated from Dubrovnik. Originally, their name had been Zucalo, which they had then changed so as to make it more easily pronounceable as it was pronounced in Dalmatia. . . .

But to return to my question, what is the explanation of the beauty, contentment, and happiness of these people? There are several explanations. One, of course, *is* the simplicity of their lives. Their food is plain, produced at home or caught in the sea. The sun-shot air they breathe could be no better. They work hard, but not too hard. Economically, they could not function on a simpler plane. What they produce they personally sell to the ultimate consumer. The depression has not fatally affected them; tourists continue to visit Dubrovnik.

Another explanation is stability. For a thousand years they have been living in the same place, engaged in the wholesome struggle with the rocky soil and the sea. They were never brutally oppressed or exploited for any length of time. Their communal and individual life was never hopeless. In the days of the Ragusan republic there was an intimate relationship between the city and the villages. Together they formed a compact economic organism. The culture of the town reached into the hamlet. Not a few nobles had children by peasant women, and the children remained in the villages. And, most important of all, for six centuries the people of Konavle, while part of the Ragusan republic, lived in peace. Until 1914 they never participated in great numbers in any war. For centuries they functioned as human beings normally should function, as tillers of the soil, fishermen, seamen, adventurers among the elements of the earth, rather than destroyers of their own species. As mariners under the Ragusan and other flags, they were constantly projecting themselves into the big world. They made contacts with western Europe and America. They were always constructive, natural, simple, a part of their environment; never became over-civilized.

The result of this centuries-old situation in the Konavle villages is that, in their hearts and minds, Konavleans, despite their narrow margin of existence, scant formal education, and semi-primitive houses, are essentially as civilized a group of people as one finds anywhere in the contemporary world.

After our initial visit to Konavle, Stella and I spent almost as much time there as in Dubrovnik.

V

In mid-September, after we had met several other people and visited other towns and villages near Dubrovnik (all more or less similar to the Konavle communities), we chanced to become acquainted with another well-known Yugoslav artist, Maksimilien Vanka ("Maxo," for short), a Croat from Zagreb, and his American wife, the former Margaret Stetten of New York. Marvelously agreeable people, we liked them at once, went swimming with them, took them to Konavle, and the four of us became fast friends. They were in Dubrovnik for only a week. They had a cottage near the town of Korchula on the island of the same name (one hundred kilometers north of Dubrovnik), where they had spent the summer and meant to stay another few weeks, and we simply *must* come with them! In September, they said, Korchula was at its best. Their cottage was right on the beach. We would love it. We would love the whole little town; it was so quiet, homely, almost purely peasant, not the least bit touristy like Dubrovnik, and ridiculously cheap. There was not an automobile on the whole island; and did we know that, according to a rumor of several centuries, Korchula was the birthplace of Marco Polo? . . . We *must* ——

At the same time I received a letter from a gentleman I hadn't heard of before, one Mr. Lupis-Vukich, secretary of an organization of returned American immigrants in Split, the largest city in Dalmatia, inviting us to come there as guests of their society and stay as long as we liked. It was one of several such invitations; but Mr. Lupis-Vukich's letter was so charming that I immediately answered him, accepting his organization's hospitality.

We accepted, too, the Vankas' invitation and the four of us took a boat for Korchula.

VI

There are few pleasanter sights, even in Dalmatia, than the town of Korchula as the ship approaches the harbor. Built upon a low, narrow promontory, most of it is a good deal older than any part of Dubrovnik. Centuries before the Christian era it was a Greek colony, later a pirates' port; then Venice took it. From Venice it passed to Hungary, from Hungary to Genoa, back to Hungary, back to Venice, then briefly to Turkey. Back again to Venice, while during the Napoleonic wars fate tossed it from France to Russia, from Russia to England, then to Austria, where it remained till the creation of Yugoslavia.

All these powers left their marks on the city, but today those of Venice are most apparent. The architecture is preponderantly Venetian. The community once had a population of 6,000, but in the sixteenth century the plague hit it, and its inhabitants today number less than 2,000. Many of the palaces and smaller dwellings have been vacant ever since the plague. In the cathedral, parts of which date back to the fourteenth century, are many curious and some valuable objects of mediæval and Renaissance art, including a painting attributed to Tintoretto. Parts of the old Venetian fortifications still stand, and the narrow, limestone-paved streets crawl up behind them from the waterfront to its climax, the cathedral.

The island of Korchula is one of the largest on the Dalmatian coast, and is in many respects typical of the islands south of Split. Once it was covered with pine woods, but Venice partly deforested it to build her galleys, and now large sections of it are overgrown by low brush and scrub trees. Were it not for the shortage of water, it could easily accommodate four times its present population of 25,000. The people make their living in stone and marble quarries on Korchula and adjacent islands, at fishing and olive-, wine- and fruit-growing, shipbuilding and firewood, which they ship in tiny vessels to Split and Dubrovnik. The Korchula quarries have been famous for centuries. Most of Venice, the whole of Santa Sofia in Constantinople, and the façades of several skyscrapers in New York are of the white stone and marble quarried on Korchula and the near-by island of Vrdnik.

The Korchulaners seem inferior to the Konavleans. They were exploited too much and fought too many wars for their various oppressors. They are not so handsome; their costumes are mixed; their manner is not so free and open as that of the Konavleans. But the general rhythm of their life is essentially the same. There is a profound agreement between them and their environment. Life is slow on Korchula, but, somehow, very sure.

Our new friends, Maxo and Margaret Vanka, and Stella and I spent three weeks roaming over the island, stopping in various villages. For hours we watched boat-builders at their tasks; fishermen endlessly mending their nets, going to sea in the evening, returning in the morning; peasants gathering in their grapes, figs, and olives; workmen sawing marble in ancient quarries—and off and on I thought briefly that I could stay on Korchula for years and watch these people at work. They seemed clumsy and slow at first glance, but by and by I discerned a grace and dignity in their motions that modern industrial workers do not possess. They live in crumbling stone houses, eat simply and sparsely, drink hardly at all—although they produce some of the best wines in the world—sing a good deal, pray a bit, sin every day, and work long hours but not hard.

Their shortcomings are many; they bathe infrequently, are not interested in comfort or progress; women carry water two miles over rocky roads in flat barrels on their backs, instead of having it piped to their villages; yet their world, on the whole, is one of true values; not perfect by a long shot, but a friendly world of huge, rough hands and decent, healthy hearts, still too primitive to be fatally influenced by goings-on in great, complicated, progressive but ill-organized countries like America.

The Vankas were splendid hosts. We swam a lot. We loafed. We ate mostly fish caught an hour before dinner, a rare cheese at half a dollar a huge ball, black bread, figs, grapes, and local caviar, and drank several kinds of Korchula wine at from five to eight cents a liter. Maxo did our portraits. We talked about everything under the sun.

In the town of Korchula we saw several stores with the name "Polo" or "de Polo" on the signs over the doors. These people were Italians of the same family as the great Venetian voyager. Some insisted that Marco Polo had been born on Korchula, others that he had merely been imprisoned there for a while.

Probably the most interesting person we met on the island was an old Catholic priest, Don Niko, as everyone called him, of the village of Lombarda, an hour's boat-ride or two hours' walk from the town of Korchula. A frank admirer of ladies, a teller of unprintable stories, an epicure, a pagan (and as such not untypical of Dalmatian village priests), the sixty-five-year-old *padre*, who looked hardly forty, was an old friend of the Vankas'. In fact, he had married them, two years before. We called on him one Sunday afternoon and he was delighted to see us.

He was just going for a walk, so he took us with him through the village, introduced us to every good-looking girl and delicately enthused about her figure. Changing the subject now and then, he told us that Lombarda dated back to 500 or 400 B.C., when it had been a Greek settlement, probably one of the first in Dalmatia, preceding even

{ 164 }

Epidaurus. The grape grown in the extensive vineyards about the village was called *Grk* (Greek); the same grape the original Greek settlers had planted there twenty-four hundred years ago! A native of Korchula, he intended to die there—"only I hope not for a long time yet. . . . Life is very good, very sweet on Korchula, here in old Lombarda."

Then he took us to the parish house and showed us how good life really was on Korchula. His pretty young housekeeper, who he insisted was his cousin, brought us a great array of bottles filled with some of the most delicious wines (dated 1895 and 1902) I had ever tasted, and platters of smoked fish and black bread. It was a jolly party.

Don Niko was the most unpriestly priest I have ever encountered. "I don't believe most things I am supposed to believe," he said. "Neither do my parishioners, not really. But they like to come to church, go through the motion of religion—so why not?" I learned he was dearly loved in the village. The people do not care if his housekeeper really is his cousin or not. They consider him a good man. He knows more about grape culture and wine-making than any other man on Korchula, is free with advice and practical help. When drought is more than usually severe and the people lack even water for drinking, he gets his friends in the Yugoslav navy ships to fill their tanks with fresh water at Split, then come down, anchor in the tiny Lombarda harbor, and pump the water into people's tanks and barrels.

At twilight-time we waited for our boat in the Lombarda harbor to return us to Korchula. The sea was pink and gold, and the fishermen of the village were just going out in their boats, all painted a rich purple—that being Lombarda's color, for nearly every fishing town or village has a special color for its watercraft.

The men rowed slowly, rhythmically. "Hi, Don Niko!" one of them cried to our host, waving a hand.

Don Niko waved back, wished them a good catch.

The scene was so Dalmatian, so deeply beautiful. I shall never forget it—that pink-gold water, those purple boats, men in the boats, hunched far over, working their oars— the vineyards and the gray old houses above the harbor, and the good old rogue, Don Niko, pleasantly mellow with wine, saying goodby to us, making us promise we would look him up again next time we came to Korchula. . . .

In the morning we sailed for Split.

VII

Mr. Lupis-Vukich, who awaited us on the quay in Split when our steamer moored, turned out to be as nice a person as his letter had distantly promised. A man in his early sixties, but, like most Dalmatians his age, younger-looking, he had been in the United States for twenty-odd years, had published and edited a Yugoslav-language newspaper in Chicago and written articles for American magazines, and spoke fluent English—or I should say American. Uncommonly quiet-mannered for a Dalmatian, almost matter-of-fact, intelligence and level-headedness written all over his face, he greeted us simply, then said there was considerable excitement in town.

"We have two newspapers here," he explained; "they've reported your arrival, and now the boys—the reporters— want to see you, as do some other persons, among them the governor of the province and the mayor of the town. There are two official automobiles with chauffeurs at your disposal as long as you stay; you can take your pick. . . . Two or three evening parties already are tentatively arranged so people can meet you both. . . . But if you don't want to, of course you don't have to see anybody. I've been appointed to take care of you, but you can tell me to leave you alone as soon as I show you to the hotel, where we've reserved lodgings for you. And you can tell the governor and the mayor to keep their autos. In fact, you don't even have to do that; I'll tell them for you. The same goes for the newspaper boys. . . . As I wrote you, stay as guests of our organization as long as it suits you; the longer the better we'll like it. We—the Association of Returned Emigrants—suppose you came because Split and its vicinity interest you; but if you want to look it over alone, that will be all right with us. On the other hand, if you want someone to show you around, I'm at your service from now on. Anything goes. . . ."

This was somewhat like coming to Slovenia, wholly different from Dubrovnik, where they have no real newspaper and the officialdom, almost as inverted, stiffly proud, straitlaced and hidden away as the old aristocracy, had left us wholly alone, except that the mayor sent me a word of welcome, along with the notification that we would be exempt from the customary municipal tax.

We immediately liked Lupis (as I subsequently began to call him) and I asked him what he would suggest.

He smiled, "I know enough about the writing game in America to know you're not rich, so I'd suggest you stay as our guest ——"

"——and 'chisel' along," I laughed.

"——and 'chisel' along," smiled Lupis. "Stay at least a month; use the best automobile, which is the governor's, and take things as they come—for a while, at any rate."

The three of us laughed till we got to the hotel, near the quayside.

Stella and I stayed in Split and its vicinity longer than a month and, with Lupis as our guardian angel, took things as they came most of the time.

First came the mayor, who, of course, was a politician and a booster. He gave me the town's population figure (35,000) and other statistics, and the freedom of the city.

Then came a man with an invitation from the governor to call on him at his office. I went and found myself face to face with a man who looked somewhat like Woodrow Wilson: a long, intellectual face, with a tall brow, vivid eyes, and beautiful, restive hands; a man of great nervous energy and quick, avid mind. I was with him till late in the afternoon, and we discussed the depression, the United States, the Lindberg kidnapping, the theory of the decline of Western civilization, Hitler, the fall of the Roman Empire, Yugoslav immigrants in the United States, and what not. His name was Dr. Yosip Yablanovich; an appointee of King Alexander and as such, I assume, a supporter of his rule, with which I have no sympathy; none the less, personally a deeply likable man. Later I met dozens of other big Yugoslav politicians and officeholders, including the king himself, and instinctively disliked nearly all of them; if not on first meeting, on second. The governor at Split seemed rather unlike the others; palpably a civilized man, at least on the personal, if not the political, plane, and one of the few public men in Yugoslavia I hope to meet again some day.

When I returned to the hotel, there were the reporters, who the next day made a big thing of my remark to them that I was only mildly interested in the ancient walls and monuments or the history of Split, but very much in living people, their circumstances and manner of life. This statement made a hit in the town, for Splitchani, although one-fifth of them live within the actual walls, still well preserved, of the famous Diocletian Palace completed in 297 A.D., have scant interest in their antiquities. They take care of them because they seem to interest foreigners, but have no such reverence for them as one finds in Dubrovnik. The tourists who come to gape at the sixteen-hundred-year-old masonry amuse them.

But in the ensuing days the Diocletian Palace greatly interested me, none the less: and amused me, too. . . . Here are the walls, the really superb gates, the octagon towers, the still sumptuous though roofless peristyle, the numerous Corinthian columns of red granite—the remains of probably the biggest, most pretentious private residence ever built, the home of one of the greatest Roman emperors

{ 168 }

—and within these walls, over 600 feet square, is a teeming town with a market place, squares, scores of modern stores, offices, printing-plants, barbershops and workshops of all kinds, jammed in along narrow, labyrinthine passageways too narrow to be called streets, and above them dwellings of five thousand people, mostly poor Croat families who maintain their existence by working at a variety of ill-paid trades, including farming on the fields just outside the city and dock-walloping—for Split is becoming Dalmatia's leading seaport.

Split is "a town within a palace." The modern houses (meaning those built within the last six hundred years, under Venice and Austria) are erected onto the old Diocletian walls, over the old Diocletian archways and columns. Over the Emperor's mausoleum, which was also the Temple of Æsculapius, stands the Catholic cathedral. Diocletian's home town, Salona (now called Solin), three miles east of Split, was destroyed by the Avars in the seventh century, forcing its inhabitans to seek refuge in the then abandoned palace of Diocletian. Now the Yugoslav government is excavating the Solin ruins. . . . All of which seemed to me vastly ironical, downright funny. History, I thought to myself, occasionally revealed itself a great joker.

We met numerous Splitchani of all classes and many professions. With several of them, including the excellent Lupis, we became close friends. Unlike most Dubrovnikers, nearly everyone in Split was frank and open to us. Men and women were charming, interesting. Less harmonious as personalities than the Konavleans, for instance; not nearly as good-looking, but as likable. By and by, after we came to know a few of them well, it occurred to me that the history of their town—or, to put it in another way, their living within the palace of a Roman emperor—has influenced them in a curious way. The great historic joke, which is the development of the Diocletian Palace into present-day Split, has, in the course of centuries, become part of their subconscious, with the result that the town nowadays is full of humorists, jokesmiths, practical jesters, satirists and ironists, excellent caricaturists, and generally what we in America call "joshers" and "kidders."

Splitchani, with their booming harbor and growing business enterprises, lead industrious, normal lives; their city unquestionably is the most progressive and has the finest future in the Yugoslav Adriatic. But most of the time they seem to take no one and nothing seriously. They laugh at everything. Greatness, superlative qualities of any sort do not impress them. Pretense, falsity they spot at once, then he-he-he! and haw-haw-haw! They have a sharp eye for incongruities; naturally so; their community is one big incongruity. Theirs is a natural, almost perennial sense of humor. Nowhere else in Yugoslavia do people laugh as much as in Split. The tendency is to mock, knock, and look on the funny side of everybody and everything, including themselves—in fact, themselves most of all. A common expression is the equivalent of, "Lord! but am I a jackass!" Their laughter at others is free of malice; all in fun. When a man dies, it is not unusual for his friends to gather at his house and have a gay party, make fun of him, tell funny stories of all the dumb things he had done in his life. They think this is better than crying and mourning. Tragedy is generally laughed at. The saddest tales are told amid roars of laughter.

Perhaps the everlasting Dalmatian sunshine has something to do with this disposition of the people, not only of the well-to-do (who are few), but also the poor. Unlike the old-time Dubrovnikers, Splitchani are outdoor folk. From morning till night the long quayside, called the Obala, is thronged with people. Some walk, others stand or sit about, talk, josh, and laugh. This is especially true in winter, when the interior of the "Palace" often is chill and damp. The Obala, sun-drenched throughout the day, usually is ten degrees warmer than any other spot in town; so the people call it "the poor man's overcoat" and, most of them being poor, wear it as much as possible. . . . I was told that one cool day back in 1904 a young Socialist spellbinder, Benito Mussolini, came to Split from Italy and, wrapping himself in the famous overcoat, harangued the Italian workers—who then were more numerous in Split than they are today—most of the afternoon. . . .

Half of Split's population are peasants. They live in town, some right in the "Palace"; their fields, vineyards, orchards, and sheds are outside the city. Which may seem odd to a stranger, but the same is true of other towns in central Dalmatia. Trogir and Shibenik, for instance, two considerable towns, usually called cities, directly north of Split, are predominantly peasant communities.

Split has the appearance of a real city, and progress is noticeable on all sides. There is a great new park. In 1923 electricity was unknown in town; now it is generally available. The Obala is lined with beautiful palms. The streets everywhere are clean, which, I was told, was not true under Austria. There are several new orphan homes and public kitchens for destitute families, a public kindergarten, and a well-organized hygiene service. Outside the "Palace" are hundreds of new apartment-houses and several small subdivisions, all built up. This is the accomplishment of the returned immigrants—our hosts—who, as workers, fishermen, legitimate business men, and bootleggers in America before the 1929 "crash", had made several million dollars, then come back to the old country, invested their savings in Split real estate, and now live on the income.

Lupis assured me that most Splitchani loved their community, but to me all of them, excepting the mayor, only criticized and made fun of it. They went out of the way to show me the worst slums in the "Palace" and other such incongruities, and told me of the awful exploitation of Dalmatian labor in the Italian-owned cement-mills, near by. Others made sure that I did not overlook the old women on the quay carrying enormous loads of firewood on their backs while young men stood idly about. "That's us Dalmatians! Let the old hags work!" said a young lawyer to me, laughing; but really I think he was outraged by the fact that ancient custom makes it shameful for adult males to engage in such lowly, ill-paid tasks as carrying firewood from the boats, which bring it from the islands, to the homes.

Still others, momentarily serious, complained to me bitterly of the lack of political freedom under King Alexander.

VIII

Every few days, using the Governor's automobile, Lupis, Stella, and I made a trip somewhere within a day's ride of the city there and back.

There was Trogir, a good hour's ride from Split, with a population of 4,000, but so tiny that at first sight you would not believe it could house many over 400. Built along canals, it is the most Venetian of Venetian towns in Dalmatia; a Venice in *piccolo*, with streets two feet wide, squares barely large enough for a grasshopper to take a leap, mighty avenues which one covers in a half-dozen strides, houses all huddled together during the centuries for mutual protection against invaders from across the canals; and the whole business walled in, with gates and towers. Every group of houses is a profusion of sculptured niches, doorways, arches, wellheads, balconies, and iron grills. But the chief glory of Trogir is its cathedral, dating from the Hungarian possession in the thirteenth century. The campanile, finely sculptured, with its ornamental windows in the belfry framed by the sky, is Venetian Gothic. A beautiful curiosity, almost beyond adequate description. . . . The people, as I have suggested, are mainly peasant, 90 per cent of them Croat, the rest Italian, not a few of them excessively good-looking, all very pleasant, hospitable, and amusing—in many respects like the people of Split.

Then there was Shibenik, 20,000 population, a great peasant village rather than a city, with a harbor Naples can envy. Immediately to the north of it is an archipelago of small islands. The town is approached through a defile between precipitous rocks. The water suddenly expands into a vast bay that might shelter a navy. From the bay the town, creeping up a slope, looks lovely. It is also Venetian, but lacks the finish of Trogir. The streets are narrow, tortuous, angular, crudely flagged, with abrupt endings. The one building worth close notice is the fifteenth-century cathedral, a greater and finer edifice than the Trogir one, with three apses, built entirely in stone in a way that, were it not so beautiful, would make it primarily an architectural stunt. . . . The people are nearly all Croats, huge men and women, rather slow-moving, ungainly if one compares them to Konavleans, but very alert. Their fields, groves, and vineyards outside the city are models in intensive cultivation. To see a thousand of them going to or coming from church is a sight never to be forgotten. Unlike in Split, national costumes are almost general in Shibenik. Men wear tiny orange-and-black caps and heavy, durable pants and jackets of coarse brown homespun. Over a scraggy shirt-front comes a fold-over, collarless vest with silver buttons of handmade filigree. Their sandals, which at first glance appear simple, actually are a complexity of folds and thongs. On cool days they sling across their shoulders a gaberdine with long, loose sleeves and a capuchin hood. The women of Shibenik wore accordion-pleated skirts from their own looms before they were known in western Europe. Besides, they wear ample bodices, cotton kerchiefs, usually white, resembling the cap of Liberty, and sandals similar to the men's.

There were a number of fishing villages near Split where we had a chance to observe an interesting, centuries-old economic organization among fishermen. The proceeds of a catch are divided so that one-fourth goes to the boat-owner, one-fourth to the net-owner, and half to the men who actually catch the fish. This economic custom, I was told, is in effect also among Dalmatian fishermen off the coasts of Florida, Louisiana, and California. They brought it with them from the old country. . . . The fishermen in

{ 173 }

Dalmatia, as a rule, are superb physical specimens, extremely resourceful and hardworking at sea, but incline to laziness ashore. Extreme forms of physical and moral degeneration, however, are evident in once purely fishing and agricultural villages near Split, where people, eager for earnings, lately have begun to work in the Italian-owned cement-factories, just outside the city.

And, finally, there were the several villages we visited in the Dalmatian highlands—Dalmatinsko Zagoryé, as the mountain region immediately in back of Split, Trogir, and Shibenik is called in Slavic. Primitive in the extreme, both in comfort and socio-economic organization, they are vastly unlike the communities along the coast or on the islands.

Zagoryé (literally, "behind the mountains") is a gray, barren, arid land, almost as unproductive as Montenegro, hot in the summer and in the winter swept by winds that sear one's skin and push one's breath back into the lungs. Rainfall is meager, but, as almost throughout the Karst region, water comes from numerous underground sources, making every other valley a swamp or semi-swamp, infested by malarial mosquitoes.

On every stretch of level ground or some ridge above it is a huddle of stone houses, anywhere from ten to a hundred, most of them as unfit for human habitation as the musty wooden shanties of the "nigger towns" and white-trash communities in Mississippi and Alabama. Many have no windows, ceilings, beds, or tables. Food is cooked— where they have any—over a fire built on the floor, which often is bare ground. The smoke finds its way out through the door, a special hole under the roof, or cracks in the walls. Frequently there is only one room under the roof, which on winter nights shelters not only the half-dozen or more members of the family, but also from ten to thirty sheep and goats.

The people are Croats. They have been living and dying there, under the heels of various foreign rules, for centuries. Now the Turks terrorized them, then Hungary,

{ 174 }

Venice, or Austria exploited them to the limit, giving them no chance to become educated or in anyway to improve themselves.

Malaria has raged in Zagoryé for five hundred years. Until lately no one there knew what it was. They called it "the shivers," and through the centuries millions died of it. Only in the last ten years has the Yugoslav government hygienic service, badly handicapped by insufficient funds, begun to take serious steps against the disease; but, at best, it will take decades, perhaps centuries, to raise the people from the level to which half a millennium of exploitation, disease, and neglect has pushed them.

Lupis-Vukich said to me, "Our foreign rulers, especially Venice, left us the cathedrals in Trogir and Shibenik; up here, only degeneration."

Degeneration in body and spirit is evident in most of the valley villages and hamlets. People have little ambition or initiative; in fact, it is a miracle that anyone is alive there at all. In sharp contrast to Konavle, one encounters few good-looking people.

The farther into the mountains one goes, however, the less degeneration one finds. One explanation is that the malarial mosquitoes do not reach up there; another, that the agents of Venetian, Turkish, Hungarian, and Austrian imperialism never got around to seek out the settlements so high up and so far from the highways, and compel them to pay exorbitant taxes and fight their wars.

But all the communities, those in the malarial valleys and those in the mountains most difficult of access, are extremely poor. We were in hamlets of from ten to fifty houses where all the families together did not have the equivalent of one American dollar in cash. Of course, the depression which made it impossible for people to sell their sheep and goats was a factor in this poverty, but not the chief one. Zagoryé is a land of perennial economic crisis. In the best of times few people use salt or petroleum. They eat their mutton unsalted. Sugar and coffee are undreamed-of luxuries.

People generally eat very little, and most of them, naturally, are very thin. For light at night they burn kindling-wood.

In the high-mountain villages the people are extremely proud. They accept no aid which might smell of charity from anyone. I was told that toward the end of winter, when they frequently begin to run short of food, adults, particularly men, all but entirely refrain from eating. To keep their stomachs from growling and feeling empty, they strap flat, specially shaped rocks close over the abdomen. This also helps them to carry themselves upright and, as one of them put it, "to keep our heads clear." Children either die very young or live; if they survive, they often live past a hundred—not only in the mountain, but, less frequently, of course, in the malarial centers as well.

The people of the malarial villages are pitiful; those beyond the reach of mosquitoes and foreign imperialism, however, are a colossal breed, thin but hard, not handsome, nor the opposite, proud, seldom ill-humored, suspicious and even contemptuous of people like ourselves who come to them dressed in city clothes, but also capable of fine Slavic hospitality and politeness. In some ways they are as impressive as the Montenegrins. Uneducated, they have a sound instinctive culture, which one does not notice unless one gets close to them. In their basic natures they are, in fact, cultivated, refined, capable of deep graciousness and great gentleness.

Despite the centuries of neglect and exploitation (perhaps because of them), they have in them a terrific power. All the onslaughts of mediæval and modern imperialism on their natural culture have failed to rob them of their national character and integrity. In Zagoryé one finds customs which the Old Slavs practiced in the third century, and hears song and expression sung and used in the heart of Russia. And now and then, as if suddenly giving vent to their bottled-up creative energy, they produce an artistic genius like Ivan Mestrovich or a scientific inventor like Nikola

Tesla, who is a native of Lika, a region very much like and adjoining Zagoryé.

They are *siroté*, poor people, and not ashamed of it. Here and there, in the more healthful, non-malarial villages, they possess lively imaginations and have embellished their hard plight with poetry. They are formal Christians, but really pagan. In a remote mountain hamlet an old woman told me of a conversation she said she had "overheard" early one morning between the Moon and the Sun.

The Sun had just risen and the Moon, which was still up, said, "Oh, good morning, Sun! You know, I must say I admire you; you're up so regular and early every morning. Don't you find it hard to be so punctual?"—"Oh no, Moon!" laughed the Sun, gently. "I like it."—"You *like* it?"—"Yes, Moon; it's no trouble to me at all to be up like this every day. God comes to my bed every morning— God Himself in person—and He shakes me and wakes me, and says, 'Get up, Sunny, get up in the sky, high up and all around the sky, over the Earth, and linger there awhile and shine bright and warm. I've made the Earth and all that is on it, but it's not a very good job. I've bungled things a bit down there and must find some way to right them. Meantime the Earth is full of *siroté*, poor people; you know whom I mean—the folks in Zagoryé, for instance— who get the worst of everything down there. So while I try to figure out something to straighten things out on Earth, go up, Sunny, go up now, high and all around the sky, and shine bright and warm on my *siroté* in Zagoryé and every other place; for the Earth is full of them.' . . . God talks to me like that on waking me; every morning he talks to me in his beautiful, sad voice; and so, to help Him out in his trouble, I up—and here I am! . . ."

IX

Early in November Stella and I returned to Dubrovnik, stayed there another five or six weeks, then took a notion to go to Bosnia—to Sarajevo.

CHAPTER X

A City Suspended in Space

FOR TWELVE HOURS THE LITTLE "CHOO-CHOO," AS Stella affectionately called the tiny train we had boarded at Dubrovnik, hissed and shuddered up the narrow-gauge track, first through the gray twisted gorges and under overhanging cliffs of the Dalmatian coast range, then into the desolate alps of Herzegovina, and finally into the green mountains of Bosnia.

From Dubrovnik we set out with one locomotive. Somewhere in Herzegovina we picked up another one. Then, at a station near the base of a high round mountain about two hours before we reached Sarajevo, we took on two more, one to help the first to pull in front and the other to shove from behind. There were as many engines as passenger-cars; but even so, going up this final and steepest incline, we made only six or seven miles an hour.

It was mid-December, but, except for the highest peaks which we saw from the distance, no snow had fallen yet in Bosnia, and toward sundown the mountains were very beautiful. Over the dense pine forests loomed fantastic crags, sculptures of millions of rainstorms and bolts of lightning. On crests, here and there, stood the broken walls of ancient Turkish forts and romantic-looking *kule*, or towered castles, of one-time Moslem beys who once had ruled Bosnia. Below us were tight little ravines alive with rapid streams and veil-like waterfalls.

Huddled in defiles and against ridges were primitive thatch-roofed villages. Occasionally we saw a girl or older woman in vast balloon-like pantaloons and embroidered jacket, busily spinning thread from the loose ball of wool, flax, or tow on her distaff while watching her sheep.

Our car was in the middle of the train, and at sharp turns which followed one after the other we could see all four locomotives. They whistled every few minutes; apparently one to the other, for there were no crossings. "I suppose the three in front," conjectured Stella, "are whistling to urge the one in back to push harder and the one in the rear answers they have a nerve and should pull more in front."

After an hour's going with four engines I remarked that it seemed as if we were climbing a rope or something.

"I was thinking the same," said Stella. "I almost feel the exertion of pulling myself up. I've been trying to keep it a secret, but I'm getting tired. . . . It's as though we were climbing up a rope that an Oriental fakir had tossed in the air—like Douglas Fairbanks in 'The Thief of Bagdad,' years ago. Remember?"

I nodded.

Stella rather liked the rope idea and continued to play with it. "Climbing up—up—up to a place hung in the air ——"

"—a place suspended in space," said I, simultaneously with her.

We knew, of course, that Sarajevo was an Oriental town —or predominantly so—somewhere on the top of where we were headed. At the moment, however, we did not realize how very close we came to describing not only the physical position, but several other aspects of the city, where on a nice day late in June, 1914, a young man had assassinated the heir to the Austrian throne, thus striking the spark for the world conflagration, the consequences of which are daily more apparent. How truly Sarajevo is a city suspended in space we knew only after we had been there awhile.

When we arrived, around seven in the evening, Sarajevo was lost in a cold, thick, unstirring fog. Riding from the depot in a slow, lurching hotel bus, we saw nothing but street lamps, which seemed miles away; and occasionally a headlight suddenly emerged from the white mass.

But it was just as well. Both of us were dead tired from the long "rope-climb," as we were referring to our rail journey by then; too tired to be interested in anything save a hot bath and sleep.

The next morning I awoke at daybreak and for the first time heard a muezzin call the summons to prayer. One of Sarajevo's ninety-nine mosques was only two blocks from our hotel.

The muezzin, drawing out his call, had a rich, beautiful voice; it drifted in through the open windows with a fine, melodious tremor. This was the Orient. By a freak of history, here in Slavic Bosnia, was this westernmost outpost of the East; an island of Islam within a sea of Christianity, almost no farther from Berlin or Paris than from Constantinople or Angora.

Although I did not understand his words, the muezzin's summons, as he repeated it several times, was dramatic and, as I say, beautiful; but at the same time it slightly rasped against my inbred Westernism. However, I presently got over the effect of the muezzin's call. Outside was a fine day. The sun was remarkably warm for that altitude in December. I learned later that this was extremely unusual weather. As a rule, Sarajevo has terrific winters, spring often is late, autumn long and beautiful, summer the best part of the year.

After breakfast we went walking through the modern part of the town. I wanted to see the spot where Gavrilo Princip had assassinated Archduke Franz Ferdinand and his wife. The waiter in the coffee-house had told me how to get to the little bridge over the River Milyatska where the incident had occurred, but, on reaching the river, we discovered several small bridges only a few blocks apart and all alike.

I stopped a young man who, while buttoned up in an elegant English overcoat, wore a red fez tilted at a rakish angle on the right side of his head so that the tassel dangled over his ear; and, explaining to him that we were strangers in Sarajevo, asked if he could point out to us the historic bridge.

"This is the one, right here," he said, smiling courteously. "You may be standing not three meters from where Princip fired the shots."

I asked him a few other questions, which he readily answered.

"There is nothing else to indicate the spot," he said, as we started to walk across the street from the bridge, "except that plaque there on the wall." We came to a two-story house.

I read the Serbian inscription on the gray marble plate—

ON THIS HISTORIC SPOT

GAVRILO PRINCIP

ON

ST. VITUS' DAY, JUNE 28, 1914

HERALDED THE ADVENT OF LIBERTY

Narodna Obrana

I translated it to Stella and explained to her that Narodna Obrana was a Serb nationalist organization of which Princip had been a member; while the young man, I noticed, was discreetly looking us over. He smiled faintly, glancing at a copy of the Paris edition of an American paper I carried in my overcoat pocket. He studied our faces and gradually his faint smile broadened, became more pronounced.

"He's good-looking," murmured Stella.

He was good-looking, excessively so, as I had myself casually noticed a minute before. Six feet tall, broad-shouldered and well-built otherwise, he carried himself erect with just a touch of bravado or recklessness in the general aspect of his personality. This bravado, I suspected already then was partly a matter of the way he wore his fez.

He looked to be twenty-three or -four, but, as he told us later, was twenty-six. His face was a composite portrait of a half-dozen Hollywood film actors. His hair was black; his eyes ditto, and very lively, friendly, and agreeable. His upper lip was symmetrically decorated with a tiny black mustache, most carefully trimmed and brushed. In his attire, save for the fez, he was a walking treatise on what a well-dressed man should wear in London or New York.

"Is he a Moslem?" wondered Stella.

"I suppose so—with that fez. But be careful; he may know English as well as you do." That possibility had just occurred to me, for the young man's smile had rapidly enveloped his whole face and a mischievous gleam appeared in his eyes.

Then he broke into a hearty laugh, and Stella and I joined him. During the previous months, elsewhere in Yugoslavia, we had suddenly and in various strange and amusing ways encountered people who spoke or understood English.

"Yes, I'm a Moslem," he said, after a while in good, if somewhat rigidly pronounced, English. "My name, if you will permit me to present myself, is Omar Hadji Alich."

"Well," laughed Stella, "I've always wanted to know some one named Omar. May I call you just Omar?"

"Of course—certainly."

The three of us were friends in no time. We laughed. Somehow it did not occur to either Stella or me to introduce ourselves; but then Omar said, smiling:

"I believe I know who you are. Your pictures were in our newspapers last spring, when you arrived from America, and I've just read in one of this morning's papers that you arrived last night."

The information had doubtless been given to the newspaper by the hotel or the police; for everywhere in Yugoslavia one is reported to the police as soon as one registers in a hotel.

"It is very funny," Omar continued, "but I was just thinking about you when you stopped me on the bridge. . . . What was I thinking, and why?" He laughed again. "Oh, that is too long a story to be told on a winter morning on a sidewalk. I understand from the papers that you plan to be in Sarajevo three weeks or a month. I hope you will come to my father's store—an antique store in the Bazaar, where I have to be during the day (I manage the place), or that you will let me see you evenings. Then I shall tell you. . . . Perhaps you can come with me now? My little brother is already in the store; he has made a fire."

He was very eager, in a restrained way, that we should come; and, having nothing else to do, we went.

I wasn't sure I had heard his full name correctly, so I asked him to repeat it. Then he explained that Omar had been his grandfather's name; Hadji signified he had made his *hadj*, or pilgrimage to Mecca. On his father's side, he continued, he was of Turkish ancestry, but considered himself a Slav, a Bosnian, a Yugoslav. "My forebears," he said, "came here from Turkey in the sixteenth century, soon after the Turks had taken Bosnia. Originally our family name was Ali, but my great-great-great (three times) grandfather Slavicized it into Alich."

I said that that was rather ironic. The Turks had conquered the Slavs of Bosnia politically and economically, and made it necessary for them to embrace Islam; but, in their turn, the Slavs had Slavicized the Turks.

Omar smiled. "In fact," he said, palpably trying (and succeeding with ease) to interest us, "this lovely Bosnia of ours is just one great irony; at least as I look at it. For example, it is rather funny and peculiar, is it not, that, although the Slavs once upon a time were the greatest enemies of Islam and fought against it for a thousand years, Bosnia—this purely Slavic country—now is one of the

{ 183 }

strongholds of orthodox Islam? The reforms of Kemal Pasha do not reach here. Hundreds of thousands of Slavic Moslems here in Yugoslavia are better Moslems, in the old orthodox sense, than most Turks in Turkey.

"Sarajevo itself is an extremely ironic town. Here, so to speak, began the Great War, which caused profound changes in the world. Russia went Bolshevik. Austria was broken up. Italy became Fascist. Germany has Hitler; Turkey, Kemal Pasha. Several new countries, including Yugoslavia, came into existence. America has a terrible economic depression. And so on. But Sarajevo, up here on this plateau surrounded by hills and mountains on all sides, remains essentially the same as it was in 1914.

"You must not misunderstand me. I was born in Sarajevo, and I love the town; at least, a great many things about it, now and then. You have no idea how beautiful, how romantic, it looks from any one of these mountains around it; you must go up and see. The numerous minarets, when you see them all at once, make it really a rare sight. Begova Djamia"—built in the fifteenth century by one Ghazi Huzgrev-beg, which we were passing at the moment —"is one of the two or three most beautiful mosques in the world. We have other things here which can be described only in superlatives. But"—hesitating an instant—"off and on I have an unhappy feeling about Sarajevo; which probably comes from the fact that I am young." He smiled, then his face turned serious again. "I feel that we are terribly far away from the rest of the world, from the vital processes of culture, civilization, progress.

"You see, my father sent me to an English school on Malta, then to Constantinople, where I also studied English and learned French and German. Lately, running my father's business, I have made some friends among the foreigners, tourists, especially the English and Americans, who come to the store. They send me books and magazines; and, reading these publications, every once in a while I

{ 184 }

realize that we here in Sarajevo are . . . well, hanging between sky and earth."

Stella and I looked at one another.

"But I'm afraid," smiled Omar, "that I am suddenly telling you too much, on your first day in Sarajevo. What I am saying is perhaps too involved and obscure for one to understand who doesn't know Sarajevo. . . . Here we are!"

Over the door of a low-eaved, slightly lopsided little building in the center of the Bazaar section of the town I read the Serbian sign—"Mehmet Agha Alich, Oriental Antiques."

"My father's name," said Omar, opening the door for us. "Agha," he replied to Stella's question, "is a title of respect. If you stay here two or three weeks, you no doubt will meet my father. He is a very fine man."

III

The store, a small, low-ceilinged place, was the neatest antique shop I had ever seen. It was full of near-Eastern junk—old silver and copper goblets, vases, trays, and pitchers of exquisite forms, with Arabic inscriptions from the Koran; bejeweled guns, hangers, yataghans, and poniards of many categories, each with a gory history; Turkish, Persian, and Bosnian brocades, drapes, rugs, and garments with rare embroideries dating back to the tenth and fourteenth centuries.

A handsome boy of twelve or thereabouts, also with a little fez on the side of his head, was putting wood into a round-bellied iron stove as we entered. "My brother Meho," said Omar.

"How—do—you—do?" said Meho, with long pauses between words, and grinned at the end.

"He speaks only a few words of English," said Omar, then told him, in Serbian, to go to a near-by *kafana* and fetch us coffee.

I protested that we had just breakfasted, but Omar said it was customary to serve coffee to everyone on all occasions.

Over his desk was a shelf of books, mostly English, with several copies of American magazines. Omar remarked that most of his library was at home, then told us of some of the books he had read recently—novels by Galsworthy, Tomlinson, Sinclair Lewis, and Ben Hecht, poetry by Edna St. Vincent Millay, and Wells' *Outline of History*.

Meho returned and placed a little copper tray with a tiny cup of syrupy Turkish coffee each before Stella and me.

"But won't you have any?" Stella asked Omar.

"You will forgive me," he answered, "but I can't. This is ramadan, the annual thirty-day fast period for all Moslems. It began yesterday. We must not eat, drink, or smoke anything from sunup till sundown. Ramadan comes every nine months, which constitutes our lunar year. This year, fortunately, it comes during winter, when days are short. It is comparatively easy, after the first few days, to fast and not smoke from five-thirty in the morning till four-thirty in the afternoon, as is the case this year, but not so easy in the summer, as it happens every few years, when the day—up here in the mountains—is from four in the morning till eight-thirty in the evening."

On his desk were two or three Christmas cards with American postage stamps on the envelopes. I remarked on them. Christmas was less than a week off.

"Yes," grinned Omar, "I received several of them this year. American tourists, mostly ladies, come here, and some of them, I mean the ladies (may Allah bless them!) are very charming. Occasionally, when I have time, I take one of them out, to show her the Sarajevo she would not see otherwise, because I am interested in America ——"

Stella and I laughed.

"No, really"—Omar laughed, too—"I really *am* very much interested in America, and I learn much about that country from American ladies who come here. But when they return to America they forget I am a Moslem—true, not a very good one, as my father often sadly reminds me; still, a Moslem. Or maybe they send me Christmas greetings only as a jest. . . . But this year the cards began to come at the start of ramadan, so I take their messages to mean 'Best wishes for a successful fast'!"

Tourists being scarce in Sarajevo in December, Omar had no business; but this suited him perfectly. "I really love some of this 'junk,' as you call it," he smiled; "and some of the people who come to buy the finer brocades, carpets, and costumes do not seem equipped with a strong enough sense of appreciation of Oriental beauty and workmanship to be entitled to own them. This may be snobbery; if so, I am sorry, but that is how I feel."

Stella thought that whatever it was it was all right.

"Then, also," continued Omar, "I am glad business is poor just now because you arrived in Sarajevo and I was so fortunate as to be on the bridge." He paused, then speaking directly to me, continued: "You probably do not realize what I shall tell you—and you probably will laugh—but we have here in Sarajevo a club called the Anglo-American Club (I am its treasurer), which consists mostly of young people—Moslems, Christians, Jews—who know a little English and have been waiting for you to come here almost ever since you arrived in Yugoslavia last spring—in May, was it not?

"We have been reading about you in the newspapers when you were in Slovenia and in Split, and we wondered when you were coming here. . . . Allow me to explain why we were so eager to see you. You are a citizen of the United States and you call yourself an American, but you were born a Yugoslav and we consider you a Yugoslav. You live in America, a country that has been exciting our imaginations for a century. There you have become a writer in the English language. We have read your books; they are in our club library. To us you are a rare phenomenon. You are one of us, 'a leaf from a tree in our mountains,' and by becoming an American writer you became, whether you like it or not, a link between us and America. This means a good deal to us.

"And that is not all. This lovely, picturesque Yugoslavia of ours, which an American lady from California said to me looked like an immense Hollywood cinema lot, with most of the population dressed in national costumes like so many actors and actresses in a drama—well, this is a small and new country, still in the process of formation. . . . We are part of the general European mess. Regardless of what we, the people of Yugoslavia, do within our narrow borders, we do not have the complete and final decision as to our destiny. We are caught in the dynamics of international politics of the big powers. Our future depends a great deal on the moods of statesmen in London, Paris, Geneva, on what may develop in America, Russia, Italy. As a country we are—how do you say it?—oh, yes, betwixt and between; not a very comfortable place to be in.

"And then we here in Sarajevo have our special situation. Our horizons are limited by these mountains. It is like living on the bottom of a kettle. Our population is 70,000, almost equally divided among Moslems, Catholics, Orthodox Christians, and Jews. This has been essentially a Moslem-Jewish community for 400 years; in recent decades, first under Austria and now under Yugoslavia, numerous buildings were built in the modern section of the town; but in general the culture and color of the city still are Moslem-Jewish: Oriental, mediæval.

"But we are too far west. We are a bit of Asia in Europe, a curiosity, a scene from *A Thousand and One Nights*. People come from afar to look us over; and it is fortunate for us they come. Tourism helps; for there is no really sound economic reason why there should be a large town here. We have no big industries; our narrow-gauge railroad connections are poor; the city is too inaccessible. We have a carpet-factory, a brewery, a tobacco-factory; but they employ only about a thousand people altogether. The provincial government employs a few hundred more. That is all.

"The basis for the development of Sarajevo to its present size was laid in the Middle Ages, when our Moslem fore-fathers made the place an outpost of Islam because of the military advantage of these mountains. Starting a big town up here was all right then, from the viewpoint of mediæval Moslemism; but, to use an American slang phrase, it is not so hot today when we are isolated from the great Moslem world of the East and our urges are becoming more and more social and economic, in the Western sense; when it is daily more apparent, especially since this world business crisis began and even tourism is commencing to fall off, that there are too many of us up here. . . ."

Subsequently I learned from other sources that over 20 per cent of Sarajevo's inhabitants—Moslem, Christian, and Jewish—lived in acute poverty and another 20 per cent, perhaps, not far removed from it.

IV

We saw Omar almost daily. Intelligent, sincere, unaffected, with a lively sense of humor, he was always good company and unfailingly pleased when we stepped into his store, or went walking with him about town or in the mountains, or let him take us to some coffee-house or restaurant.

We wandered for hours through the labyrinthine streets, alleyways, and arcades of the great *tcharshia*, or Bazaar section, full of tiny shops operated by Moslem and Jewish artisans and merchants. . . .

Most of the shops in the Bazaar are not like Mehmet Agha's antique store, which, unlike the others, aims to attract tourist trade, but mere open-front wooden sheds, without doors or windows, low-eaved and dilapidated, in which one may see wrought and sold several thousand different articles by some of the best handcraftsmen in the world.

Here an *opanchar* (cobbler) is making primitive sandals of red, green, and yellow leather, laced with thongs like moccasins. Here a hatter is shaping fezzes between two metal forms under a heavy press. When he pulls them out he caresses them delicately with his hands. The fezzes are red and black, the latter color being intended for the Jews.

Another shopkeeper offers new rugs which are Turkish and Persian in technique but Slavic in design. The establishment next door is a jewelry store and one can watch men making filigree earrings, tobacco and vanity cases, trays and bric-à-brac-boxes, pins, buttons, bracelets.

There are shops which display great collections of heavy socks, muffs, and mittens knitted by peasant women in the villages, containing all the colors of the rainbow. Other sheds are veritable museums of every kind of primitive tool and implement since the days of the Prophet. From under the eaves of food stores depend festoons of green and red peppers, garlic, sweet onions, and a certain aphrodisiac vegetable called *bamya*. Beneath them are open sacks of beans, lentils, cornmeal, and flour; baskets of prunes and other dried fruits, nuts, eggs, and kindling-wood.

There is an entire district of coffee-shops, for coffee in Sarajevo, as elsewhere in central Balkans, is an important item. As Omar suggested, it is served everywhere on all occasions. The best Mocha, Java, Hodeida, and Brazil beans are roasted and ground into the finest powder in little coffee-mills manufactured in special shops in the district, or—this is said to be ever better—pounded in a primitive contraption called *stupa*, a hollow log of hard wood with the center of it burned out. Coffee-roasting and -grinding, as well as coffee-cooking, has the status of an art in Sarajevo. The *tcharshia*, like the more or less Occidental sections of the town, abounds with coffee-houses, which serve only coffee at one or two dinars a cup the size of a large thimble. The coffee is very strong, but what one first notices about it is a vague and delicate flavor I can describe only as Oriental.

Another large district is devoted to bakeries and kitchens. Here housewives bring their bread to be baked, tradesmen in the Bazaar their pots of stew to be cooked, at so much per loaf or pot. . . . To Stella and me this was one of the most interesting sections because, as already stated, we happened to be there during ramadan. The Moslems broke their daily fast at four-thirty, and by then most of them were ravenously hungry. At four o'clock the merchants in the business-sheds had their food-pots and bread delivered to them, but did not touch anything till the sunset gun was fired from one of the mountain-sides; whereupon all together they dug into the stew and broke the loaves, simultaneously lighting their first cigarettes and gulping down their first cup of coffee since before the dawn.

One street of the Bazaar, the farthest from Begova Djamia, runs for blocks up an incline. It is the braziers', silversmiths', coppersmiths', tinsmiths', and blacksmiths' quarter, where hundreds of hammers pound glowing metals into plowshares, steelyards, field and house tools of all kinds, boilers, kettles, pots and pans, trays and pitchers, and one is unable to hear one's own words. But one stops and looks in amazement. Here is the handcraft age in full and vital operation, as vital as anything in Sarajevo. Hundreds of various articles of startling workmanship—and in many cases of beauty—are made before one's eyes by essentially the same methods that have been employed by Near-Eastern artificers seven centuries ago.

The merchants, busy making things, make no attempt to sell anything. Some post their prices, others merely display their wares, then wait patiently, almost indifferently, till the prospective buyer, tarrying in front of their shop, addresses them. It can hardly be said they do a lively business, but they eke out an existence on the purchases that the Bosnian peasants make on market days.

They need little. Some of them wear the same clothing for ten, fifteen years; then the garment is cut up and used to patch other clothes. In the winter their business-booths are as wide open as in the summer. A few of them have a pot of burning charcoal near them, while others hardly even bother buttoning their waistcoats or shirts. An enormous sash wound 'round and 'round their middle is the central heating-plant for their whole body.

Many of them have been working and doing business in the same shed for thirty, forty, fifty years. Their fathers and great- and great-great-grandfathers had been in the same trades on the same spots. Omar took Stella and me to a primitive barber shop that has been run by the same family for 230 years. He showed us an apothecary shop owned and run by an old Jew with a far-away look, selling the same sort of herbs and strange powders, concoctions and leeches, that his forbears sold five hundred years ago in Spain. We visited a 400-year-old *han* (Turkish hotel) in charge of an ancient Moslem who had had the job for nearly half a century.

According to Omar, these men, Jews and Moslems alike, are all extremely honest. Honesty is not a mere policy with them; it is in their blood. They trust one another and everybody else. When the muezzin calls to prayer the Moslems pull their legs from under themselves and, without so much as thinking to board and bolt up their shops, hurry off to the nearest mosque. "They believe," said Omar, "that while they pray to Allah, Allah protects their interests—and it seems to be true." Despite the widespread poverty, there is almost no thieving or other crime in Sarajevo.

But more interesting even than the shops and their *maistori* are the people jamming the streets and alleyways, especially on market days, which come every Wednesday.

First one notices the Moslem women, who, unlike the women of modern Turkey, are still veiled and wear *zari*, long, loose cover-all mantles of cheap material which completely disguise the wearer's form, while under the cover-alls the well-to-do women wear the latest fashions in Western clothes. Some of the veils are very thin, and occasionally one catches a glimpse of a pair of enormous orbs (for already as little girls they artificially augment their eyes) or a smile.

The poor Moslèm women who stop one at every few steps and ask for a coin appear to wear, in the coldest of weather, clothes but little thicker than their veils. One or two I saw barefoot on frozen ground; others had only wooden clogs on bare feet. Some of these female beggars are "divorced" women—that is, their husbands, for one reason or another, had driven them out of their homes.

Next one notices the enormous Bosnian mountaineer-peasants from the vicinity of Sarajevo who come in to sell their calves and sheep, firewood and other products, and make their simple purchases. Some of them are six-feet-six or seven, thin and rawboned, with colossal fleshless hands and faces. They walk with the peculiar stride of mountain men. Nearly all of them, Christian and Moslem, wear homespun clothes, crude boat-like sandals, and fezzes or turbans. Their breeches have enormous baggy seats, which often reach below their knees. They are men of incredible strength and endurance. Carrying huge burdens, they walk all night from their villages to get to the Sarajevo market place by morning and realize their ten or fifteen dinars, which is the equivalent of fifteen or twenty cents, then walk back again.

One sees curious-faced *hodjas* (Moslem priests, judges, and generally learned men) with white and golden turbans; little Jewish women with a headgear covered with gold coins, the same that their ancestors wore in the ghettos of Madrid and Granada five centuries ago; Yugoslav army officers in foppish uniforms; Moslem lawyers, doctors, politicians, and modern business men wearing, like Omar, aside from the fez, complete Western outfits; and orthodox Serb Christians and Bosnian Catholics who look like the general run of people in any European city.

We took, as I have said, several walks into the mountains about the city. The view from there was indescribable—a chaos of East and West, fantastic, weird, yet beautiful.

"Yes, it is lovely," agreed Omar; "and, as I have said, I love Sarajevo—oh, very much; but I wish I were in your boots, free to come, stay three weeks or a month, see the place, then go again—to America, back into the great lively, moving world. . . . I guess this is because I am young and know American and English ladies (may Allah damn them!) who send me interesting books to read—what?"

He laughed; we laughed with him. But I was sorry for him, as was Stella. He told us he was trying to induce his father to send him with a carload of their antiques to the Century of Progress Exposition in Chicago, but Mehmet Agha only shook his head, "We can't afford it."

V

Mehmet Agha, whom we met on our second day in town, was a solid middle-aged man, ultra-conservative, wearing the old-fashioned Moslem garb—great baggy breeches, embroidered waistcoat, fez and all. His eyes crinkled up in a sharp gaze, but, actually, within the limits of his conservatism, he was one of the kindliest men.

His friends dropped into the store, among them some of the leading men in Sarajevo—business men, politicians, doctors, judges. There we met also Omar's three brothers-in-law. One of these was a *hodja* and Sheriat (Moslem) judge who had married Mehmet Agha's daughter, Fata-hanum. He, of course, always wore a priest's garb with the white turban. The second brother-in-law was a business man; he was the husband of Hata-hanum; while the latter's sister, Sultania-hanum, was married to a government official.

Each of these three couples, we learned, already had several children. Omar had three more sisters at home, Sahiba, Aisha, and Saima, as yet too young to marry; and in addition to Meho, whom we had met on our first morning in Sarajevo, two more brothers, Ahmed and Husrev; which altogether made ten children.

I remarked to Mehmet Agha that he had a large family.

He nodded, smiled, and quoted an old Slavic-Moslem adage: "A household has never too many coffee-cups and children." In fact, he never spoke to me without quoting some ancient proverb.

Perhaps the most interesting man Stella and I met in Mehmet Agha's store was a high priest from Mecca, one Said Emmin Akaad, who claimed to be a direct descendant of Mohammed. He wore a resplendent satin robe and a turban of golden cloth. His face had a weird Oriental loveliness. He was, perhaps, in his early fifties, spoke no Slavic, but knew a few words of English, in which he imparted to me bits of Oriental wisdom that have since escaped me. He was a *bedel*. An old man unable to make his *hadj* before he died had asked him to come to Sarajevo, take a portion of his cash, then return as his proxy to Mecca. I was told he made several of these proxy-pilgrimages between Sarajevo and Mecca every year; of course, at so much per.

One night Omar took us to the Anglo-American Club, whose chief purpose is the study of English and the procurement of books from England and America. It was a surprise party. Some fifty persons were packed in two small rooms—young Moslems of Omar's age, Orthodox Serbs, men and women, a half-dozen Jews, and two or three Catholics; business people, government clerks, journalists, teachers and students—all avidly, quiveringly interested in the United States, the world beyond the Sarajevo mountains, in American literature, art, films, music; social, racial, religious, and sex questions and problems; immigration, racketeering, labor, and politics—and in Stella and me personally.

The party lasted all night. By the end of it Stella and I were exhausted from answering their questions. When Omar succeeded in getting us back to the hotel, the muezzin was again calling his morning summons to prayer from the minaret of the near-by mosque.

Thereafter, if we wanted to rest during the day, we had to leave word at the desk that we were not in. Always there was somebody waiting in the lobby to tell me something, to beg Stella to send them a certain book or fashion magazine from America, in return for which they brought her gifts of all sorts, for in Yugoslavia it is forbidden to send money out of the country and many persons are unable to order anything from the outside. Young authors brought me their books and asked me would I take a little time off from my own work to translate them into English and get them published in the United States. Always somebody was waiting in the lobby to tell me something about Sarajevo or the political situation in Yugoslavia as it affected Bosnia or the Moslems; to urge me, when I went to Belgrade, I should seek to meet Alexander and "tell him the truth," namely that 95 per cent of the people were dissatisfied with his *diktatura*. Young newspaper men came for interviews, much of the same thing that we had had in Lublyana and Split. A worker, who I think was a Communist, called on me to say that in certain small sweatshops in the city women operatives, working fourteen hours, earned only ten cents a day, and lumber workers in the great Bosnian forests earned even less. Men and women—Moslems and Christians and those who seemed proud to declare they were neither—who had lately come out of prisons, where they had served terms because of their opposition to the dictatorship, came to tell me their experiences and what they had seen others endure at the hands of King Alexander's terrorists and sadists. . . . This went on during our entire stay in Sarajevo.

But, as in Slovenia (and, to a lesser extent, in Dalmatia), it had little to do with me, at least not directly or in any basic sense. It was the same thing as in Lublyana six months earlier. Many educated, intelligent people in Sarajevo, as elsewhere in Yugoslavia (and, for that matter, all over Europe), felt they were "betwixt and between," hung in space, more or less frustrated, momentarily uncertain of their future; while I—with my "success" in America, my ability to return there whenever I liked, my Guggenheim Fellowship, and my American citizenship which protected me against anyone in Yugoslavia who might wish to put me in prison for political reasons—was good luck and romance personified.

VI

On another night Omar took us to a performance, in the state-operated theater, of a Bosnian tragedy, "Hasanaginica" ("The Wife of Hasan Agha"), based on an old folk-poem dealing with the fate of a Moslem woman whom, due to a misunderstanding, her husband divorces by the simple procedure of ordering her out of the house. It is one of the most interesting and moving pieces of Bosnian literature: a Moslem theme treated in the spirit and form of Serb tragic poetry. Goethe learned Serbian to be able to translate it into German.

But to us the performance, given in Serbian, was no more interesting than the audience, which consisted largely of well-to-do orthodox Moslems and the younger generation of heretics. It was a full house; the Sarajevans go to see the play over and over again. There were several hundred Moslem women who lifted their veils when the curtain went up, and by glancing about during the acts one could see some pretty and even beautiful faces. Simultaneously with the drop of the curtain they put down their veils again.

During the intermissions, which are long, it is the custom to go to the *kafana* in the theater lobby and drink coffee and smoke. There Omar introduced us to more of his young Moslem friends and acquaintances. Some of the boys, he told us, were even more "modern" than he was; they no longer wore the fez. We met also two or three modern Moslem girls, one exceedingly beauteous, who refused to wear the veil and sported the latest Parisian fashion in clothes.

I was impressed by the fine materials and elegance of most of the Occidental clothes worn by these young Moslem heretics, and it occurred to me that they, including Omar, wore such excellent suits and gowns—many of them doubt-less costlier than they could afford—in a pathetic effort to justify their heterodoxy in their own eyes, to feel better in the face of the orthodox opposition of their elders, and at the same time propagandize their cause. I mentioned this to Omar; he smiled and said, "Perhaps."

One evening he took us to a *tekia*—a dervish monastery —in one of the oldest sections of the town, where we wit-nessed the devotional ceremonies of a group of holy men and their disciples. Chanting, they swayed and contorted their bodies, gradually raising their voices and increasing the tempo of their movements and prayers till they worked themselves into something akin to a cataleptic fit and drove Stella and me to the verge of exasperation. Though he showed it less, Omar's exasperation with these doings per-haps was even greater than our own.

VII

The last night of our stay in Sarajevo, Omar invited us, in his father's name, to his home, which was a rambling, walled-in house, several hundred years old and built around a large cobbled courtyard.

In his stockinged feet (for Moslems go shoeless in their homes) Mehmet Agha greeted us formally, perhaps with the same words and manner his forbears had used centuries ago when visitors came, then ushered us into a large sitting-room where a number of guests, friends of the family's, already were assembled. This was the only room in the house I saw. Its furnishings were essentially the same as when the house had been built—very simple and tasteful, beautiful in an Oriental way, with rugs covering every inch of the floor as well as the ottomans along the walls. In front of each guest was a tiny table for coffee, preserved fruit, and water. On one of the walls was a collection of ancient Bosnian firearms; on another, an exquisite Damascan rug.

Hospitality in a Sarajevo Moslem home, even in families of pure Slavic blood, is not the spontaneous, almost orgiastic business that one has to endure in Christian homes in Yugoslavia, but extremely formal and restrained. One sits and talks, exchanging more or less stereotyped remarks. The youngest sons of the family stand one in each corner and come soundlessly to take one's empty coffee-cup or water-glass and return it filled, or light one's cigarette.

Stella was the only girl in the room. After a while Omar asked her to come upstairs to the women's quarters to visit his mother, two grandmothers, and unmarried sisters; and so while I spoke with Mehmet Agha and his friends about things in America and my impressions of Yugoslavia, she conversed with the women, Omar acting as interpreter.

As she told me afterward, they received her in a room similar to the one downstairs, somewhat less formally than Mehmet Agha had received us below. They looked at her a long time.

Zarifhanuma, Omar's mother, a large woman in enormous red silk pantaloons, huge braids hanging down her back, and many jewels on her fingers, wrists, and throat, smiled and asked her. "How long have you been away from your mother? How many brothers and sisters have you?"

Stella told her, then they all limbered up a bit and began to question her on how American women did their housework, and when she told them about vacuum cleaners, electric washing-machines, automatic gas-heating, frigidaires, and other such conveniences of the American home, their large eyes became even larger and they shook their heads in restrained wonderment. What did women in America do with their time?

Umhihana, Omar's eighty-year-old maternal grandmother, remarked: "You have a beautiful complexion. How do you make your face creams?"

Stella laughed, "I buy them in a store."

Whereupon, on Omar's urging, Zarifhanuma and her young daughters showed her the concoctions—all homemade according to centuries-old formulæ—with which they kept their skins smooth and soft: jars of *surma*, an Indian cosmetic used by adult Moslem women in compliance with a passage in the Koran, to blacken their eyelids; vessels of Oriental perfumes and öils with which they anointed their persons; and receptacles of *hrmza*, a homemade odorless paste for removing hair.

Young Sahiba, who was fourteen, showed her her *tshezlyuk*, or hope chest, full of silken garments and jewels.

When Mehmet Agha came upstairs for a minute, all the women in the room except Stella rose and stood till he told them to sit down. They rose again when he started to leave.

Although they asked about American women, their interest really did not extend to anything beyond their homes and families, the intimate methods whereby they kept themselves as lovely as they could as long as possible. Yet as far as Stella could make out, they were happy women; and Omar assured her that, in their own way, they actually were happy. "Perhaps, happier," he added, "than most American women, if I may judge by those I have met or read about."

Neither Stella upstairs nor I downstairs was exactly comfortable; the restless, dynamic West was too strong in us; and so we did not stay long. Our parting, while not uncordial, was as formal as our arrival.

VIII

Omar saw us back to our hotel. We walked in silence a good part of the way. It was rather late of a cold and foggy evening, with almost no one in the streets.

"You have a very charming home, Omar," said Stella.

He smiled. " 'Very charming,' *but*—you were going to say 'but,' were you not?"

"No, I wasn't, really," said Stella.

"But there is a 'but,' " said Omar; "there are many 'buts,' from my angle. My sisters are good and nice, but they are not, say, like Leora, Martin Arrowsmith's wife *in*

Sinclair Lewis' novel, or like Kay Francis or Greta Garbo, both of whom I saw in films recently—or— Oh, well!" He laughed.

We were both sorry for Omar Hadji Alich. We were leaving the next morning. He had said several times the past few days how much he hated to see us go. Because I was a native of Yugoslavia, we were for him a more vital contact with America, the large world beyond, than most visitors to Sarajevo. I tried to make light of our parting, but was awkward about it. "Oh, you're just young, Omar," I laughed. "You've been hinting, yourself, that that was the trouble—your youth. When you get older, you'll probably settle down and not only continue wearing the fez, but put on breeches with baggy seats hanging below your knees, go to the mosque three times a day, and marry a nice Moslem girl whom you will require to wear a veil, or maybe become a dervish."

Omar smiled. "I do not think so. There is much that is charming in our life, but we are mediæval, over-conservative, unspontaneous, stuck in a historical and geographical rut. . . . We need something drastic to push us out of the rut. It may be that something will come along and do that. It may be the forces that were released here in 1914 will finally reach back into these mountains and make a change in our situation. But," he laughed, "I *am* young and it is hard to sit in an antique shop and wait, just wait for something big to happen to us."

He paused, then continued:

"If I did not love my father and my whole family as much as I do, I would have gone long ago—to England, to America—anywhere. But our family ties are very close, very strong and, in their own way, beautiful. They are part of our old social, religious system. If I went and threw off all my background (assuming that I could), it might kill my father. He loves me and is unhappy about me even now, although my heterodoxy is comparatively mild."

Near the hotel a semi-Oriental sweet shop was still open;

and although already overloaded with gifts of all sorts, we begged him to curb his generosity, Omar pulled us in and bought quantities of Oriental sweetmeats, handing the bags to Stella. "This is silly, I know. If you eat all this, you will be sick, and I shall not mind if tomorrow you throw it all away; but this is all I can do for you now, before we say good-by. Pathetic—no?"

We laughed a bit, then walked the rest of the way to the hotel in silence. Our train was leaving very early in the morning for South Serbia and we had forbidden Omar to get up to see us off at the station.

He said: "All day I have rehearsed nice things I would say to you when we parted tonight; now it seems anything I might say would be rather inadequate. . . . Please think of me a little in America now and then. I am very sad." He smiled.

He kissed Stella's hand, then shook mine. We parted.

CHAPTER XI

"Here the Clock Was Set Back"

THE OFFICIAL AND CIVIC CIRCLES IN SARAJEVO WERE as eager to make our stay there pleasant as had been those in Split, and succeeded as well. On the suggestion of the local Rotary Club (and, by the way, every larger town in Yugoslavia has a Rotary Club), the mayor of the city, a Moslem whose fez made him look like a middle-aged American business man on the way to a Shriners' convention, presented to me a beautiful album of pictures of Sarajevo and vicinity. The governor of the *banovina*, an Orthodox Serb, gave us his automobile and chauffeur whenever we wished to go somewhere.

I liked neither His Honor nor His Excellency, either personally or politically, but it would have been difficult, not to say totally unwise, to refuse their gifts and favors. In the first place, we liked very much a Mr. Urosh Ducitch— a Serb from Herzegovina and returned immigrant from the United States, now head of a small bank and a moving spirit in many Sarajevo activities, and (notwithstanding the fact that I disagreed with his politics) possessing a deep personal charm, rare kindness and sincerity, who, after we became acquainted with him, took it upon himself to personally arrange our trips into the rural sections of Bosnia and into Herzegovina. He was, I think, a friend and fellow Rotarian of the governor's. In the second place, we wanted to see as much of these ex-Turkish regions as possible, and our limited funds would not have permitted us to pay for motor transportation as we did in Montenegro: for distances in Bosnia and Herzegovina are considerably greater than those in the Black Mountain. And in the third place, the elegant automobile we used was not the governor's personal property; it belonged to the *banovina* government, in other words, to the people of the province, many of whom disliked the governor, an intimate friend of the Belgrade dictatorship's, much more than I did, and for more concrete reasons.

At any rate, having thus rationalized our use of the governor's car, we visited during our stay in Sarajevo, when not with our young Moslem friend, Omar Hadji Alich, numerous peasant communities along the highways within a radius of about 150 kilometers of the city. Here and there we hiked to one of the mountain villages off the highways which were inaccessible by auto. Occasionally the kind and agreeable Mr. Ducitch came with us; at other times another Herzegovinian Serb, Professor Obren Vukomanovitch, of the Sheriat (Moslem) Gymnasium in Sarajevo, or one of the Sarajevo newspaper men joined us; and once or twice we went alone with the chauffeur, who also knew the country well. In a couple of places we stayed overnight. We came in close contact with Orthodox Christian, Catholic, and Moslem peasant people—and by the time we left Bosnia for South Serbia I realized the truth of what an elderly Serb journalist, who visited me at the hotel soon after we arrived in Sarajevo, had said to me:

"Here in Bosnia and Herzegovina, as in South Serbia"— to give his words in free translation—"the clock was turned back by the invasion and victory of the mediæval Turks. When the Turks came, there was a considerable Christian-Slavic civilization here. Bosnia was a rich, independent country ruled by native kings. The Turks stayed over four hundred years. Half of that time the clock of progress, so far, at all events, as the peasant masses were concerned, ran back, then stopped. There was a long feudal period, minor wars, and local terror. A few decades ago Austria supplanted the Ottoman Empire and the clock was wound up again—however, not to go forward, certainly not for the rural masses, but still farther back. The Hapsburg rule helped the Moslem feudal lords to exploit the people. . . .

"As a result of Gavrilo Princip's *atentat* in June, 1914, which was a revolutionary act in behalf of the masses and which set off the World War and led to the creation of Yugoslavia, Bosnia and Herzegovina and nearly all of South Serbia now are 'free'—free from Turkish and Austrian oppression and exploitation, at all events. Yugoslavia, of which these lands now are parts, is not a perfect state; much is wrong with it; but basically it is all right. With all its imperfections, the present state of affairs here is a distinct improvement on the state of affairs, say, twenty years ago. . . .

"After the 'liberation' the clock was wound up again and made to go ahead. Here in Bosnia the great estates of the Moslem feudal grandees have been cut up into small farms and given to their one-time serf-peasants. With that we not only made the clock of progress go again, but, I think, set it considerably ahead.

"Since then, however, the clock has been going very, very slowly. It is still far, far behind-time. In the last decade there has developed here in Sarajevo a small but powerful new-rich class. They are mostly former Moslem landowners, whom the new Yugoslav government paid more for their estates on dividing them among the peasants than they were worth, and Christian Serbs, who are 'in' with the Belgrade regime and in cahoots with foreign (chiefly French) money-imperialists, and the two groups together are beginning to exploit our vast natural resources, especially the immense forests of Bosnia, to their own and the foreigners' further personal enrichment; while hundreds of thousands of peasants, who form 90 per cent of the population in these parts, get nothing out of this. If the peasants become lumber workers, their pay, as you know, is next to nothing. . . . The system under which we live is essentially no better than were the systems under the Crescent or the Double Eagle. The big idea is still exploitation of the country by a few people while the masses are separated from their natural resources. No one now in power in Belgrade or here in Sarajevo has any vigorous interest in the uplift of the peasant, who is still very primitive; and part of the peasant's primitiveness is his profound conservatism, which tends to obstruct rapid progress even where the government and the upper classes are not in silent (perhaps unintentional and unconscious) conspiracy to keep him poor and backward. . . .

"Many of the village communities here in Bosnia—and you don't have to go far from Sarajevo to find them—are still no farther advanced culturally and economically than tenth- or twelfth-century; while in sections of Herzegovina and through most of South Serbia, as you will see when you get there, people live no better than people lived in the Balkans and Asia Minor two or three thousand years ago. . . ."

II

Scenically or physically, Bosnia, Herzegovina, and South Serbia (the latter frequently also referred to as Old Serbia or Macedonia) are very unlike one another.

Herzegovina is part of the rocky, barren Karst belt. To the south of it is Montenegro; to the north the Dalmatian Highlands. It is more desolate than Tsernagora and, during winter, swept by severer winds than those blowing over Zagoryé. Its dominating physical feature are the Dinaric Alps, the grayest, most awesome range of mountains either Stella or I had ever seen. Once, as we drove and hiked over them, Stella remarked, "Mountains on the moon probably are something like this."

What little vegetation there is on the ridges is coarse, poor, hardly fit for goats; but over them graze also herds of sheep and *bushé*, a small, scrawny breed of cattle peculiar to Herzegovina and northwestern Bosnia. Water is scarce. Karst-like, streams tumble out of one hole, run on the surface awhile, then vanish into another hole. Fertile *polya*, ("fields") are few, small, and far between, most of them suitable only for raising maize and tobacco. Beside each "field" is a crude, primitive settlement, but one comes upon hamlets, utterly heartbreaking to see, even where no soil is available for cultivation, and people subsist mainly on sheep and goat cheese and meat.

In sharp contrast to Herzegovina, most of Bosnia is humid, green, and lush; mountainous, but full of valleys, big and little, and gently sloping ridges on which agriculture is feasible. In its northern parts one comes upon extensive plains with deep, rich soil, crossed by lazy, muddy rivers. The high, rolling mountains are covered by dense pine forests, which, along with the forests of Slovenia and Croatia, make Yugoslavia Europe's leading timber country. Besides, entire ranges of mountains are literally stiff with coal and ore deposits, which, although Turkey and Austria began to exploit them, are as yet little developed. As in other parts of Yugoslavia, mineral waters bubble out of every third mountain. Indeed, Bosnia may be potentially the richest part of southeastern Europe; but you would never guess it from observing the circumstances of the peasants, especially those living high in the mountains. In the midst of stupendous natural wealth the masses live upon a low level. Thousands of families, not only during the depression periods, but normally, use no sugar or salt, no matches or petroleum.

South Serbia is mountainous, too, but less so than Bosnia or Herzegovina. Most of its ridges, while not rocky, are bare of trees. The country was deforested by the Turks; below ground, however, great wealth remains—iron, copper, zinc, lead, bauxite, sulphur, antimony, chrome, and even gold and silver.

The people of all these regions are mostly Serbs, but not the same kind. The Herzegovinians are "pure Dinaric," an indigenous product of the Dinaric Alps. In their general physical features they are very much like the Montenegrins; if anything, perhaps even taller and leaner, more wiry and stronger. There is almost no Turkish blood in them; after they had surrendered to the Sultan's authority, the Turks left them, unlike the people of opulent Bosnia, very much to themselves.

The law of the survival of the fittest is even a tougher proposition in Herzegovina, especially in its northern parts, than in Montenegro. One-third of babies born along the Dinaric Alps die of exposure and lack of food before they are two years old. (One Herzegovinian told me, "Here in our country, if children do not die, they live," but in saying this he was not cruel, merely realistic.) Another third of Herzegovinians succumb to T.B. and malnutrition between the ages of five and twenty. The rest, as likely as not, live to be ninety or a hundred, and through most of their lives exhibit incredible capacity for suffering, extreme poverty, and hunger.

We came upon men, young and elderly, who haven't had what in America is considered a square meal all their lives, whose garments were of the simplest, roughest homespun, whose dwellings were unworthy to be called huts, whose formal schooling was none, yet who unmistakably were superior individuals. Their language is purer, more poetic even than the Montenegrins'. They are keen, eager, mentally quick; their manner is alert, aristocratic. If they have anything at all they do not let you, a stranger, go away without giving you a gift. Going about, we accumulated several balls of goat cheese, pots of sheep fat, and chunks of smoked mutton. One man gave us a bottle of mead. From another man I learned he hadn't eaten for several days, but when I offered him a little money he refused to accept it unless I let him do something for me. All Herzegovinians seem fanatically honest. They are sober, somber, restrained. Pure Slavs, with, as I say, almost no admixture of Turkish blood, they are innately civilized, capable of great instinctive kindness and gentleness. They have in them vast mental, physical, and spiritual powers. They can work twenty-four hours at a stretch at the hardest physical labor imaginable without resting or eating. They can run (not walk) uphill for hours. Their bodily movements are agile and graceful. Their faces, like those of people in other Yugoslav regions, are exciting with a strange beauty, a beauty that has behind it no end of hardship stoically endured. Their eyes glow with a strange pride.

Herzegovinian, like Montenegrin, students in Belgrade go through four years of university education on the equivalent of two or three cents a day; some eat only every other day. Educated Herzegovinians almost invariably become leaders in whatever field they take up. But no matter how high they get or where they live, they always remain Herzegovinians. Their love for the gray Dinaric wasteland is to an outsider something fantastic to contemplate. Behind that love, of course, are centuries of suffering endured by them at the hands of nature and their oppressors, and dramatized by them in folk poetry.

The Bosnians—approximately half of whom are Moslem and half Christian (Orthodox and Catholic)—differ considerably from the Herzegovinians. Many are as tall as the Herzegovinians, but heavier, not as straight or agile and alert; slow, sluggish, Oriental. There is no excusable or inevitable starvation in Bosnia. The Herzegovinian is essentially a simple, intelligent animal engaged in a terrific, never-ending struggle with nature. The Bosnian is complicated. About one-third primitive and pagan, one-third Byzantine Christian, one-third mediæval Moslem, he is full of slow but powerful and conflicting urges. His historic experience with the Turk, as already suggested, has been deeper than the Herzegovinian's. Also, living in a more comfortable region, the Bosnian could indulge in Moslem and Christian metaphysics, in the building of edifices to Allah and Yahweh, which in the course of time commenced to dominate his personal and communal life, made him less gentle, less fine than is the more pristine Herzegovinian; operated, in fact, to make him cruel and blood-thirsty.

Bosnians are horrible enemies in war. In the World War tens of thousands of them fought on the Austrian side, and single Bosnian regiments kept back and defeated entire divisions of Italians.

The Bosnian tills his voluptuous, rolling fields with a semi-sexual passion. Plowing, he is apt to talk endearingly to the black soil, make love to it. In the spring, I was told, it is not uncommon to see Bosnian peasants halt their oxen, drop to their knees or lie prone, spread their arms in embrace, and kiss and caress the dirt; while in Herzegovina one may see tall, gaunt men abruptly cease their digging to kneel and pray.

The South Serb or Macedonian peasant, in many respects, is a mingling of the Bosnian and the Herzegovinian. He is shorter, but almost as quick, lean, and tough as the Herzegovinian, in his inner nature more complicated even than the Bosnian. Upon his primitive Old Slavic make-up history has impressed powerful Byzantine and Turkish influences. For centuries he was oppressed and exploited far worse than the Bosnian. Also, for centuries, like the Dalmatian highlander, his body has been fighting malaria, especially in the valleys where rainwater rushes down from deforested mountains and creates swamps. There is considerable Turkish and Avar blood in his veins.

When Yugoslavia was organized, there were over a half-million wooden plows in use in Bosnia, Herzegovina, and South Serbia. One hundred thousand of them still remain; the others have been replaced by steel plows. That is great progress. There has been some advance also in other respects. Malaria and other diseases are being fought systematically by the government. Roads have been improved. But even so hundreds of thousands in these regions live on no higher plane than lived the peasants in the days of Christ and even Homer. They exist on crude bread, green peppers, and water-buffalo milk and cheese. They are primitive not only outwardly but inwardly.

III

I have briefly described the position of orthodox Moslem women in Sarajevo. Christian women there, as in other larger towns in Bosnia, live in more advanced circumstances; that is, the few who are comparatively well-off; but even in the home of so civilized a man as our friend Mr. Urosh Ducitch, both his wife, who is the daughter of a former Montenegrin general, and his mother rise when he, the head of the family, enters the room, and remain standing till he sits down, and get up again when he rises to leave. Mr. Ducitch, no doubt, would prefer if his women-folk did not respect him so formally; but they live in a country whose customs and traditions pertaining to relations between the sexes, based on the Moslem and primitive-pagan idea that woman is inferior to man, are still very strong.

I have described, too, the woeful position of women in Montenegro. In Bosnia and Macedonia it is even worse. A Christian Serb in a Bosnian village apologetically introduced to us his wife, "Excuse me, my woman,"—and she was pleased he did not entirely ignore her. In South Serbia it is not unusual to see a man riding on a donkey while his wife walks behind him, carrying a huge burden.

In both Bosnia and Macedonia we saw men strike their wives, who suffered the blows calmly, without resistance. Witnessing such scenes, Stella and I were moved to go to the women's defense, but, actually, for a Bosnian or Macedonian woman to be struck over the head by her husband is equivalent to an American woman being reproached by her spouse, "Please don't do that, honey!"

In Herzegovina, Bosnia, and South Serbia, especially in the last named, woman is practically man's slave. She is trained in childhood to submit to her brothers' will and consider them superior to herself. In sections of Macedonia the young man still buys his bride, then owns her body and soul—only, she is not considered to have a soul.

Quite generally, throughout these lands, the woman's paramount function is childbearing and work, work, work. She attends to the hardest, dirtiest, most important tasks. She produces at least three-fourths of everything her family consumes. She spins the thread, weaves the cloth, and sews and embroiders the clothes worn by her husband and children and herself. She does all that by hand, according to methods employed elsewhere in the world several thousand years ago. She hunts for roots, leaves, and grasses out of which, following ancient formulæ, she makes her own dyes. The costumes she fashions often are incredibly fine in technique (similar to that used in ancient Egypt, Peru, and Mexico) and beautiful in design. Although illiterate, she is really an artist. She makes her own pots and pitchers out of clay she digs out of swamps and river-beds. In all seasons she works, without receiving any credit, from early morning till late at night. At thirty she looks middle-aged, but in spite of all the hardships and maltreatment often lives to be eighty.

If she doesn't bear a child every year, or gives birth to too many girls, it is just too bad for her. The successful woman is one who bears eight or ten boys. But in thousands of cases childbearing is almost an incidental function. I was told of a Bosnian woman who, sent by her husband to fetch a load of wood from the forest, returned with a new girl baby; whereupon the man gave her a tongue-lashing for not bringing also the load of wood!

In sections of Bosnia and Macedonia, where childbearing is considered a low function, the woman must not give birth in the house, but crawl for that purpose into the barn or hay-shed. Elsewhere custom, based on some pagan close-to-the-earth mysticism, requires her to bear children on bare ground. No wonder, then, that infant mortality is high.

Against all this there is, so far as I could discern, little rebellion on the part of village women. In cities and towns, however, one comes upon educated young women of the post-war generation who burn against the injustice and social unsoundness of the dark-age system which oppresses their rural sisters. There is no feminist movement in Yugoslavia such as we know in America or England, but my impression was that these young women tend strongly toward Communism. They feel that the Belgrade regime, from the king down, has no vital, consistent interest or intelligent program to improve the socio-economic conditions in the backward sections. They hear of sex equality in Russia and believe that only drastic government action initiated by far-sighted, consistent social engineers can liquidate the archaic system which keeps two or three million women in Yugoslavia on the social level of domestic animals.

IV

Of the three regions considered in this chapter, South Serbia is by far the most interesting. There the past, harking back to Alexander the Great, the ancient Celts, Greeks, Romans, and Byzantines, the Old Serbian Empire and mediæval Turkey, hangs on heaviest.

From Sarajevo, as I have said, we went to Skoplyé, an ugly but lively, almost booming Balkan city of 70,000 on the River Vardar, in the heart of Old Serbia. Its history goes back two thousand years B.C. It is the commercial and political center of a great tobacco, grain, cotton, opium, and mining country. Half the town is new since the World War, but crudely, haphazardly constructed. The Moslem quarter is much the same as that of Sarajevo, only far less agreeable to the eye and nostrils. Many streets are still unpaved, uncobbled. The ruling class, small and closely allied with the Belgrade hegemony, consists of a few new-rich individuals of the racketeer type, while the overwhelming majority of Christians, Moslems, and Jews alike live in extreme poverty. On market days, when peasants come in with their produce, the city is an indescribable stew of Balkan humanity.

The governor of the South Serbian province, whose capital is in Skoplyé gave us his official car; then for two weeks, usually accompanied by well-informed faculty members of the Skoplyé University, we rolled over impossible roads in a world left far behind by time. In Macedonia, more so than in Bosnia, one sees things, customs, and modes of life of from one to four thousand years ago still vital in everyday life of great masses of people.

On the market place in Skoplyé, for instance, we saw for sale wooden plows, a variety of primitive instruments for striking fire, and contraptions called *drndala*, used for shaking and fluffing wool and cotton, made exactly as in the time of Alexander the Great. In the Skoplyé bazaar, as in Sarajevo, we found the handcraft age in full swing.

In two weeks I gathered enough curious facts to fill a small believe-it-or-not book. One day on the market place in Veles, a town just south of Skoplyé, I engaged in conversation a middle-aged peasant from a mountain village and discovered that, although not unintelligent otherwise, he did not know what the word "nature" meant. Primitive and closely a part of nature, he had no perspective on it, no word for it; was wholly uncognizant of it.

In a peasant house we came upon a man and his wife engaged in a strange ceremony. Under a worm-eaten beam of their roof they had placed a tub of water, and while the man struck the beam with a stone, causing the worm-dust to fall into the tub, the woman stirred the water with a large wooden spoon. When I asked the man what they were doing, he explained that, though they had been married nearly six months, she was not yet pregnant and, therefore, would drink the water mixed with worm-dust to help her conceive. She had already tried another form of anti-sterility magic—bathing in a tub of water polluted with the placenta of a woman who had just been delivered.

Another proof of the country's extreme primitiveness came to my notice one day as, walking on the outskirts of a mountain hamlet, I saw a woman pick up a chunk of dirt from the field and eat it. It was a case of geophagy, and

Dr. Milenko Filipovitch, a leading Yugoslav anthropologist whom I met in Skoplyé, told me that, as in most primitive countries, the practice was not uncommon in South Serbia, and Bosnia too, especially among pregnant women.

In a village an hour's drive from Skoplyé we witnessed one Sunday a girls' *kolo* marathon. *Kolo* is the Serbo-Croat national dance in which anywhere from a dozen to a few hundred persons move rhythmically in a circle, to the beating of a drum or the blowing of fifes. In this instance the girls danced all day, hour upon hour, some from early forenoon till nightfall, without pausing, while the young men and their fathers looked on. It was an endurance test, for in Macedonia a man marries a girl more for her physical prowess and stamina than anything else.

On another Sunday afternoon we were guests in the home of a family counting sixty-eight members. It was one of the few remaining family *zadrugé*, or collectives, in Serbia. We met about forty of the members, including the *stareshina*, or head of the family, a patriarch of seventy and absolute ruler of the group. The enormous household, with a considerable tract of ground and a twenty-room house, was all but self-sufficient economically. Every member above ten had his or her special duty to attend to. Six women and girls, supervised by the *stareshina's* wife, did nothing but cook and bake. Eight other females only spun, weaved, sewed, and embroidered. Five men and boys attended to all the sheep, goats, buffaloes, cattle, and horses. One man was the family shoemaker. And so on. Eleven families lived under the same roof. The husbands were all the *stareshina's* brothers, sons, and grandsons; their wives had married into the *zadruga* from near-by villages. As recently as thirty years ago these family *zadrugé* were numerous in South as well as North Serbia and Bosnia, but new social forces, which lure young men into the world, are inimical to them and they are breaking up. The tendency seems to be toward independence, individualism.

Many of the primitive collectivist customs, however,

persist. It is quite common for two or more peasants in a village to own one plow or one pair of buffaloes, and help one another at field work. When two or more need the animals or the implement simultaneously, they throw dice. Dice are used also in dividing property when a family *zadruga* splits.

The water buffalo, resembling the Indian buffalo, is a common domestic animal in South Serbia and parts of Bosnia. It is far more economical than the ordinary ox, more patient, capable of endless toil on little food, and the cow gives rich if somewhat pungent milk, suitable for cheese-making.

A good deal of opium is produced in Macedonia, but there are no opium addicts.

V

What one notices first of all in South Serbia are the marvelously picturesque, elaborate, and varied costumes. Nearly every community has some peculiarity in dress. As a general rule, however, the garments are of coarse, rough wool or cotton. Silk, also a home product, is worn in certain sections on festive occasions. Taken separately, the garments, those of both men and women, are baggy and ungraceful; but each person wears anywhere from four to a dozen pieces, and together they produce a harmonious, even beautiful picture. Some places women wear from three to six skirts and over them an apron, each garment heavily embroidered with complicated Egyptian-Byzantine-Slavic designs. A well-dressed South Serb woman seldom wears less than thirty pounds of clothes even when working in the field, and in many places over sixty pounds. The embroideries frequently are so thick that parts of the garments, when new, are stiff almost beyond bending and can be comfortably worn only after numerous washings.

The men's garb, comparatively simpler, includes only a pair of baggy white linen trousers or tight woolen breeches, a blouse or waistcoat, a shirt, and a sash, which is the most important article of attire; it takes the place of pockets, almost unknown among the Macedonian peasantry. Men wear home-made *opanke*; women go shoeless most of the time.

In a village near Bitol, the southernmost town in Yugoslav Macedonia, we came upon a costume which makes all women over sixteen years of age look pregnant. Around their waists they wind a forty-foot cord, weighing close to fifteen pounds. The explanation for this curiosity goes back to the fifteenth century, when the Turks came. It seems that the commander of the Ottoman force in that vicinity ordered his soldiers not to attack pregnant women, whereupon all the women and girls wound rags and ropes about themselves. The present-day cord is a relic of that.

In another region, also not far from Bitol, the Turkish commander, with a different attitude in this respect, ordered his men to kick every Christian woman who looked to be with child, causing miscarriage. The result was that women in that section adopted as part of their garb a heavy shield-like plate fitted over their middle, and their great-great-(etc.)-granddaughters today still wear the shield, considerably smaller, strapped in front of them as an ornament.

Elsewhere, for ornamentation, women wear great strings of coins. Moslem women's attire in South Serbia is approximately the same as in Sarajevo; only here and there, for reasons lost in antiquity, they wear an elaborate, grotesque outfit consisting of immense black overalls, a hood and cloak, which drapes and makes the whole body appear utterly shapeless.

All Christian peasants and some Moslems have embroidered somewhere on their clothes little blue circles, supposed to counteract the effect of the Evil Eye, in which they still believe, as they believe in dragons, werewolves, and vampires.

The Macedonian technique of weaving and embroidering employed by Christian peasant women, as I have suggested, goes back several thousand years. Their looms probably are no better than, if as good as, the old Egyptian looms. It takes a woman from four to eight months to make for herself a comparatively simple costume, such as worn, let us say, in a village near Skoplyé, and over a year in villages near Bitol. She usually spins, weaves, sews, and embroiders at night, after working all day in the field and forest. It is a horrible slavery, and I, for one, though not unmindful of the beauty of homespun and hand-embroidered garments, have no sympathy with people who decry the passing of national costumes elsewhere in Europe.

VI

In South Serbia one finds some of the oldest, oddest-looking villages in the world, those in the hills being naturally the most interesting. Set in little hollows, they straggle up the slope, each a complete community unto itself, largely independent of any large town, and, in its everyday existence, beyond any superior authority. Every stranger, especially if he wears Western clothes and comes in an automobile, is regarded with distrust. After he overcomes that attitude he is invited to stay as a guest of the community. Most villages have communal guest-houses, or at least one or two rooms reserved in some private house for strangers.

The stone houses, plastered with clay, are crude, seldom exceeding one story. Many seem on the verge of collapse, but one learns they have been that way for three or four hundred years. Windows are small but numerous. Glass is a luxury. They have wooden shutters, which keep out light as well as air. Doorways are low, roofs elaborately tiled, and eaves enormous. Inside one finds nothing but a chest or two, which contain the women's costumes, a few straw mats and night rugs or blankets. Food is cooked over an open fire. Stoves for heating are undreamed-of. In winter people sit indoors bundled up in their voluminous clothes.

Women, of course, work their looms and embroider even

in coldest weather. To keep their fingers from freezing, they erect special workshops in the courtyard which consist of a large frame ingeniously made of branches and twigs, shaped like a large army tent and thickly plastered with buffalo manure, with only a small opening to admit light and air; and inside these curious sheds they do some of the finest, most artistic weaving, sewing, and embroidering imaginable. The chemical action of the manure keeps them warm.

This might suggest that the people are not clean. As a matter of fact, Stella and I never ceased wondering how they managed to keep their clothes so white.

We came upon all sorts of taboos. One must not sleep under a fruit tree or burn wood of a fruit tree. One must not wash laundry, bathe children, or knead bread on Wednesday, Friday, or Sunday. The origin of these and similar folk-laws are traced to ancient mythology and magic and to the historical experiences of the race. Saturday is "the day of death," a bad day to begin anything. Equally bad is Tuesday, for it was on a Tuesday the Serbs were defeated on the Kossovo Plain.

A good time to start a new enterprise is at full moon, which notion probably is pagan in origin. When a domestic animal falls sick, the peasant builds two fires in the courtyard, then leads the beast between them. The best headache remedy is to bathe one's forehead in a bowl of water containing a few sunflower seeds; the next best, to smear one's brow with crushed onions.

Arriving in a village near Strumica, not far from the Bulgarian border, we saw a crowd gathered in front of a house, and on inquiry learned that a young man who lived there had married the day before, and these people were here to see if the bride's skirt was bloody. When assured that she had been a virgin, they began a *kolo* dance, which had an obvious sexual tinge.

Had the bride not been a virgin, she would have been sent

{ 219 }

back to her parents mounted on a donkey, disgraced, her marriage annulled.

VII

Every second or third village has a state *gendarmerie* station, which—from the viewpoint of the Yugoslav government—is necessary because the Macedonian Question is still unsettled, and probably will remain so till some sort of Balkan federation is formed and Macedonia, now split among Yugoslavia, Bulgaria, and Greece, becomes an autonomous state within the union. Now Bulgarian *komitadji* are wont to raid villages in Yugoslavia, and there are violent feuds among neighboring communities dating back for centuries.

But a stranger is as safe in Yugoslav Macedonia as almost anywhere. There is no crime even where poverty is greatest. The explanation is that in the Old Serbian Empire and, later, under the Ottoman rule, thievery was punished by cutting off the culprit's arm or gouging out his eyes.

Poverty—due to the people's backwardness, which, in turn, must be ascribed to ages of oppression and exploitation, and now to the lack of any comprehensive, consistent and aggressive program on the part of the Belgrade regime to lift and revitalize the masses—probably is the paramount social fact in South Serbia. As in parts of Montenegro, Herzegovina, and Zagoryé, no salt, no matches, no petroleum. Thousands of peasants do not see the equivalent of a dime in two or three months.

In a village not far from Skoplyé I asked a group of peasants how they managed. "Where do you get money when you really need something badly, when you must go to the city and buy, let us say, needles so your women can sew and embroider?"

A grizzled old peasant, revealing a toothless mouth, laughed, "When we need a few dinars to buy something in the city which we need and cannot make ourselves, we go into the woods, which the government owns," making a gesture toward the mountains, "and we say to the state forester, who is a decent sort, that we are poor (*siroté*) and he should stop his ears and not hear the sound of our axes. So he stops his ears, goes on the other side of the mountain, and we chop a little wood and put it on our donkeys or horses, such as we have; then we take the wood down to Skoplyé, where one of two things happen—we either sell the load or we don't. If we sell it, we have ten or fifteen dinars, then we buy what we need. . . . You see: we work a little, we steal a little, a little God gives (*i tako zhivi se*) and so we live!" He laughed again.

This may seem a contradiction to what I just said about the people's honesty, but when the old peasant said "steal," he didn't actually mean *steal*. The wood belonged to the government, hence to the people, to him. Another line of reasoning is this: Through its agents who come to buy their tobacco crop the government exploits them, paying them as little as possible, simultaneously forcing them to buy a copy of the official biography of the king-dictator which, in five chances out of ten, they are unable to read. Therefore, to chop government wood is playing a grand trick on the government. . . . This sort of "stealing" does not degrade their character or self-esteem.

Near the Albanian border we found a village where the peasants refused to use iron points on their wooden plows, maintaining that metal was "bad for the soil." In another village we found peasants who would not remove stones from the fields. "Stones are to my soil," one of them told me, "what bones are to my body."

VIII

We visited a number of malarial villages, which we found much the same as those in the Dalmatian highlands.

In two of them we came upon little colonies of political exiles—young students, teachers, journalists, and other intellectuals, peasants, and workers from Slovenia, Croatia, Dalmatia, and other more civilized parts of Yugoslavia, who had been arrested and imprisoned for active opposition to King Alexander's *diktatura*, and later sentenced to live a few years, or till they died, in primitive malarial villages, where they must report to the *gendarmerie* every two hours day and night. Some were Communists, other Agrarians, still others Croat Nationalists. Because of malaria, sleeplessness, and bad food, most of them were ill and emaciated, but, with one or two exceptions, full of spirit. Under the influence of conditions as they observed them in South Serbia, the Agrarians and Nationalists tended toward Communism. Like the modern women in Skoplyé and other Macedonian towns whom I mention earlier in this chapter, they appeared to think that only drastic action under a dictatorship established for the benefit of the people could begin to "liquidate" the dark-age backwardness and pauperism of these once Turkish regions.

CHAPTER XII

The Epic of Kossovo

JUST BEFORE QUITTING SOUTH SERBIA FOR BELGRADE, Stella and I visited what, historically and culturally, doubtless is the most significant place in Yugoslavia—the Plain of Kossovo, a few hours' auto-ride from Skoplyé. It really is not a plain, but a vast mountain valley, a thousand feet above sea-level, high peaks all about it. Strewn with ancient little towns and villages, the region is rather bleak-looking late in January, when we drove through it, although in the summertime, we were told, parts of it are vividly beautiful with fields of blooming opium poppies.

To understand Yugoslavia, one must know Kossovo, not the place, necessarily, but what happened there five and one-half centuries ago, and how that event affected the Yugoslavs—and, for that matter, the entire world. Kossovo is historically significant not only for Yugoslavia, as it now exists, but for the world at large. It can be said that, were it not for Kossovo and the strange inspiration that the Serbs and other Yugoslavs drew from it, there would have been no Sarajevo and possibly no Great War as Europe and America experienced it between 1914 and 1918.

II

In the thirteenth and fourteenth centuries, as I have suggested in connection with Galichnik and Montenegro, Serbia was one of the most civilized, progressive countries in Europe. Its culture was a rich, picturesque mingling of the native Slavic "heart culture," Orthodox Christianity, and borrowings from the arts of Byzantium.

Byzantine arts, of course, were then already deep in decay, but Serb painters and architects of as early as the eleventh and twelfth centuries, with their fresh racial energy, revitalized and adapted them to the Slavic temperament; and even today, all over Old Serbia, one may visit scores of churches and monasteries built six, seven, eight hundred years ago whose architecture and frescoes, a few of the latter almost unmarred by either Turks or time, are downright startling in their artistic vigor and technical execution. There is no doubt that over a hundred years before Giotto painters in Serbia had solved the most difficult problems of perspective and knew how to give their figures subtle and intricate expressions. These mediæval Serb paintings and buildings are now being scrutinized by European art students and archeologists, whose general opinion is that they were the immediate precursors of early Renaissance painting and architecture, particularly painting. One theory is that Old Serbian monasteries and frescoes influenced the early Renaissance artists and architects through Dubrovnik, which in the fifteenth century continued to have regular contact with central Balkans, including South Serbia, although those regions by then already were firmly under the Turkish heel. Be that as it may, certain it is that in the fourteenth century Serb artists occupied the foremost position in Europe. Viewed today, some of their works seem almost modern. . . . Here I may only mention the existence of these significant art treasures in Old Serbia; to deal with them exhaustively would require a book as thick as this one. . . .

Along with a well-developed art, Serbia of that time had a legal code, written by Tsar Dushan, which, in humaneness and common sense, was a distinct improvement on Justinian's code. The artisans of Skoplyé, Veles, Tetovo and Prizren (many of whom later fled to the mountains and initiated communities like Galichnik) were among the best in the world. There were beginnings of a native literature.

Ornamentation and design flourished: and the present-day costumes are partly a result of that glorious period, which reached its climax during the reign of Dushan, between 1345 and 1356.

Dushan died in 1356; whereupon dissension among the clans commenced to afflict the country and Turkey, taking advantage of this internal situation, began to threaten its independence, and, finally, in 1389, dealt it a death-blow in the battle on the Plain of Kossovo. The entire South-Slavdom participated in the conflict. Serbia itself, which had lost vast numbers of men in preceding battles trying to stem the Turk, threw in all its remaining man power. In the great emergency the clans were more or less reunited. Bosnia and Herzegovina, Croatia and Dalmatia, sent their contingents, and there is no doubt that Slovenes also were present as volunteers. Moreover, mercenary troops came from Italy, Germany, France, and the Christian clans of Albania. Yet all these forces were greatly outnumbered by the Turks. Sultan Murad (or Amurath) brought 300,000 men from Adrianople, whereas Tsar Lazar of Serbia had less than 100,000. These armies inundated the whole valley. The butchery lasted twelve days and, following an act of treason by one of their own chiefs, the Serbs and their allies were crushed. The nobility was wiped out. Tsar Lazar was captured and beheaded, after which his son-in-law, Milosh Obilitch, one of the few survivors of the battle, rode into the Ottoman camp in full daylight and slew the Sultan in his tent.

With Serbia vanquished, Bosnia and Herzegovina lost their independence soon thereafter, and thus the entire Serb nation, save the Montenegrins, was beaten into dependency upon the Crescent.

Kossovo put a deep and terrible impress upon the Serb imagination. For a decade the nation was stunned by the horror and political consequences of it all; then, gradually stirring in their anguish and humiliation, the plain folk began to make tales and *pyesmé* (song-poems) permeated with a discreet and manly melancholy, describing the battle; and, in the course of a century evolved a cycle of legends of crude beauty and vigorous pathos. Out of their suffering and consciousness of defeat the people created the epic figures of Tsar Lazar; Milosh, who slew the Sultan; the Ganelon-like Vuk Brankovitch; the tender, lovely Maiden of Kossovo; the famous Kralyevitch Marko; and—to mention but one more—the Serb Mother who, in her superhuman strength of character, bearing the sorrow of the battle in which she lost her husband and her nine sons, symbolizes both Serb womanhood and Serbia as a whole.

For centuries these spontaneous folk creations—a good many of them available in inadequate English translations —were sung and recited by illiterate peasants throughout Serbia, Montenegro, Bosnia, and Herzegovina, high in Zagoryé, along the coast of Dalmatia, and in Croatia, usually to the accompaniment of primitive one-string instruments called *guslé*, their influence finally penetrating even to Slovenia, and thus becoming the paramount factor in keeping alive—indeed, in intensifying—the idea and spirit of South-Slav freedom from foreign domination, and of unity.

Probably the most striking, certainly the most popular, of these folk creations was the great, almost endless ballad dealing with the exploits of Kralyevitch Marko, a member of the mediæval Serb nobility who, however, was what we might call a "tough guy"; a hero similar to such characters as Roland in the Charlemagne cycle of romantic tales, the Spanish Cid, the Persian Rustum, the Russian Ilya Murometz, and, to an extent, the American Paul Bunyan.

The original Marko was an unscrupulous freebooter whose acts prior to Kossovo were partly responsible for the fall of the Empire; but the Serb people, no doubt ignorant of his true quality at the time, made him into an epic personality whom Goethe called "the Serb Hercules." A Gargantuan drinker, he is at the same time a champion of the common people, a faithful warrior of his country against the Moslems. He participates in the battle of Kossovo, is one of the few survivors, then lives to the age of three hundred, drinking, fighting, riding his great steed Sharatz, and, in his tender moods, seeking peace in the company of a *villa*, a nymph of the wooded mountains, whom he calls his sister. His death is somewhat of a mystery. One version has it that, like the Slovene legendary messiah, King Matyazh, Marko really is not dead, but asleep in a great cave, Sharatz beside him eating wheat out of an immense bag. When the steed will have consumed all the grain, Marko will rouse himself, remount his horse, and emerge to give battle to all the enemies of his people and rid the country of every wrong and injustice.

Most of the *pyesmé*, especially those dealing with the decline and fall of Serbia, contain a terrific power. Reading them, or, better yet, hearing them sung or recited in the original, one marvels at the tremendous "guts" and realism of the people who made them up. They are history, not only "learned by heart by a whole nation," as it has been said, but history intensified, purified, and beautified in the creative, poetic fire of a strangely potent race. Besides being history, the song-poems are also a vast depository of the wisdom of Balkan Slavs and a moral code expressed in vivid images. Among terrific scenes of butchery and bloodshed, one finds great spiritual tenderness and melancholy, passages of pure heart-interest, amiable thoughts of young girls, dialogues of love which attract by a penetrating charm, a seeming naïveté full of subtlety, and highly communicative and contagious emotion. One thing is sure: had they not produced these *pyesmé*, the Serbs would have passed out under the Turkish yoke—and with them probably the other Yugoslavs, who were under Venice, Austria and Hungary. The poems and legends, more than any other factor in their life under Turkey, helped the Serbs, in spite of endless persecutions and massacres, to conserve their national character (even where, as in Bosnia, great numbers of them embraced Islam) and recuperate their energies so thoroughly that at the beginning of the nineteenth century they gradually reconquered their political autonomy in northern Serbia; which in time led, little by little, to the Balkan Wars of 1912 and 1913, to Sarajevo in 1914, to the outbreak of the World War, to the breaking up of Austria, to the formation of a great Yugoslav state. Composing and endlessly singing and reciting the ballads of the Serb Mother, of Marko and the many other legendary figures, they created about themselves a Homeric atmosphere and developed an "unsubduable soul," a sense of power through tragedy. They turned defeat and slavery into a promise of victory and liberation. They became great and strong in adversity. They were something like the Jews; only, it seems to me, tougher, manlier, more earthy. There was nothing soft or maudlin in their sense and acceptance of tragedy, in their emphasis upon the tragic. While their young sons were being taken from them to become janizaries and their daughters abducted for the seraglio of the pasha, they sang their old songs and made new ones.

In the nineteenth century a native scholar, Vuk Stefanovitch Karajitch, started to write down the old song-poems and legends of his people. Goethe learned Serbian to read and translate them. Jakob Grimm declared: "They would, if well known, astonish Europe. In them breathes a clear and inborn poetry such as can scarcely be found among any other modern people."

III

Now that Serbia has liberated her territories, and Sarajevo, the World War, the Turkish and Austrian empires are things of the past, and Yugoslavia is an actuality, the epic of Kossovo has largely fulfilled its political rôle in the Balkans and in Europe. But the great, crude folk masterpiece, I think, is vastly interesting today *as a key to the*

Serb and generally the Yugoslav national character and background; as the essential part of a powerful social complex of a great people occupying a strategic position on the map and in the politics of our world.

In the various *pyesmé* we find descriptions of mediæval Serb manners, clothes, and food, and learn that women as women were about the same in Serbia two or three hundred years ago as were (and are) women the world over. Here are the words from the song of a young girl as she laves her face and speaks to its reflection in the water:

> "O my fair white face, if I knew that thou were to be given to an old husband I would go to the green forest, I would gather there all the wormwood, I would press out all its bitter juice, and I would bathe thee with this juice, O my fair white face, so that all the kisses of my old husband might be bitter. But if I knew that thou were to be given to a young husband, O my fair white face, then I should go into the green garden, I should gather there all the roses, I should press out all their perfume, and I should lave thee therewith each night and morning, so that the kisses of my well-beloved might be sweet to him and his heart might be rejoiced."

All through the epic we find passages dealing with the people's love of their native place, which frequently is a very narrow form of patriotism, an unintelligent fanaticism leading them to hate their neighbors and fall victim to demagogic politicians, who exploit that patriotism to their own selfish advantage.

In poetry of their own creation the Serbs reveal themselves as extremely clannish, which, to a lesser extent, is true also of the other Yugoslavs. Family is a cult. A man's first duty is to those of his own blood. If he attains to a position of power, he must help his brothers, cousins, uncles, and in-laws in every way possible, regardless of their merit or at whose expense. Serbs probably are the greatest nepotists in the world, and have revealed themselves as such in their own folklore.

In the vast epic we find also numerous suggestions that unscrupulousness and patriotism are not incompatible in practical life. To gain power, one is traditionally, according to the example of the greatest legendary heroes, allowed to resort to almost any trick, any method. To the ambitious and aggressive, the *raya* (rabble) usually is something to love and despise at the same time, to exploit and use as a means to power and self-fulfillment. There are characters in the epic story of Old Serbia who, as political and military leaders of the people, are capable of the noblest, most heroic deeds, while simultaneously they exploit the poor and helpless to the limit. Some of them, including Marko himself and the nine Yugovitches, sons of the glorious Serb Mother, are not beyond downright gangsterism and the meanest, lowest cruelties imaginable, but at the same time are great men in point of patriotism when their country, due largely to their own shortcomings, finds itself in a critical situation. For years the nine Yugovitches squabble for power, rob the King, who is their brother-in-law, and plunder the state; then, of a sudden, seize their lances, mount their steeds, hurl themselves against the enemy on Kossovo, and perish heroically.

A close study of the great Kossovo lore reveals another great weakness of the Serb people—and not the Serbs alone, but all the Yugoslavs. They have a hard time in getting along among themselves. Their leaders almost invariably are opportunists, rather than men of principles and programs. They act on the theory—historically, natural enough—that they are surrounded by enemies and cannot wholly trust anyone who is the least bit unlike themselves. In common with other peoples of the world, the Yugoslavs are having the devil of a time in developing in their minds an image of the fact that—to quote from Professor H. A. Overstreet's recent disquisition on what would be healthy patriotism—they are "a group . . . surrounded by other groups, all of them essentially human and all of them seeking, by mutual interchange of what is true, good, and beautiful, to carry on with an increasing success this strange adventure of life." Where the interests of one group clash with those of another, the two are apt to become bitter enemies before making any attempt to iron out their difficulties.

For centuries, as the Kossovo epic so tragically records, the Yugoslavs have had within them two powerful urges— one toward union, the other toward discord. The first, despite their clannishness, has been strongest in the common people, who are all God's *siroté*, poor people, and as such have a great deal in common; while the second has usually come from their leaders and would-be leaders seeking momentary political and economic advantages for themselves.

IV

From Old Serbia, as I have suggested, Stella and I went to Belgrade, a full night's ride by rail from Skoplyé. We went immediately after our trip to Kossovo.

Prior to that, in Dalmatia, in Montenegro, in Bosnia and Herzegovina, and finally here and there in Old Serbia, I had read various anthologies of the Kossovo epic, and listened to *guslari* (bards) singing old *pyesmé* to the accompaniment of *guslé*; and, after arriving in the capital of the one-time Kingdom of Serbia and the present Yugoslavia, and thence proceeding to Croatia, I tried to bear in mind both the positive and negative phases of the Serb and generally the Yugoslav character as revealed and (perhaps unconsciously) self-criticized by the nation itself in its matchless masterpiece.

ILLUSTRATIONS

The page numbers given with the captions accompanying each illustration refer to related passages in the text.

DUBROVNIK (RAGUSA) ON THE ADRIATIC
(See pp. 8 and 150)

VINTAGE-TIME IN DUBROVNIK
(*See p. 150*)

A SCENE IN CARNIOLA (SLOVENIA)
(See p. 13)

MAIN STREET IN A SLOVENIAN VILLAGE ON A SUNDAY AFTERNOON

(See p. 94)

CARNIOLAN GIRLS
(See p. 19)

INTERIOR OF A SLOVENIAN VILLAGE HOME

(*See p.* 21)

GRASS WIDOWS OF GALICHNIK
(*See p. 115*)

MONTENEGRINS
(See p. 131)

A WOMAN OF MONTENEGRO

(*See p.* 141)

Fishermen going to sea at sunset

DALMATIA

Women carrying water

(See Chapter IX)

MEN OF DUBROVNIK

PEASANTS FROM SHIBENIK

(See Chapter IX)

THE QUAY ("POOR MAN'S OVERCOAT") IN SPLIT

(See p. 166)

NEEDLEWORK IN DALMATIA
(See Chapter IX)

DALMATIAN HIGHLANDERS

GIRLS OF KONAVLE

(See pp. 157 and 174)

FACADE OF THE CATHEDRAL IN SHIBENIK
(See p. 173)

SARAJEVO
(*See p.* 178)

THE BAZAAR SECTION OF SARAJEVO
(See p. 189)

POPOVO POLYÉ, A FERTILE FIELD IN HERZEGOVINA

BOSNIAN COUNTRYSIDE

(See p. 206)

A MOUNTAIN VILLAGE IN SOUTH SERBIA
(See p. 218)

GIRLS OF SOUTH SERBIA
(*See p. 215*)

SOUTH SERBIA: PEASANTS DANCING KOLO

(*See p. 215*)

A FAMILY COLLECTIVE IN SERBIA

(See p. 215)

KALAMEGDAN PARK, BELGRADE, OVERLOOKING THE CONFLUENCE OF THE RIVERS
DANUBE AND SAVA

(See p. 235)

CROAT PEASANT WOMEN
(*See p.* 268)

CROAT PEASANTS LISTENING TO STEPHAN RADITCH IN 1928
(*See* p. 274)

A VILLAGE IN CROATIA

(See p. 270)

CROAT SHEPHERD
(*See p.* 270)

CROAT CHILDREN
(See p. 269)

CROAT WOMEN ON THE MARKET-PLACE IN ZAGREB
(See p. 287)

IVAN MESTROVITCH

OLGA MESTROVITCH,
A PORTRAIT BY IVAN MESTROVITCH

(See p. 296)

"MEMORIES," BY IVAN MESTROVITCH

DR. ANDRIYA STAMPAR ("DOCTOR HERCULES") AND ONE OF THE
600 VILLAGE HEALTH STATIONS HE ESTABLISHED
THROUGHOUT YUGOSLAVIA
(See p. 308)

KING ALEXANDER
(See p. 325)

PART THREE

Belgrade and Croatia

CHAPTER XIII

A "Boom" Town

WE LEFT SKOPLYÉ IN THE EVENING AND, GETTING A compartment all to ourselves, with room to lie down, slept through most of the night, for the clatter and swaying of Yugoslav trains have a monotonous rhythm highly conducive to sleep. Our slumber was interrupted two or three times by detectives and gendarmes who, on all lines leading to Belgrade, examine the passengers' passports and other papers of identification every few hours.

The next morning, on waking at daybreak and looking out, we found ourselves passing through a country which reminded me of southern Connecticut and parts of upstate New York. The season was midwinter, the trees were bare, there was no snow yet, and a sharp wind blew; but even so the region, with its low, rolling hills and extensive valleys, looked very beautiful. Stella said, "It must be lovely in spring and summer."

It was Shumadia, the great section of northern Serbia immediately south of Belgrade; one of the best parts of Yugoslavia, both in land and people. We went through towns which reminded us of American communities. There evidently had been much economic progress here in recent years. Everywhere we saw new bridges, new buildings, new power plants.

The explanation is that the land there is naturally rich and that, ever since the War, the Belgrade politicians have favored northern Serbia with especially big appropriations. A large portion of German war reparations was turned, quite properly, to public works in Serb territories south of the capital, and at the same time—very unwisely, from the viewpoint of political harmony in the new state—the provinces formerly under Austria-Hungary were ruthlessly taxed to provide additional subsidies for business enterprises in Shumadia, in which the dominant Belgrade politicians, of course, were personally interested.

This progress, however, benefited mainly the business class. The peasants as a class probably are little better off today than they were twenty-five years ago. Long before the war, rural Serbia had a well-developed system of local coöperatives (*zadrugé*) which in many cases were captured after the War by aggressive modern business men, who thereupon usually managed them to their own narrow advantage; and now Shumadian peasants, including those within a half-hour of Belgrade, are in the same boat with peasants elsewhere in Yugoslavia. During 1932 and 1933 thousands of homes in northern Serbia used no salt, sugar, or matches. There was no market for their hogs, sheep, and other products. During the few prosperous years after the war, the people, especially those closest to Belgrade, had ceased weaving homespun; now that depression had gripped the whole country, they lacked money to buy store-made clothes and found it difficult to go back to making their own garments.

But despite this poverty, the Shumadian peasant is a grand, proud character. Unlike the *selyatsi* in most other sections of Yugoslavia or the peasants of near-by Hungary or Rumania, where feudalism still exists, the Shumadian has been a free tiller of the soil for over a century, ever since northern Serbia regained its independence. He had never been a docile serf. His manner, therefore, is at once democratic and aristocratic, always civilized, sometimes remote. He is unfailingly polite and hospitable, even when he does not entirely accept or trust you. To a Shumadian, ideal life is to live in a house of his own on a little hill overlooking a valley which includes his fields, have a few well-fed beasts in the barn, good tools and implements, a wholesome, diligent wife, seven or eight children, and one or two close friends among his neighbors whom he can trust in all respects. Like all Serbs, he is clannish, narrowly patriotic. He has a deep, mystical love for the soil. He is proud of his nationality, as he may well be; he loves Serbia as the Russian loves Russia, but wants everybody to mind his own business and leave him alone. He can endure endless discomfort and wrongs, but can be terrible in his wrath and righteousness. While it is true that he has in him a streak of Slavic mysticism, he is, next to the Czech and the Slovene, the most realistic and progressive Slav. As peasant, and also as a Serb, he is the perennial opportunist, but, as long as he operates on a small scale, tries to be fair and honest toward everybody. He is the purest Serb in Serbia proper. Except here and there, he never mixed with Turks, Rumanians, Bulgars, gypsies, or Jews, who have been numerous in Serbia during and since the Turkish occupation.

This cannot be said of the average business man, with whom the peasant must deal. He usually is the local politician, closely allied with the Belgrade moguls, who gets the peasant going and coming. The provincial Babbitt, as his Belgrade brothers, is in six or seven cases out of ten not a pure Serb, a pure Slav, but part Rumanian, part Turk, part Bulgar (Bulgars are part Tartars), or part Jew, and in some instances a mixture of all these strains, which, by and large, intensifies his opportunism and other dangerous flaws of the Serb and Slavic character, and makes him an aggressive and unscrupulous rugged individualist and a great success. He is a Balkanite, with curious, centerless dark eyes, which can be warmly ingratiating one moment and coldly cruel and calculating the next.

Two of these provincial Babbitts entered our compartment at a station an hour from Belgrade. They were short, fat, overdressed, bediamonded, distinctly unattractive individuals, almost sinister-looking; utterly unlike the lean, tall, handsome peasants who, probably lacking the price of train fare, their feet shod in simple sandals, strode capital-ward on the road that for a short distance ran parallel with the railroad track. Chiefly because of these two Babbitts, it was a keen relief to both Stella and me to get to the end of our journey.

But, alas! during our stay in Belgrade we met the same type of person at every turn.

II

I had been hearing for months that Belgrade was a big city, a veritable metropolis; none the less, its size and apparent modernity amazed me. To come there from the heart of Old Serbia was like stepping from the Middle Ages into the twentieth century.

Belgrade, to my notion, is one of the most interesting cities not only in the Balkans, but in Europe. By this, let me hasten to say, I do not mean that it is beautiful or picturesque, or exceptionally agreeable to live in because of some other virtue. It is none of these things. Nor does it teem, as do many other Yugoslav towns, with historical monuments and curiosities. Its history reaches back to the third century B.C., but there are few traces in the city, as it stands today, of anything that existed prior to 1919 A.D. It is new practically from top to bottom; busy, bustling, and noisy. It is, so far as I am aware, the only considerable "boom" city in contemporary Europe and, in my belief, destined eventually to become one of the world's great and important centers.

I visited Belgrade for the first time as a boy of thirteen, back in 1912, shortly before the First Balkan War, a year prior to my going to America. At that time it was the capital of Serbia, with King Peter on the throne. I came there with an excursion group of young Gymnasium students from Lublyana; and Belgrade, with its 65,000 inhabitants, was one of the largest communities and the only capital of a state I had seen until then. But, actually, old Belgrade was little more than a vast Balkan village strewn over the triangular foreland, which suggests a whale's back, at the dramatic confluence of the rivers Danube and Sava. Half the buildings, I recall (though before my return from America I had almost forgotten I had ever been in Belgrade), were low, lopsided, semi-Turkish dwellings with projecting eaves and roofs of crude, irregularly shaped dark tiles. The plaster walls of many of them, apparently, hadn't been whitewashed for a decade. The windows were few and small; here and there broken panes were pasted over with paper.

Two-thirds of the streets were uncobbled. They were dusty in dry weather, muddy and slippery when it rained. Some of the sidewalks were mere wooden planks. Other sidewalks were strings of stepping-stones, used when streets became streams of muddy water. Aside from the half-dozen or so government cars, there were no motor vehicles. Over the cobbles past the royal palace, which was the biggest and handsomest structure in town, trundled ox-carts.

Peasants, venders, and swineherds from near-by and more distant villages and towns, as well as some of the city folk, wore the various Serb national costumes. The Moslem population was no longer numerous, but one still encountered turbaned men and veiled women at almost every turn, and from the minarets of the four or five remaining mosques the muezzins continued to call the faithful to prayer three times a day.

The hotel where our excursion group put up had no running water in the rooms, but plenty of vermin which kept us from sleeping. Most of the other hotels in the old town probably were no better.

Two and a half years later the Austro-German artillery demolished more than half of the houses I had seen there on my first visit. Most of the government buildings were ruined and even the royal palace was damaged. The old Turkish quarter along the Danubian riverside was a melancholy mass of crumpled-up walls and wreckage of all sorts.

By the end of 1915, when the Serbs finally surrendered

{ 239 }

their capital to the numerically and technically superior armies of the Central Powers, thousands of Belgrade families had preceded the remnants of their army southward into exile. In 1916 two epidemics of typhus, brought there by Austrian soldiers from the Russian front, swept through the town, and by the end of the hostilities in 1918 the native population dwindled to 25,000.

For three years the military forces of the Hapsburgs and Hohenzollerns held Belgrade, along with the rest of Serbia, and before leaving it, after the Allied-American victory, blew up the power-plants, the water-works, and most of the machinery that could not be moved onto the barges and taken up the Danube to Hungary and Austria. From undestroyed private houses they removed all serviceable furniture, linen, silverware, china, pans, and pots—and in recent years it has happened that Belgrade families, passing second-hand stores in Budapest and Vienna, suddenly recognized their pre-war beds and pianos in the display windows, and were served meals in restaurants and private homes on plates they recognized as their own.

By the end of those three years Belgrade was virtually a dead city. Hardly a store was open. Women thought themselves lucky if they had a needle and a few yards of thread. Leading citizens of the town walked around wrapped in old quilts, frayed carpets, threadbare blankets, flags, curtains, and ordinary sacking.

No other city, with the probable exception of Liège and Verdun, suffered more in the World War than the capital of Serbia.

III

Yet today, as I say, Belgrade is a "boom" town—and this in the most thorough sense of that 100-per-cent American phrase. Its population figure is rapidly nearing 350,000, which is over five times higher than the record figure it attained in its history before the war. Some of the suburbs now are larger than the entire community was twenty years ago, while the center of the city is a vast complex of wide cobbled and asphalted thoroughfares and squares, of five-, six-, and seven-story government, private business and bank buildings, palaces housing foreign legations, large modern hotels, modernistic apartment-houses, elaborate private residences, markets, and department stores.

The streets, for the most part, are clean and orderly. On weekdays the ones running through the heart of the city are almost as jammed with taxies, private machines, buses, and tramways as the main streets of the average American center of equal size. The ox-cart has all but disappeared.

Turbaned men and veiled women are no more. Only once in a great while does one see a fez. One small dilapidated mosque is left, and its *hodja* either is too old to climb up the minaret, or he figures it is futile to yell over the din of traffic that streams by the edifice. The bazaar section on the Danubian side of the whale's back is the only part of Belgrade where the Oriental atmosphere still predominates—but I suspect it is artificially maintained by Christian officials of the local tourist bureau.

Many peasants, venders, migratory laborers, and drifters who come in from Shumadia, from central Serbia, Macedonia, Bosnia, and the Albanian mountains still wear their local national costumes; but fewer every year. The city people, almost without exception, sport Occidental clothes, in many cases carefully and expensively tailored in accordance with the latest Parisian or London styles.

The first impression of present-day Belgrade, as one rides in a taxi from the railroad depot to the hotel, is unfavorable. The city's natural position at the coming-together of two great rivers is an enviable one, both commercially and scenically; but, as I have hinted, the town is not beautiful. In fact, it is not too drastic to say that at its current state of development it is the direct opposite.

Here and there one catches glimpses of handsome buildings, but the young metropolis as a whole is ugly, inharmonious, afflicted with all the aspect of the typical American "boom" town. At every turn one sees evidences of rapid, haphazard, inorganic growth.

Registering at the hotel, one finds out that Belgrade is a "boom" town also when it comes to prices. It is the most expensive city in Yugoslavia, which, taken as a whole, was an incredibly cheap country to live in while we were there. In Zagreb, the chief urban center of Croatia (where we went from Belgrade), for instance, two persons could get a suite of rooms equivalent to the best available in any first-class hotel in Chicago or New York for a dollar and a half or, at most, two dollars a day for both. The same accommodations in Belgrade were from three and a half to five dollars a day. In Zagreb a delicious, over-abundant eight-course dinner, which included roast goose, duckling, or turkey, cost from thirty to thirty-five cents. The same spread in a Belgrade restaurant came close to a dollar, and the food was not half so tasty and well served as in Croatia.

If one remains in Belgrade for a while, the unpleasant first impression persists and deepens in one. At the same time, however, if one knows the language of the country and has letters of introduction to representative residents of the city, as happened in my case, Belgrade becomes an intensely fascinating place.

To Americans who chance to visit it the city is interesting even if they don't know the language and have no letters of introduction. At the United States consul-general's office I met a man from Chicago, one of whose first remarks to me was, "You know, although I don't understand a word of Serbian, or whatever language they speak here, this town reminds me of back home. It's like Chicago was thirty years ago."

Despite the depression, Belgrade's "boom" was showing no signs of diminishing. The residential suburbs stretched toward the foot of the Avalla Mountains, while, across the Danube, the industrial towns of Zemum and Panchevo, both part of the Belgrade municipality, were developing by leaps and bounds.

I met dozens of people in the city whose psychology was essentially the same as the psychology I had observed in Los Angeles in 1924, or thereabouts. They told me, as though the fact was a matter of paramount importance, that in 1932 over 15,300 new structures had gone up in Belgrade, including 498 store and office buildings, 25 coffee-houses and restaurants, 15 lecture and meeting halls, 154 warehouses, and 57 large garages. They maintained that, barring another war such as the last, Belgrade would pass the half-million mark in ten years, while in ten more "this will be another Paris."

Considering that Belgrade is in Europe—and not only in Europe, but in the Balkans—its development in the last fifteen years, I think, is nothing short of amazing. Behind that development is the great virility of the Serb people, with their "unsubduable soul"; the same virility that we find in the Kossovo ballads; the same spirit—only temporarily perverted by the circumstances and the system under which it now functions.

After the Serbs regained the ruins of their principal city and tiny old Serbia suddenly bulged out into great Yugoslavia, tens of thousands of men, women, and children returned home from three years' exile. At the same time people from Croatia, Dalmatia, Slovenia, Bosnia, and Macedonia commenced to pour into their new capital as fast as railroads could bring them. Missions came from France, England, and the United States. The city had practically no water, no fuel, and no electricity whatever. It was winter-time.

And then there happened, on that triangular spot between the two rivers, something for which I know no better analogy than what occurred in San Francisco after the fire in 1906, when a new and greater city rose out of the ashes within a few years.

IV

A prominent Serb journalist, who has been living in Belgrade since the autumn of 1918, graphically described to me what transpired there after the first winter following the Armistice.

"Of a sudden," he said, "the place became a veritable bedlam of construction activity. Thousands of people were simply frantic to rebuild their homes. Other thousands were equally anxious to quickly erect great apartment and tenement houses, store and office buildings, hotels, warehouses, which they might rent at high rates.

"There was an acute housing crisis. I remember a minister of the government of the new Yugoslav state who, throughout 1919 and part of 1920, slept on a couch in his temporary two-room office. He couldn't get a private room for love or money. Some of the big stores you now see on Prince Mikhailo's Avenue twelve years ago were only stands on the sidewalks (which were not really sidewalks), or else their proprietors were mere peddlers carrying their wares on trays strapped from their shoulders.

"Of course, most of the people who wanted to build, having lost everything in the war and suffered great privation during the years of occupation and exile, lacked money even for a decent suit of clothes, but their passion for property had been enhanced by their recent experiences, and now they begged, borrowed, and stole everything in sight to finance their building projects. For years there was political chaos in Yugoslavia, accompanied by a wild scramble for government jobs; and most of those who got the good jobs stole enough in a couple of months to erect homes for themselves, which were better than their pre-War dwellings, and finance the building of a couple of apartment houses, a hotel, an office building, or a warehouse.

"I hear you have graft in American cities. Well, you have nothing on us here in Belgrade twelve or fourteen years ago! But perhaps at the time that was the only way for the city to rise out of the ruins; and in saying this I am not trying to be cynical.

"There started an orgy of speculation in property values. The prices of lots doubled, trebled, overnight. This was especially true of parcels right around the royal palace, where the government owned building sites.

"The city and the new state governments—especially the latter—urgently needed new quarters and lost no time in building them. While the great palaces you now see on King Milan's Avenue were being erected, many important divisions of the various ministries had their offices in tents and in hastily-put-together wooden shacks. . . . Where did the government and the city get the money? Well, some of it was borrowed in France, England, and the United States. Some of it came from Germany and what was left of Austria, in the form of reparations. Much of it, particularly after 1921, was extracted—quite heartlessly and brutally; we may as well admit it—from the peasants in the former Austrian and Hungarian provinces.

"Anyhow, from the early spring of 1919 to the end of 1922, or even later, there was so much debris-clearing and building in Belgrade that, in dry weather during summer, one couldn't see half a block ahead for the dust that filled the air. Thousands of masons' and carpenters' hammers, the rattle of thousands of wheels, the frequent dynamite blasts, and shouts of workmen contributed to making the city a tumultuous chaos.

"There was a scarcity of trucks and wagons, shovels and other necessary tools, so the people—some of whom you now see driving about in Mercedeses and Packards—were picking up the debris and carrying the stuff off in improvised baskets on their backs and shoulders. Of course, much of the wreckage was used over again in laying the foundations for the new buildings, in putting up the new walls.

"The municipal and state governments, after attending to the water, light, and fuel problem, tried to make a city plan, and finally did succeed in putting something on paper that looked like a plan, but they might as well not have bothered. While the politicians and architects were talking over the details, the town grew with terrific vitality. New homes and buildings sprang up almost overnight. The work went on day and night. It was an epidemic of hasty construction. In this respect, too, your American builders had nothing on us a decade or so ago. Everybody wanted to beat the other fellow and thus gain some advantage over him.

"The result, alas! is what you see—ugliness. Cement buildings predominate, partly because cement lends itself to quickest results, but largely because part of the German reparations came in the form of cement—tens of thousands of sacks—much of which, of course, was appropriated, stolen, for private building by those who momentarily happened to be in high authority in the government.

"Here and there you see a building that doesn't look half bad on the outside; inside, however, it probably is full of serious deficiencies. Too much space is wasted on stairways and corridors. Or the rooms are too large or too small. Or too few windows. Or they forgot to put in a lift and then, when they thought of it, installed a contraption which now noisily runs up and down through the stairshaft—when it is not out of order!

"Some of the hotels put up immediately after the building epidemic struck us have no running water in the rooms, and there is a bathroom only on every other floor. Many of the otherwise elaborate private residences but lately acquired modern plumbing and lighting.

"I suppose the best thing about the town as it stands today is that nearly everything was built quickly and inefficiently, and within a decade most of the structures that now dominate our streets will have to be torn down and replaced. Some of the more recent business buildings in the main sections of the town and the suburban private residences already are better built, both as to design and from the viewpoint of modern comfort."

Twenty years ago it could have been said that in Belgrade East and West met and mingled. It would have been hard to determine which of the two was predominant. Today, as already suggested, it is plain that the West is rapidly pushing out the East.

One or two confectionery stores on Prince Mikhailo's Avenue still sell Oriental sweetmeats. But the display windows of other shops on the street, which is the center of Belgrade's shopping district, are totally Western. There are the latest styles in ladies' dresses and gowns, lingerie and stockings, hats, gloves, and footwear; gentlemen't haberdashery stores, with London neckties, hand-tailored shirts, tuxedos, dinner jackets; flower shops and American drug stores; book stores selling reading-matter in Serbo-Croat, Slovene, French, German, and English; agencies of most American and European makes of automobiles, tires, typewriters, radios, frigidaires, and sewing-machines.

At first I wondered who was buying all these things, but presently we began to meet men and women who, to all seeming, were very well-to-do. They were the ministers and other higher officials of the government, army generals, merchants, bankers, industrialists, and their families. There is a considerable new-rich class. Fifteen years ago, and even more recently, most of them were penniless. Today they have large winter residences in town or in the suburbs, cars and chauffeurs, three or four other servants, and summer villas in the country.

Most of them are Serbs, though few are really of the pure, dignified Shumadia stock. The Serbs had a tremendous advantage over the Croats and Slovenes when Yugoslavia was formed, and made the most of it. Of the three main racial groups that the doctors of Versailles bundled together into one state, the Serbs alone had had experience in practical politics. Besides, Belgrade, though it became the capital of all the Yugoslavs, was *their* city. Also, their great military victories in less than seven years had touched their minds and characters with megalomania, which is not inexcusable; while the privations they suffered in the World War, as already hinted, had intensified their instinct for property and wealth.

The Croats and Slovenes, when they were united with the Serbs, were rather timorous. Many of them had fought on the side of Austria. Then, too, by and large, they were more cultured and refined, less aggressive than the Serbs had been even before the war. And so right from the start—naturally, inevitably—the Serbs took all the best jobs in the central government and generally in the administration of the new country. In this they had the support of King (then Regent) Alexander, who is also a Serb, in some respects a typical Serb of the upper class.

Then other phases of the Serb character and national culture which, as suggested before, are a matter of long historical development, naturally and inevitably came into play. Here I shall mention just one of those phases—or rather, I shall quote a Croat I met in Belgrade, who had great admiration for the Serbs, though sharply conscious of their faults.

"In many respects," he said, "the Serbs are a marvelous people. In martial heroism they proved themselves second to no nation. In personal contact they are kind, gracious, hospitable to a fault, which is characteristic of all Yugoslavs and, in fact, of most Slavs. But in one vital way they differ from other Slavs, and especially from the Croats.

"Both the Serbs and the Croats have been under foreign domination and oppression for centuries, but the effect thereof upon our characters has been dissimilar. We Croats, who are Catholics, are eternal yearners for what we conceive to be 'justice' (*pravica*). For hundreds of years we have been exploited, humiliated, abused; and, somehow, I don't know just how, we developed into a most simple, naïve nation. We expect and long for fair play. We believe in the triumph of 'what is right.' We—I mean the masses,

{ 248 }

the peasants—hold that no one should be harmed and deceived; everybody should be free to work in his field or forest, at his job. However, when we are exploited by others, we merely complain and passively resist the forces of injustice and evil, as we conceive them. We lack aggressive fighting qualities and the will to oppress others.

"The Serbs were in political and economic bondage to the Turks for five hundred years—unwillingly, of course, with all the inner power of resistance that is characteristic of them. Except in Montenegro and parts of Shumadia" (where great bands of them lived for centuries in the wooded mountains), "they were physically helpless against their brutal masters and exploiters. They were deprived of all human and legal rights. Their one defense was *podvala* —cunning, deceit—which they practiced against their oppressors through the centuries until recently, when circumstances made it possible for them to liberate themselves; but meanwhile cunning has become an art with them and part of their nature. Their Kossovo epic, as great as it unquestionably is purely from the literary standpoint, was a form of *podvala*. They fooled the Turks. The Turks didn't know what those songs and legends really meant even when they understood the words. They probably thought the Serbs were a little crazy to glorify their defeat. . . . In my mind, the Kossovo epic is first of all a piece of great political subtlety—a bit of colossal propaganda, cunning as anything. And cunning, as I say, has become second nature with them.

"Of course, this in a generalization. In Shumadia one finds great masses of plain people who are naïvely frank and direct. By and large, however, talking to a Serb, you can never be sure whether he believes you or not, although he may appear sincere. His nation has been deceived and exploited so long by other nationalities and adherents of other religions that now he believes and trusts only an Orthodox Christian Serb. I have reason to say that the average Serb will sooner trust an Orthodox Serb of dubious character and honesty than a Croat or Slovene of proven high character and unquestionable integrity. In fact, Serbs of one region generally don't trust Serbs of another.

"Then, as you know, there is their traditional clannishness. All of us Slavs are clannish, but with the Serbs it is a fanaticism. Two second cousins in Serbia are closer than two blood brothers or a father and son in France or some other Western country. They adhere to one another through thick and thin. If one Serb gets ahead, his first impulse, which he never disobeys, is to help all his relations.

"Now take the Serb distrust of everything and everybody that is not Serb, couple it with the Serb clannishness, and you have a general explanation why, after the Serbs had initially occupied the commanding positions in the new Yugoslav state, all big government jobs were immediately filled with Serbs; why Slovenes and Croats were and are kept out of them; why most of the non-Serbs who have government jobs are mere clerks; why a Croat or Slovene, no matter how able, is almost invariably elbowed out of a high position, if he accidentally attains it; why at this moment all the 130 army generals and six of the nine provincial governors are Orthodox Serbs; why Yugoslavia was made into a centralized state instead of a federation of autonomous states; why Belgrade today is a stronghold of a Serb political and economic hegemony which has the entire country at its mercy, and which supports the dictatorship of King Alexander, who is one of them, has encouraged them in their characteristic Serb pursuits from the start, and is an autocrat by nature; and, finally, why Yugoslavia is, momentarily at least, in danger of breaking up."

VI

Yugoslavia, I think, was not in any real danger of breaking up, but otherwise the Croat was largely right. In fact, not a few Serbs, who—exceptions to the above-quoted generalizations—had not tried or had failed in the attempt to become rich and powerful in the post-war "boom," expressed themselves to me much more severely concerning the economic-political-military ruling class of Belgrade than he did.

One evening I sat in a Belgrade café with an English-speaking professor of the Belgrade University. When two new guests entered and all the waiters in the place rushed to assist them in removing their enormous fur coats, he said to me: "You see the man on the left? An ex-Minister of Justice," mentioning his name. "He was in office eight months, years ago, and in that time increased his wealth from nothing to 150,000,000 dinars"—nearly $3,000,000. "The man on the right is his brother-in-law, formerly an important official in the Administration of Forests. Now he's a millionaire, too. A couple of robber-barons!"

I became acquainted with a good many of the "robber-barons" and their brothers and cousins and brother-in-laws. I met four ministers of the government, two or three generals, a number of private bankers, merchants, industrialists; and on meeting them for the first time not a few of them struck me as very pleasant persons indeed. They were interesting, superficially cultured; some of them rather amusing, absurdly proud of their high positions in the country and their possessions.

They reminded me very much of American boosters. On hearing that I might write something about Yugoslavia when I returned to the United States, they took Stella and me around in their fine automobiles to show us the new bridge across the Sava, the new docks along the Danube side, the great park at Kalamegdan. They pumped me full of statistics of growth and progress, past and potential, which to them were the most significant figures in the world. They had no interest in the old Kalamegdan fort at the point where the Danube and the Sava meet, although the ruins date back to the seventh century. Their interest was only in new things, in the future. Few of them had any understanding of the present; any cognizance of what really was the situation in the country, in the provinces. They simply knew that they were on top of the world, and anyone who said that conditions were no good—*"ne valya"*—was a fool.

Driving me through the suburbs, they remarked exuberantly, "Four years ago there wasn't a building hereabouts. . . . You see the row of houses over there? My brother and I built them. All but two are sold."

I went to their heavily tapestried and carpeted offices. One of them told me the inkwell on his desk cost 25,000 dinars, and was very proud of it.

In their residences they served elaborate teas and lavish dinners. There were domestic and imported liqueurs, wines, champagnes, mineral waters. There were caviar, Javanese citrus fruits, London marmalades, Swiss and Dutch cheeses.

Our hosts were childishly boastful of their French furniture and paintings. Some told me how much they had paid for them. They spoke bad French among themselves and self-consciously imitated the French in social etiquette. Belgrade, which before the war had been under the influence of Petrograd, now was not only under the politico-economic but also the cultural sway of Paris.

At first, as I say, I liked some of them personally; they amused me. On second or third meeting, however, they somehow appeared to me less charming, less amusing, downright sordid, but more and more interesting. Stella disliked most of them from the start. She said, "They give one a pain." I discerned a feverish uneasiness in their manner. Their boasting and boosting sounded less convincing. Their speech and manner were hectic. Their personalities struck me as incongruous.

They were a product of a "boom" town, which, in turn, was their creation, but they did not feel at home there—not really, not yet. In this they were typical of "boom"-town people in the United States, perhaps everywhere.

But Belgrade is not an ordinary "boom" town. In the United States "boom" towns spring up where oil has been struck or a new railway opened up. Belgrade began to "boom" in consequence of a political event in world history. It is the capital of a new country, which, since its inception has been in political agony, and that agony—now, it seems, rapidly coming to a climax—must be ascribed primarily to the personal go-getterism and lack of broad, sincere statesmanship on the part of those who had seized power at the beginning and have been keeping it largely to their own enrichment to this day.

After a while, going a little deeper into the matter, I realized that, in its essence and secret life-springs, Belgrade was not a purely Serb or Yugoslav city. It was the capital of a country which was not wholly free and independent. With other so-called "small" countries in the Balkans and eastern Europe, it was an important factor in the French and the English (particularly French) military-diplomatic systems in European politics, aimed against Italy, Germany, and Russia, especially Russia; and these rather silly, showy self-conscious people with dark, centerless eyes, whom I was meeting in government and private-business offices, at house parties and hotel dining-rooms, and who took Stella and me driving about the city, really were little more than local executives of the Western powers' imperialist designs, though some of them perhaps were unaware of their rôle. With King Alexander as their chief, they ruled and terrorized their country, keeping it in line for an eventual new war which England and France might deem necessary to wage against Italy and Germany, or just against Germany; or, with Italy and Germany, against Russia. England and France were giving them loans to keep up their army, police force, and terrorist machine; and meanwhile French, English, and other foreign money-imperialists were sinking their golden hooks into the great natural wealth of the country, exploiting its mines and forests, exploiting the native workmen, under the protection of the terror rule which their money supported.

In fine, Yugoslavia was not unlike Cuba was under Machado.

And as I realized all this, the people I was meeting in the high-toned offices and private homes began to get on my nerves. One day, when one of them, driving us around, suggested that I write about Yugoslavia so that American capital would be attracted to my native country, I had to summon all my powers of self-control not to haul off and hit him. The same self-control was necessary on a number of other occasions, for I wanted to stay in the country awhile longer.

One such occasion was when an official of the government press bureau asked me if I did not need some "help" in order to write my book and get it published, hinting I might be able to get one or two thousand dollars; the idea being, of course, that in return for such "help" I would promise to write favorably of the Belgrade regime. I told him I was a very rich man and did not wish to augment the Belgrade government's annual difficulties in balancing the state budget.

Another instance calling for self-control was when an old Slovene politician, highly cultured and not without personal virtues, but closely allied with the Belgrade ruling clique, took me to a sumptuous lunch in the best hotel in town to tell me of my brilliant future if I would "coöperate" with my native country—*i.e.,* the Belgrade government. I told him that I liked my native country very much, meaning the people, and meant to write of it accordingly. I made the luncheon unpleasant for him by asking him such questions as why several hundred ex-ministers of the government (of whom he was one) were receiving salaries although long out of office. Was it possible they were thus bought to support the regime?

Still another occasion on which I had to suppress a violent impulse was when a man came to my hotel and told me that two ministers of the government, both of whom I had met a few days before, had decided to recommend me to His

Majesty the King for a decoration—the Order of the White Eagle, to be exact—but, before sending in their recommendation they wished me to indicate whether or not I would accept such an order. I said no.

VII

Both Stella and I, after the first week in Belgrade, began to feel extremely uncomfortable. That we stayed there nearly three weeks was because I wanted to find out as much about the town as I could.

We continued to meet people. To some of the "big shots," as I began to call them in my mind, I deliberately mentioned that in my travels over Yugoslavia I had observed widespread pauperization of peasants, workers, and the lower white-collar class; and when I did that, our charming, amusing hosts suddenly became less charming, unamusing, and abrupt. Yes, they admitted, the depression was bad, but times would improve. It was evident they were afraid and basically ignorant.

I asked them about the *glavnyacha* (police headquarters) in Belgrade, where political opponents of the dictatorship, not only Communists, but mild Republicans and Peasant Party adherents, were being "examined"—*i.e.,* tortured in special torture-chambers by specially picked sadists. I asked them, was it true? They all denied that anyone was being tortured in Belgrade or anywhere else in Yugoslavia, "except maybe the Communists"; but they knew that I knew that over 15,000 "politicals," men and women, had passed through the *glavnyacha* and at least half of these had been tortured, scores of them to death, in order to preserve the *status quo*.

Such questions, of course, along with my refusal of the decoration and "help," did not make me very popular in the higher circles. Two ministers of the government failed to take us to lunch, as they had said they would when we first came to Belgrade. There were no more drives about the city in high-priced cars. And so, by and by, I began to have lots of time to see more of the people I really wanted to see, both for themselves as persons and for the authentic information they could give me.

With most of these I had been put in touch by men and women I had met during the previous months in Slovenia, Dalmatia, Bosnia, and Old Serbia; others had written me suggesting I get in contact with them when I came to Belgrade. The majority of them were opponents to the government—Republicans, Green (peasant) Internationalists, and underground Communists—professors, students, journalists, lawyers, government officials, a few army officers, and private individuals. None of these can I mention by name or describe, for the dictatorship is likely still to be in power after this book appears.

Talking with them and checking one against the other, I learned a great many things I could not have learned otherwise. I was told, for instance, that the inner circle of the ruling group in Yugoslavia consisted of less than one hundred families, most of them Serb, or rather Serb Balkanite. They were the new plutocracy, headed by the king. "Their urges, their psychology," a Belgrade professor said to me, "are the same as the urges and psychology of your American racketeers. Every once in a while gruesome crimes occur in our upper circles. They kill one another over business deals. They hire men to do away with their competitors. Rich men are found mysteriously dead; only not often enough! Our king is a glorified Al Capone. To stay in power, he employs, on the whole, the same methods—terror." The next-to-the-inner circle comprised about five hundred families, or from twenty to thirty thousand persons, for Serb families even in the upper social strata, counting cousins, uncles, and in-laws, are enormous.

The standing army (180,000 men) had over 130 generals in active service, all Serb Balkanites, all drawing huge salaries. In Belgrade we met a general every few steps. They were the main support of the *diktatura*, an intrinsic part of it. They administered the terror discipline which kept the army together. They saw to it that most of the non-commissioned officers in permanent service were not Slavs, but a sadistic breed of semi-savages from along the Albanian border in South Serbia, who beat and tortured the recruits drafted from Slovene, Croat, and Shumadian villages. They sent Slovene and Croat soldiers to regiments stationed in Old Serbia and Montenegro to keep down the Macedonians and the Montenegrins, and Serb soldiers from Bosnia, South Serbia, Montenegro and Herzegovina to Croatia and Slovenia to keep down the people there.

In addition to these various strata in the ruling class, there were in Belgrade (or elsewhere, under the control of Belgrade) a few hundred Croat and Slovene politicians, mostly renegades of former people's parties (now outlawed), who had allied themselves with the Balkanites in power in Belgrade in order to benefit themselves economically at the expense of the people in Croatia and Slovenia. These were probably the most disgusting of the lot—bootlickers, spies, cheap intrigants, and flunkeys. Among them one encountered also exceptionally cultured men, but that did not prevent them from being obvious snakes-in-the-grass.

I learned that, in common with the rest of Yugoslavia, most of the Belgrade population, including at least three-fourths of the 80,000 state and city employees, were against the existing system and regime; not openly, of course, for, to exist at all, they must keep their petty jobs.

The incomes of the overwhelming majority of people in Belgrade (as in other Yugoslav cities) were pitifully low. Two-thirds of the government employees, including postal clerks, teachers, and lower-grade professors, drew less than the equivalent of fifty dollars a month. Thousands of white-collar family men received less than twenty-five dollars a month, while rents in Belgrade were almost as high as in the average American city of its size, and clothing was higher and food only a little cheaper. I heard of state employees holding responsible positions, not only in

Belgrade but in other towns, who were too poor to be able to afford underclothes. At public functions they often wore their shiny dress suits over bare skin. Only army officers, high officials, the gendarmerie and the secret terrorist police were paid well and regularly. One state employee told me he had not been paid for two months. "But please," he added, quickly, "don't tell anyone I said so. Should the wrong person learn that I told you this, I would be guilty of minor treason and arbitrarily dismissed from the service."

When I told these things to Stella, she said, "No wonder that at night they have to have a gendarme with a fixed bayonet on every other corner in the high-class shopping district! I should think the people in such circumstances would crash the display windows and try to get next to those enormous loaves of Swiss cheese."

VIII

The three weeks we spent in Belgrade were by far the least pleasant part of our stay in Yugoslavia. Not, of course, entirely unpleasant. We met people, mostly Serbs, who were as nice and broadly civilized as anyone we had met in Slovenia or Dalmatia. Besides charm and intelligence many of them had also a great vitality which the average Slovene or (as I subsequently observed) Croat lacked. Talking with them, I had a feeling that Serbs, with their superior energy and many-sided *élan*, inevitably would be the leading racial group in Yugoslavia for a long time to come, probably until the three branches, Serbs, Croats, and Slovenes, finally merged into one nation and developed a just and sound social order. They dare more. They can and are willing to endure more for their ideas and principles. It is a matter of general knowledge in Yugoslavia, for instance, that under sadistic treatment in the torture-chambers of the Belgrade *glavnyacha* Slovenes and Croats "break" sooner than Serbs. Everywhere I came some one told me the epic story of the death of one Bracan Bracanovitch, a Serb revolutionist who a few years ago fell into the hands of Belgrade terrorists. He was a veritable giant, nearly seven feet tall and built in proportion. When they brought him to the *glavnyacha* he suddenly burst the shackles on his wrists and the chains on his ankles, then for nearly an hour tossed around the office sixteen gendarmes and secret agents. That they did not shoot him then was because they thought they would extract from him information about his fellow revolutionaries. Finally they succeeded in tying him up and kept him tied up the rest of his life, while they subjected his body to the worst imaginable torture. With sticks of hard rubber they pounded the soles of his feet into a bloody mess. They put live coals under his armpits and tied his arms close to the body till the coals became cold in his blood. They stuck needles under his nails. They broke all the joints of his fingers. They did things to him I cannot print. They told him to tell what they wanted to know, but to all their questions he hurled colossal curses upon their heads, such as but a Serb can utter. He taunted them by laughing while they beat him, and even while the coals sizzled under his armpits. He told them what was going to happen to them and their king and everyone around him when revolution swept over the Balkans. He never lost consciousness. They threw him into a cell, emptied a couple of revolvers into him, then the Minister of the Interior issued a communique that Bracan Bracanovitch had been killed by the police when he "attempted escape during examination" in the *glavnyacha*. I carefully authenticated this story, and every time I heard it I thought that the nation that produced such a man—quite apart from the merit of his ideas, if you wish—was a nation to reckon with.

In one way or another, it seemed to me, the Serbs were bound to dominate not only Yugoslavia, but more or less the whole Balkan situation. Momentarily the wrong type of Serb was at the helm in Belgrade; but the current socio-economic order favors that type; the present ruling group,

I was confident, carried within itself its own death germs and eventually was bound to be displaced by the constructive, decent element in Serbia which is far more numerous than the other, and which, in the long run will give the Croats and Slovenes a show at governing their countries and contributing their talents to the improvement of the general character of Yugoslavia and the Balkans.

Belgrade, I believed, was bound to grow in importance. Some day it may be the capital of a Balkan federation.

I was deeply impressed by the Serb intelligentsia in Belgrade. Some of the new writers, whom I met individually and in group, were colossal fellows, though, for the time being, not so much as writers as persons. Though many of them lived in extremely taut circumstances, vitality simply oozed out of every cell in their beings. They imitated French forms of literature and turned out reams of stuff, mostly bad, yet highly promising because of its terrific, if as yet undisciplined and uncrystallized, creative vigor. They were experimenting, trying to discipline themselves. They were all extremely serious and hard-working. They were beginning to think along social lines. In them was the same racial energy that created the epic of Kossovo.

But the group that impressed me most were the students, especially the university students, several thousand of them in Belgrade, the bulk of them peasant boys; two-thirds of them Serbs from Voyvodina, north Serbia, Old Serbia, Montenegro, Herzegovina and Bosnia; the other third Slovenes and Croats. Many did not know where their next meal was coming from. Some, as I already have mentioned, ate only every other day. Not a few had no permanent sleeping-quarters. They studied in parks in the summer, in libraries and often unheated "clubrooms" in the winter. They put up for the night wherever they could. Some worked nights as waiters, street-sweepers, laborers, and clerks. Perhaps half of them supported themselves. Every morning most of the milk in Belgrade was delivered by students.

The government helped, as a rule, only those who were for the regime and willing to spy on the political activities of their fellow students. These were few.

Nearly all university students in Belgrade—and this goes also for university students in Zagreb and Lublyana—were active politically. At least 90 per cent of them were anti-regimists. Leftism was widespread among them. They staged anti-regime demonstrations at every opportunity and got clubbed by the police, jailed, put through torture-chambers in the *glavnyacha*, exiled to malarial villages in Macedonia.

Every few days, while we were in Belgrade, the streets were strewn with leaflets attacking the king-dictator, and everyone knew that the students had scattered them. This usually occurred on windy days. Students threw the leaflets from house roofs, then wind carried them all over the city, while gendarmes and plain-clothes men, who swarmed the thoroughfares, tried to catch them in midair and snatched them out of the hands of people who picked them up from the sidewalks.

IX

Toward the end of our second week in Belgrade it became obvious to me that a number of people in various official circles were a little worried what sort of book I would write about Yugoslavia. The queen's lady-in-waiting—Madame Shverlyuga, a woman of incisive personality and studied graciousness, which missed by a hair to pass as genuine—arranged to have Stella and me invited to a tea so she might put me through a long examination as to what I planned to tell in America. Others came to discreetly inquire what I meant to bring out in my writings about the country. Would I deal with the political situations? Officials at the press bureau wondered audibly. I gave them vague answers. To some I said that for the time being I wasn't sure just what and how I would write. I hinted that folklore interested me very much. But they realized that I was interested in politics more than folklore and not in sympathy with the dictatorship; so some of them tried to explain and justify things to me. They told me what a great statesman King Alexander really was—"and personally very charming, really; very democratic. . . . You should meet him," they said. "You *must* meet him. When you will see the king you will know that he really is a great man. Everyone is impressed by him."

People outside the regime urged me, too, "You *must* meet him!" Several had said that to me already in Dalmatia, in Bosnia, in Old Serbia. "And when you see him," the anti-regimists had added, "tell him the truth about the situation as you see it. He doesn't like to be told unpleasant things by strangers, nor anyone else, but he can't do anything to you." Others had warned me not to antagonize him; people in Yugoslavia died in sudden "accidents," and an accident could happen to an American citizen as well as a subject of the Kingdom of Yugoslavia. Some told me he was a "strong man"; others maintained he was a mere tool in the hands of the military-economic clique in Belgrade. An ex-minister of the government whom I met in Bosnia considered him very capable. A former member of the Parliament said he had the personality and ability which would make him a good second lieutenant.

Naturally, I was curious, more than curious; so when persons in government offices in Belgrade suggested that I seek an audience with His Majesty, I said: "All right. How does one get an audience?"

Then a very nice official of the press bureau, a Dalmatian, whom I liked personally and who was eager that I should do the king no injustice in America, took me to the chancellery of the royal palace, where I signed my name in the beautiful Visitors' Book and was introduced to the secretary to the Minister of the Court. The gentleman from the press bureau told the secretary, among other things, that I was the author of a couple of books published in America, including one entitled *Dynamite*.

Watching the soldiers, officers, and gendarmes as they passed in and out, I sat in the big anteroom until a liveried flunkey invited me to enter the office of the Minister of the Court.

I found myself before a tiny, youngish man of serious mien, solemn voice, and searching Byzantine eyes, who had a Serb name but did not look like a Serb at all. He said he was glad to see me, but did not really seem so. I think he considered me a great nuisance. He begged me to sit down, then asked me various questions, which I answered; and my answers moved him to remark, "Oh, I suppose you're not a Yugoslav any longer; you're an American," and from his tone and expression I gathered that that was not in my favor at all.

I said nothing. My tactics were to say as little as possible. I knew His Excellency the Minister did not like me, and I thought he probably was acute enough to feel that I did not like him. We spoke in Serbian. It was awkward.

He said, "I understand you wrote a book called *Dynamite*. What is it about—*Dynamite*?"

I said, "About violence between capital and labor and about the development of racketeering in America. A more or less objective study."

"I see," said His Excellency, scrutinizing me, nodding his head slightly. Then: "I understand you desire an audience with His Majesty the King," and saying this, he turned eyes, suddenly very pious, at the picture of Alexander which hung on the wall directly above him.

I said yes, I did desire an audience.

"His Majesty just now is very much occupied," said His Excellency. "His Majesty is the hardest-working man in the kingdom. However, on my part, I shall do what I can. To-morrow I shall inform you approximately when—and if—

His Majesty," turning another pious gaze at the portrait, "will receive you."

I said, "Very well, Your Excellency." The little man, somehow, struck me as very ridiculous and it added to my amusement to call him Excellency. I made a move to rise and go, for I had an inner giggle which threatened to split my face into a laugh, but he made a gesture detaining me, then continued:

"If you are so fortunate as to be received by His Majesty," again looking up at the picture in a way that I had to smile, "you will meet a man in the prime of his life, at the apex of usefulness to his state and his people—a man who has spent the years of his young manhood in camp, at the battlefront with his soldiers, but who today, by the grace of God, none the less, is at the height of his physical and mental powers. If you are so fortunate as to be granted an audience, you will meet a man who, though a monarch, is a man of the people, a great democrat, a man of simple taste, profound intellect, broad culture—" And so on for several minutes.

I thought to myself, "This is blurbiage, and dumb blurbiage, at that." For a minute I did not care if I met the king or not and, simultaneously amused and disgusted, got out of the chancellery as soon as I could.

The next day a gendarme (!) brought me a message from His Excellency the Minister of the Court, informing me that His Majesty the King (I visualized him lifting his pious eyes as he had dictated the letter) was unable to receive me for at least a week, possibly ten days. Could I wait?

I replied I could not wait that long. In four days I had to be in Zagreb, Croatia, where I had promised, weeks before, by mail, to give a lecture on depression in America and had to meet a number of people with whom I had been corresponding the past few months. I said that I might return to Belgrade in three or four weeks. Could I get an audience then?

Just before we left for Zagreb, the same gendarme brought me another note from the Minister of the Court, to the effect that an audience might in all likelihood be arranged for me three or four weeks hence. His Excellency begged me to inform him when I would return to the capital.

CHAPTER XIV

Trouble in Croatia

THE TRAIN-RIDE FROM BELGRADE TO ZAGREB TAKES TEN hours. We went in the daytime, so we might see the country, the plains of the great Sava region which, with the Danubian and the Tisa River basins in Voyvodina, immediately to the north of Belgrade, had fed the armies of Austria-Hungary during the war.

A good deal of snow had fallen all over northern Yugoslavia early in the winter; now, however, in the last half of February, the vast stretches of level ground were bare and dull brown under the feeble sun. None the less, there was a fascination about the wide, gently undulating landscape, with its villages behind clumps of leafless poplars, the fields free of hedges, walls, and fences which give Slovenia, for instance, the idyllic appearance of a park. This looked to be a real country, like the plains of Missouri, Illinois, or Indiana. Here were the great open spaces of the otherwise mountainous and hilly Yugoslavia. Every once in a while we glimpsed the broad, slow-moving Sava; eight months before we had seen it as a rapid mountain stream tumbling through the gorges of Upper Carniola.

This was Croatia-Slavonia, usually referred to merely as Croatia.

A gentleman, with whom we became acquainted on the train said (speaking in German, so Stella could understand): "But you should see this country in the spring or summer. The air then is very clear and bracing even in hot weather. In May the fields, purple with violets, emanate an overwhelming sweetness. To breathe here at that time of the year is for a sensitive person a delight almost too much to experience; I'm not exaggerating. Early in June, the meadows are ablaze with wild flowers—white, yellow, red, scarlet, and sky blue; mignonettes, huge poppies, snapdragons, harebells, stonepinks, forget-me-nots, and thyme. . . . I am a professor of botany and zoölogy, and Croatia is as though specially made for me. In the wooded mountain regions, down where Croatia touches Bosnia and the Karst, the flora is even more varied; and as for the fauna, there probably is no place like this section of the Balkans. In the mountain forests all sort of wild things abound—marmots, polecats, chamois, bears (four or five different kinds, amazing fellows!), roebuck, wild boar; golden eagles, vultures of all sorts, pheasants, and partridges. . . ."

What one especially notices in Croatia, however, as in other sections of Yugoslavia, are the costumes—very different from those in Dalmatia or Montenegro, where the people, particularly men, go in for dashing effects which express and reflect their spirited natures. The lowland or inland Croats, as already suggested in comparing them with the Dalmatians and the Serbs, are not dashing or spirited. There is a profound softness in their blue eyes. Their hair and complexions are fair. They are, for the most part, pure Slavs. They came to the Balkans from the Carpathians. For centuries, between brief periods of independence which constitute some very glorious pages in Croatian history, they were under foreign domination, but always passively and effectively resisted every rule of exploitation and, in their own peasant way, while enduring endless humiliation and hardships, helped to break up the Dual Monarchy.

The Croats are real peasants, four millions of them, peasants in body and mind—slow, plodding, persevering; sad, idealistic, naïve, muddled, tragic-minded, not easily articulate, superstitious; always complaining, but, in the curious mingling of pagan and Catholic faiths, with their constitutional distrust of everything not of their own making, infinitely patient and quietly strong—in brief, full of positive and negative traits. And this curious character is reflected in the national dress.

The men of the plains, none of them very tall or otherwise impressive, wear wide trousers of white homespun linen, shirts and blouses of the same material, conservatively and often tastefully embroidered around the sleeves and collars. No matter what the weather or how muddy the roads or dirty their work in the fields, they always wear white, yet few ever appear soiled or bedraggled. In the wintertime, men wear heavy sheepskin coats or mantles, usually decorated with beads, hog tusks, and tassels. Their headgear in the summer is a broad-rimmed black hat; in cold weather, fur caps. Here and there they carry slung from their shoulders a large pouch (*torba*) frequently over a foot deep and almost as wide, made of finely woven horsehair and variously decorated. It is the receptacle for their personal articles—pipes, money, religious charms, food, knives, and flasks of *slivovitsa*, or prune brandy.

Several Croat peasant women assembled on one spot make an unforgettable picture. Their knee-high white-linen skirts worn over two or three petticoats are yards wide, gathered into countless pleats, and starched on holidays and Sundays. Over the skirts come aprons, beautifully embroidered with blue and red thread. The torsos usually are incased in stiff, zouave-like sheepskin jackets full of buttons and bead decorations, or wrapped in knitted shawls of thick, soft baby-lamb wool. On their heads they wear white or colored kerchiefs, silk or linen, tied under their chins, sometimes turban-fashion around the head. Their stockings, like the men's, are of thick, coarse wool knitted in fancy designs, yet fit to endure steady wear for years, and below the knees they wear elaborate garters with ribbons and tassels in various colors. All of which, of course, is produced and fashioned by women themselves in their fields and homes. As in South Serbia, they make their own dyes out of saffron and juices extracted from the willow bark and wild-pear-tree roots. Men usually shear the sheep, but women dress, spin, weave, and dye the wool or hemp. Men sow the flax, but women gather it and steep, dry, spin, weave, and bleach the linen.

In late years great numbers of peasants in the northern sections of Croatia have given up the colorful homespun apparel, but perhaps two-thirds of the women and half of the men still wear national costumes, just as their ancestors wore them for the last thousand years. This is due, in part, to the economic backwardness of the country, which in turn must be ascribed to centuries of exploitation by foreign rulers and, since 1919, to the lack of any honest, comprehensive, and aggressive program on the part of the Belgrade government to stimulate rural progress; and then to the fact (not wholly separate from the above causes) that the people, though quite civilized in manner and not unintelligent, still are primitive and pagan, and as such believe in various supernatural forces apart from those officially recognized by the Catholic Church, and in symbols which attract the good forces and repel the evil ones.

Thus, for instance, thousands of Croat peasants, like their fellow countrymen in Old Serbia and Bosnia, still believe in the Evil Eye; and to fight it, women embroider their garments with little blue or red circles. Married women, to conceive more readily, wear jackets on which they had embroidered ears of wheat, symbolizing fertility. After conception, they put on a cap with two hornlike points over the temples, to ward off evil spirits which may have designs upon their potential children.

Women affect different ornaments at various stages of their lives. In early childhood girls wear miniature reproductions of their mothers' costumes. On reaching puberty they don dresses with red ornaments. When they marry, green and blue ornaments are added. Widows wishing to remarry wear costumes with blue-green embroidery. The stripes on their sleeves signify how many children they have.

Symbols extend to other things than clothing. The married woman's pillow-cases are embroidered with figures resembling ears of grain, so she may be fertile. Pregnancy achieved, she sleeps on a pillow decorated with little roosters, symbols of maleness, so the child may be a boy, for in Croatia, too, boys are preferred to girls.

If a woman fails to bear a child after she has been married, say, for two years, women relatives, who keep their eyes on her, bring her gifts of hard-boiled eggs beautifully decorated with ears of wheat. If she does not conceive after eating several of these, her husband receives gifts of eggs decorated with figures of roosters. In all this, of course, there is nothing erotic.

Eggs adorned with oak leaves, symbolic of strength and long life, are presented to old men. When a Croat peasant plows, he puts an egg, exquisitely embellished with wheat ears or some other symbol of fertility, at the start of the first furrow, and another egg at the end of the last, plowing both under.

Superstition, usually accompanied by some folk or social custom, touches every phase of Croat peasants' life. When newlyweds retire, the wedding guests break a pot at their door and shout, "Boy!" When a child is taken to church to be christened, the mother must walk three times around a table so she will have plenty of milk to nurse it.

In some villages they say, "When your baby is learning to walk, don't worry about its hurting itself if it falls: for the Mother of God"—some places a *villa*, or nymph—"goes before it and drops an invisible pillow in front of it whenever it stumbles."

If an infant gets an upper tooth before a lower one, he will not live long, and the other way around. A child born on Friday is unfortunate. If a girl catches a blind mouse and puts it into a man's pocket, he will fall in love with her and, blind to all her faults, worship her forever. If a strange woman enters a house, asks only for water, and refuses to sit down, cattle and hogs will die in that household. . . .

In most Croat villages, as in many Slovene ones, the

Catholic church is the largest building. It dominates the community. The peasant homes, as a rule, are not impressive either in size or in style. They stand along uncobbled village streets, which are dusty in the summer and slushy in the winter. Most houses are wooden, for oak and pine are abundant in Croatia. Compared with the cramped quarters of the South Serbian peasantry, they are spacious enough, but usually ill-ventilated.

The front door leads into the big-room, which is used by all members of the family for meals, indoor work, prayer, and recreation. In one corner is a large oaken table with benches, in another a huge open stove, in a third a loom—a woman always working at it, working, working, weaving coarse linen or fine cambrics much according to the methods employed by the Egyptians in the days of the Pharaohs. There are two or three large chests, a bedstead, the inevitable cradle occupied by the latest addition to the family. The small windows are seldom curtained. There are shelves for pots and pans, spoons and forks (often wooden), jars of gherkins, bottles of this and that, loaves of bread, sacks of flour, baskets of dried fruit. In many cases the food is prepared over the open stove in the big-room, but separate kitchens are gradually coming into vogue. From one of the blackened rafters dangles an ear of corn, a symbol supposed to help make everyone in the household, including the animals, fertile and productive.

Upon the walls are holy pictures, a crucifix, cheap photographs of relatives who have emigrated to the United States. In prosperous homes petroleum lamps or homemade candles are lit evenings; in the poor ones, which numerically predominate, dry kindling-wood is burned torch-fashion. Few houses have more than three rooms, yet they accommodate anywhere from five to fifteen persons. Frequently two families live under one roof, the father's and the son's; sometimes two brothers stay together, each raising a family, but the elder of the two is the head *gospodar*.

Most men and boys over ten sleep with the animals in the barn or in the hayloft.

This may give a bleak picture of the average Croat peasant's home. On closer scrutiny, however, the house-furnishings, while unquestionably primitive and inadequate, appear anything but bleak. The Croats have a great love of beauty, an instinctive urge toward the artistic. Their embroideries, executed in simple geometrical designs according to ancient Byzantine and Holbein techniques, are not the only beautiful things in peasant villages. The eggs I have mentioned are decorated by the batik method. Indeed, batik, superior to the usual Malay variety, was until very recently made on fabrics in certain Slavonian villages.

The peasants' homemade earthenware has clean, lovely lines. Their tables, chairs, chests, and looms are decorated with hand-carved figures. Their plows, wagons, oxen yokes, hand tools, and beehives are beautifully painted. . . . This, let me add, is true also of the Slovene peasants' tools and implements. . . .

But I have gotten slightly ahead of my story. It occurs to me that we are still on the Belgrade-Zagreb train, conversing with the botany and zoölogy professor, and most of the things I have just told I did not find out till later.

II

Zagreb is the second largest city in Yugoslavia (150,000 population), the cultural, economic, and political capital of Croatia. Though it has grown considerably since Croatia became a part of the Yugoslav state, its general character is still Austro-Hungarian. It is as nice and civilized a town as any of its size in southeastern Europe. It is well laid out, with numerous parks, fine public buildings, and paved streets, and kept superlatively clean.

Its history goes beyond the eleventh century. For long periods it was the cultural and political center of Croatia.

Some of the most glorious, as well as the most tragic, political events in Croat history occurred there.

Like Lublyana (a few hours away), Zagreb is soaked in culture. The oldest printshop and bookshop in northern Balkans are in Zagreb. One of the earliest music societies in Europe was organized there. The town has the best university, the largest library, the foremost art academy (till lately in charge of Ivan Mestrovitch), and the best opera in southeastern Europe, and the finest ethnographic museum in the world.

And, most important of all, Zagreb is the greatest center of anti-Belgrade sentiment in Yugoslavia.

As already suggested, Serbs and Croats have in them certain temperamental differences. Besides those already mentioned, the educated Croat is innately more refined than the educated Serb. One is gentle, peaceful; the other aggressive, martial. One is polite, discreet; the other vital, dynamic, irrepressible. One developed under the law-and-order rule of the Hapsburgs, while the recent background of the other consists largely of warfare. One is idealistic, the other realistic. Their languages are almost identical, but the Croat uses the Latin, the Serb the Cyrillic alphabet. One is Catholic, the other Eastern Orthodox; but in this respect both are close to being mediæval. One tends to be bureaucratic, the other anarchistic.

With such and other differences in character, coupled with the complicated circumstances discussed in the preceding chapter, the Serbs naturally achieved and retained supremacy in the new state, though numerically the Croats are almost as strong as the Serbs.

From the start, as already stated, Belgrade imposed heavy taxes upon Croatia and other "liberated" provinces, while the Serb regions went almost tax-free and, as I have also mentioned, received additional aid from the central government in the form of subsidies for public works and private enterprises. Nicholas Pashitch, then the chief muck-a-muck in Belgrade, was an old Balkanite politician, "a fox," first and last for Serbia and Serbia only. He had never had any real interest in a united, solid Yugoslavia. To him, Croatia, Dalmatia, and Slovenia were conquered parts of Austria-Hungary.

While Belgrade spent big sums on the army and the police, Zagreb could never—still cannot—get sufficient support for its cultural institutions. For years the Zagreb University was discriminated against. There were other causes of hard feeling almost from the start, and they exist to this day. The only persons in Zagreb and in Croatia generally satisfied with the Belgrade regime were (and are) the very rich and their political flunkeys who, under the existing system in Yugoslavia and in Europe as a whole, naturally allied themselves with the big nabobs in Serbia and the foreign money-imperialists who have their money invested in Yugoslav banks and textile, mining, and lumber industries.

Out of this profound discontent in Croatia—now in its second decade—there emerged and developed, back in the early 1920's, a remarkable political leader, Stephan Raditch, an educated peasant, who for several years personified the country. To understand Croatia—and for that matter, Yugoslavia—one must know something about Raditch.

He was a native of a typical Croat village, a real peasant. He studied at the Universities of Zagreb and Prague and the *École libre de sciences politiques* in Paris. As a youth he was an enthusiastic, impulsive participant in political student activities, always brimful of enterprise, energy, and fire.

When Yugoslavia was formed, Raditch was in his late forties, fattish, robust, with a large, kindly face and pudgy hands. Extremely shortsighted and generally untidy, he looked like a cattle-buyer. Often he went about collarless, shirt open, disclosing his broad, hairy chest. At political mass meetings he appeared in peasant boots and a well-worn, soiled sheepskin coat.

He was an eccentric, a demagogue, anything but a great

mind; yet, in his own way, a genuinely big, even great man. He knew how to appeal to the peasants, whose interests were closest to his heart. He made political capital of the conflicting impulses, vague desires, aspirations, and keenly felt wants of the rural masses who had been neglected and exploited for centuries. Playing upon the vanities of the illiterate, socially backward peasantry, he gradually molded its instincts and prejudices into new political aims and tactics. He spoke in parables which reminded one of the parables of Jesus. Often he talked for three, four, five hours at a stretch, rhythmically repeating and contradicting himself, uttering no end of nonsense; but that never hurt him. If muddle-minded, he was none the less a big man in his physical and spiritual energy, his force of character and will power; in his whole personality, which, with all its faults and virtues, was a summary of the weaknesses and strength of the Croat peasant. His language was that of the people, full of rich imagery, which came from his love of nature, his appreciation of the essential dignity of peasant life, and from his profound knowledge of the human heart.

He was often tiresome; then, suddenly, he would flash a brilliant thought or witticism and begin to expound his ideas and feelings in a manner that straightway arrested the attention of all, and everybody cried, *"Zhivio! (Hurrah!)"*—though none, not even he himself, really knew what he was driving at. He talked about Woodrow Wilson, the great American; about liberty, the people and their rights, social justice and democracy. Now and then he blurted the word "republic." . . . (*"Zhivio!"*) . . . . He said the king in Belgrade was responsible for the heavy taxes and high prices which the peasant must pay; therefore Croatia ought to become a republic like France or the United States, but remain part of the Kingdom of Yugoslavia. A republic within a kingdom, why not? Weren't the Irish aiming toward a similar scheme? . . . *"Zhivio!"*

{ 275 }

Within a republic, the peasant would be "king on his own land." . . . "*Zhivio,* Raditch!"

A shrewd peasant educated to political tricks and the ways of the world, he was sincerely interested in the welfare of the masses—a combination of Gandhi and William Jennings Bryan. Campaigning, he slept in peasants' houses, ate their food. His following increased by leaps and bounds. He became a saint, a cult, a religion, a great political party. His influence spread outside of Croatia, to Slovenia, Voyvodina, Shumadia, Bosnia, Dalmatia.

His party was the Peasant Party, loosely allied with the Green (peasant) International. He was its brain and heart, mostly its heart. His aim was moderate socialism in a state dominated by peasant interests. He wanted a government which would not operate to divorce the people from the natural resources of their country, but utilize those resources to uplift the masses, improve the conditions of the villages. At first he proposed to achieve that aim by passive resistance to the Belgrade rule. His party won seventy-odd seats in the Parliament, then withdrew from that body. It was a vague, inchoate program, essentially sterile, negative; yet to millions of peasants Raditch was the one and only messiah.

Village bards, not merely in Croatia but in Serbia, began to put him into their ballads. Peasant women embroidered his name, face, and slogans on tablecloths. If word came that "Our Leader" was to speak upon a plain twenty miles distant, men and women mounted their horses or took the road under their heels and rode or walked all night to hear and see him who at long last, after centuries of social agony in Croatia, would redeem them from exploitation by the state and private interests; free them from all evil; make them "kings within a republic." He often spoke to ten, twenty thousand people assembled on some great field or meadow, all in national costumes—a sight the like of which had never before been seen in the Balkans or anywhere else.

Belgrade clapped Raditch into prison. That increased his

prestige in Croatia and elsewhere. When he came out, his immense following was more fervent than ever. He secretly played high-handed, opportunistic politics with leaders of other parties; he blabbed endless nonsense; but all that was no matter. He expressed the people, the great mob of *siroté*. They trusted him. He knew them and loved them, and they knew it.

Speaking several languages, he went to London and Paris and told all who would listen about the wrongs that Croatia suffered at the hands of that "old fox" Pashitch, King Alexander, and their crew of Serb scoundrels, who really were not Serbs, but a lot of *cincari* (hybrid Balkanites) who had no heart even for the Serb peasant, who was the real Serb. He went to Bulgaria and made himself close with Stambuliski, leader of the great peasant movement there; then, with great instinctive intelligence, talked of the necessity of uniting all the Slavic peasant countries in the Balkans—Bulgaria, Serbia, Macedonia, Croatia, and Slovenia —into a great federation of free, socialistic states in which private property would be limited and exploitation of the many by the few impossible.

He went to Russia, where Lenin himself received him. He traveled all over the country and addressed tens of thousands of muzhiks, who responded to his demagogic genius almost as acutely as the Yugoslav peasants, simply because he could make them feel that he was one of them. He spoke their language, knew them, loved them. He probably had no real understanding of the Russian Revolution, but Lenin, recognizing his power as a propagandist, suggested to him that he stay in Russia a few years and galvanize the muzhik into a conscious revolutionary element. But Raditch rejected the suggestion. He belonged to Croatia, to Yugoslavia.

On his return from Russia the Belgrade gang promptly clapped him into jail again. Then ensued a period of dirty politics. Raditch compromised, was taken out of prison and made a minister of the government. His party, stronger than ever, took its seats in the Parliament. Soon he was an ex-minister. He had made all sorts of pacts with his opponents, including Pashitch; was betrayed by them, and he, in turn, betrayed them.

He became definitely anti-Belgrade once more, while his power among the people throughout Yugoslavia increased. He entered into coalition with other anti-Belgrade groups and, as his ideas and program gradually clarified, became the most effective enemy of the military camarilla and business plutocracy around the king. He instinctively opposed the Yugoslav government's policy of coöperation with the diplomatic-military and financial interests of France and England. Though no Bolshevik, as a Slav and a peasant, he was closer to Soviet Russia than to the capitalistic powers of western Europe.

Finally, during a violent debate in the Parliament on June 20, 1928, a gangster-like flunkey of the court cabal, one Punisha Racitch, a Montenegrin Serb and member of the Parliament, suddenly drew a gun and, opening fire on the Croat Peasant Party deputies, killed two and wounded Raditch and three other men. (Of this shooting more in a later chapter.) Raditch was taken to Zagreb and seven weeks later died there.

For days, as "Our Leader" lay on his death-bed, the streets of Zagreb were jammed with orderly, quiet crowds of peasants, men and women in colorful national costumes. When word of his death reached the villages, great sobs went up everywhere and weeping peasants began to pour into the city by train, afoot, and on horseback, thousands upon thousands, to pass by the bier of their martyred messiah; then—it was on a Sunday—an endless procession of them followed his body to the cemetery. It was one of the greatest, most colorful public funerals in the history of the world.

Then Stephan Raditch really began to live. His political program, while he walked around in flesh, had been, as I say, an inchoate, negative business. His big achievement lay in the fact that he had stirred and inspired the neglected, backward peasant masses, made them politically conscious. Now, dead from the bullet of a servant of the people's enemies, he became a great hero-martyr, a William Tell, an Abraham Lincoln—a modern Kralyevitch Marko.

In direct consequence of the killing of Raditch, King Alexander and his group of generals, plutocrats, and politicians—not only in their own interest, but, as I shall show later, in the interest of Western powers' imperialistic-military plans—abolished the Parliament, established a dictatorship, and outlawed all political parties, including Raditch's Peasant Party. But they might as well have outlawed the River Sava or the seasons of the year. Secretly, under the leadership of men designated by Raditch before his death, the party continued to grow and crystallize itself ideologically. Under the pressure of dictatorial terror, it has intensified its opposition to the Belgrade rule and moved further Left. By outlawing the Peasant Party Alexander automatically outlawed most of the Croat people—city people as well as peasants; for after his death Raditch became a hero-martyr also to vast members of educated urbanites.

His death brought Zagreb and rural Croatia closer together. It made Zagreb the center of Croat revolutionary resistance to the Belgrade rule.

III

In Zagreb we were met by a crowd of a dozen people or more, about half of whom claimed us for their guests. There were our friends Maxo and Margaret Vanka from the island of Korchula, now in Zagreb for the winter, who insisted we lunch with them daily while in the city. We told them we probably would be there a month or longer. They said the longer the better; they had a splendid cook and chickens were a dime and turkeys forty cents apiece in Zagreb.

There was a committee from the Zagreb branch of the Returned Emigrants' organization who informed us they had reserved rooms for us, arranged for an automobile if we desired to drive into the country, and were at our service as long as we remained. There was the publisher who had brought out my books in Croatian translation and was eager our stay in Zagreb should meet with our satisfaction. With him were two literary gentlemen who pointed to an enormous placard on a wall announcing my lecture on America, and said all arrangements for it had been made; there was lively interest in it, and we were sure to have a full auditorium. There were the reporters, a committee from a Slovene society in Zagreb, and so on.

It was Lublyana plus Split plus Sarajevo—the climax in hospitality as we experienced it in Yugoslavia.

At the hotel the manager handed me a pile of mail, most of which were invitations to various homes and notices from all kinds of people that they would call to see me. The day before the papers had reported our impending arrival and where we would stop.

The next morning the procession began. Perhaps half the people who came to see me were discontented politically, frustrated under the dictatorship or for other causes—writers, students, professors, business men, leaders of underground labor and peasant organizations. There were returned emigrants who wished to know what was happening in America, journalists wanting interviews about the new President and the literary scene of the United States, and people who merely wanted to see me, ask me what I thought of Yugoslavia.

A banker and business man from another town, temporarily in Zagreb, sought my ear to tell me that since the establishment of the dictatorship things have come to such a pass in Yugoslavia that it was virtually impossible to make any money honestly. "The only way is to be a relative or friend of one of the ministers in Belgrade who gives you a large order for the government, whether the govern-

{ 280 }

ment needs the goods or not; then you deliver half the order, receive payment for the full order, and split with the minister." Did such things go on in America, too? . . . Finally he told me that, should the people of Yugoslavia be given a chance to vote in a free election, two-thirds of them would go Red—"most of them, of course, not because they are really, intelligently Communistic, but as a reaction to the bloody, brutal regime in Belgrade."

A peasant soldier just released from the service came to tell me how officers and non-commissioned officers had beaten him. (Stella and I, passing soldiers at drill, had seen with our own eyes officers smash privates in the face on several occasions.) "The discipline in the army," he said, "is based on fear and terror. The officers, acting on orders from above, create such an atmosphere in barracks that every soldier believes all his comrades are spying on him and doesn't dare move, let alone rebel."

Students came to tell me how the police beat them when they demonstrated against the high fees which the government, trying to reduce the number of registrations, requires them to pay on admission and throughout the year. Students had been killed by the gendarmes. Just then the Zagreb University was closed, as a punishment to the students for demonstrating.

A young radical came to ask me would I come to a certain house and see burned-out armpits and other marks of torture on the bodies of men and women who had passed through the torture-rooms of the Belgrade and Zagreb police headquarters. . . . I went. When I returned and told Stella what I had seen, she almost fainted. . . .

A high officeholder, whom I had met in Dalmatia in the summer, came and told me how low he felt when, although not in sympathy with the regime, he was ordered to appear at all official functions and enthuse for the *diktatura* and the king-dictator. He could not afford to lose his job; he had a family.

A big industrialist, with whom we had become acquainted

in Bohin nine months before, came and insisted on taking us for a ride in his new automobile costing half a million dinars. Essentially stupid, though successful in business, he was showing off and told us that he and his wife had spent the rest of the summer, after leaving Bohin, in Switzerland. The trip had cost them 200,000 dinars. Women in his factory worked twelve hours for as little as twenty cents a day!

An artist came. Could I help him get in touch with some gallery in New York which would exhibit his pictures?

People of various walks of life brought or sent me all sorts of information. (Hereinafter I mention only what I verified.) Did I know that lately anywhere from three to eight suicides occurred in Zagreb every week, and that these suicides were mostly persons of the lower-middle and proletarian classes? . . . That in the last forty-eight hours unknown mothers had left ten infants on the doorsteps of various institutions and homes? . . . That one-fourth of Zagreb's population lived in extreme poverty? . . . That thousands of people in Zagreb, in fact everywhere in Yugoslavia, ate no breakfast because they couldn't afford it? . . . That peasants in Croatia and Bosnia lately killed a number of gendarmes who came to confiscate their cattle for non-payment of taxes? . . . That the industrial suburbs were hotbeds of extreme radicalism? . . . That the average of high and low wages for industrial workers in Yugoslavia in 1932 was twenty-two dinars (twenty-nine cents) a day for ten hours' work? . . . That in the foreign-owned textile mills in the Croatian uplands female operatives received as little as forty-three dinars (about fifty-two cents) for 164 hours of work in two weeks? . . . That one of those mills, partly owned by French capital, last year profited twenty million dinars? . . . That King Alexander, through his straw men, was financially interested in some of those mills? . . . That that was also true of several of his ministers and generals?

Did I know that 80 per cent of Yugoslavia's industry and

private banking business were capitalized and managed by French, Italian, English, German, Swiss, and Belgian money imperialists, who, in their exploitation of Yugoslav workers and natural resources, had the coöperation of the Belgrade regime? . . . That, with the aid of their political friends and partners in Belgrade, these foreign industrialists got their raw materials at low cost, almost for nothing, then kept up the prices of finished goods, and finally took all their wealth out of Yugoslavia as soon as Yugoslav labor, under the whip of terror, produced it for them? . . . That some of the mining and textile companies paid, even in these times of depression, as high as 300-per-cent dividends—to investors in France, Germany, Belgium, and other foreign countries? . . . That in a few months during the winter of 1929-30 (toward the end of King Alexander's first year as Dictator) foreign interests pulled out of Yugoslavia over two billion dinars of wealth created by Yugoslav hands out of Yugoslav materials? . . . Now wasn't that a fine economy for a country. What did I think?[1]

And did I know that the landlords in Zagreb (as those in Belgrade), charging high rents and collecting over 400,-000,000 dinars in rentals every year, paid no taxes because they were in cahoots with King Alexander's regime? . . . That Yugoslav emigrants had sent home from America nearly half a billion dollars during the last fourteen years, but at the moment Yugoslavia had little to show for it because most of those dollars, after exchanging them with the people for dinars, had been used by the government to cover the trade balances in foreign countries? . . . That in the best of years half of Yugoslavia's income from her

[1] I describe the socio-economic-political conditions in Yugoslavia in some detail; they are important because they happen to be a part of the general Balkan and east-European situation, which involves 120,000,000 people, most of whom are peasants. Conditions in Bulgaria, Rumania, and Hungary are worse than in Yugoslavia, almost as bad in Poland and Austria, and but little better in Czechoslovakia. The significance of this appears when we consider the facts that all these countries verge on Soviet Russia or on one another, and that four of them are Slavic lands and as such drawn Russia-ward.

exports stayed in foreign countries to cover interest on her debts?

Did I realize that capitalism in Yugoslavia was capitalism at its conceivable worst; that industrially and financially Yugoslavia was drifting into the tragic situation which Russia escaped by having had a revolution against tsarism (of which the Yugoslav dictatorship now was a shabby imitation) and against the whole racketism of international finance capital? . . . Did I wonder that the people everywhere were seeing red and that, to keep them down, the regime had to organize all the sadism in the country and develop a terror machine (this was before Hitler's full rise to power) second to none in the whole world? . . .

Just prior to our arrival in Zagreb, grapevine telegraph had brought there the message that I was enthusiastic about the country and the people as a whole, but against the Belgrade regime; so now, trusting me, the people came and talked to me or wrote me letters, some signed, some anonymous.

Now and then, listening to them and reading their letters, my head whirled. Stella was nervous. Something might happen to me. An "accident." One or two other persons warned me I should be careful. Some of the people who came to see me might be detectives. Yugoslavia was full of them.

IV

My lecture on America, though I delivered it in my very poor Croatian, was a success. Students, government clerks, intellectuals of all sorts, men and women, mostly young, filled the largest hall in town, and hundreds were turned away. I think few speakers ever had a friendlier audience. What I told them was, to them, a tremendous fairy tale. It was not really vital with them. They were tense, waiting for me to say something about Yugoslavia. But I had been told that about sixty plain-clothes men were distributed through the hall and, in addition, uniformed policemen were inside and out. The authorities, I heard, were afraid I might say something which would snap the emotional tension of my audience and start a demonstration, a riot. They were prepared for such an eventuality. So I carefully avoided all mention of Yugoslavia; there was no use starting anything.

After the lecture a mob followed me to the hotel. One of my new friends whispered to me, "Half of these are detectives."

Then for a week or longer detectives followed me around almost everywhere I went. I suppose they were not watching me so much as those who called on me or whom I went to see. I began to suspect my mail was being opened. Later I met people who told me they had written me about that time, but I never received their letters.

One result of this was that fewer people came to see me. Stella and I had more time to look over Zagreb, to loaf in the market place where peasant women in colorful costumes were selling fruit, vegetables, and needlework. We visited with the Vankas and a few other people with whom we had become acquainted soon after our arrival in Zagreb.

A few days after my lecture I heard that government agents and regimists were spreading rumors in student circles and in coffee-houses frequented by intellectuals that I was very much in favor of the Belgrade regime; that I had tentatively agreed to accept a high position in the Yugoslav diplomatic service; that I was about to be received by King Alexander, who would decorate me with an order. One rumor had it that I had accepted a considerable sum from the press bureau. The purpose of this was to keep people from coming to see me and tell me things.

For a few days this nearly drove me frantic, for I noticed that a few people half believed this slanderous talk.

Annoyed and worse, Stella and I went to Slovenia for a few days, to visit my people in Blato and our friends in Lublyana. They were all very glad to see us. My mother was happy. Peasants in Blato told me the *kriza* was a hundred per cent worse than it had been in the spring, when I first came home. They could sell hardly anything any more. People in the cities were so poor few could afford milk, even. Exports to foreign countries had almost ceased. And what did I think of this talk about a new war starting in the spring? Would Italy really attack Yugoslavia? Or was it just a rumor spread about by the government in Belgrade so the people, thinking their country was in danger of foreign attack, would not rebel? This last question was whispered to me by a student who was a peasant's son.

They were dreadfully pathetic, helpless, these people of my native village. What could I do for them? They were in a trap, which consisted of the Belgrade terror government, the world economic crisis, and international politics which were pushing the world into a new war.

I heard the legend about Mr. Guggenheim and me was still being told. It had amused me in the spring. Now it did not seem funny any more. My head whirled. How different my village looked to me from what it had last spring! Now I knew so much more about the country, the crazy world, of which it was a part.

I began to feel extremely uncomfortable in Yugoslavia. So did Stella. Detectives did not follow me to Blato; that would have been too obvious. But in Lublyana I was always conscious of being under some one's surveillance. I hated the idea of my mail being scrutinized. But in another department of my mind I was glad that all this was happening to me. Now I really knew what it meant to live in this beautiful, naturally opulent country which was full of poverty and ruled by people who were no better than American gangsters. Talking with Stella, I commenced to refer to King Alexander as the "big shot."

We had meant to stay in Yugoslavia till May. Now we talked of going as soon as possible—perhaps the end of March—as soon as I had all the material I needed for a full book about Yugoslavia.

V

We returned to Zagreb, where in the meantime my friends had put on the grapevine telegraph that, rumors to the contrary notwithstanding, I was not for the regime. Everybody was very friendly again; but I saw as few people as possible.

Our hotel was on Yelachitch Square, the center of the town. Taking our old rooms again, Stella and I looked from one of the windows down on the square. It was a bright sunny winter morning. The square was lively and colorful with city people and peasants. Pigeons flew about. Very pretty.

Stella said, "Looking at this scene, one would imagine everything was all right in Zagreb—in Croatia—in Yugoslavia."

A half-hour later we heard shouting outside. We ran to the window. There was a demonstration of unemployed and starving people, men, women and children, everybody in rags, some of the women carrying babies in their arms, all crying: "Work and bread! Work and bread!" Seven or eight hundred of them, marching four abreast—a long line.

The sidewalks filled with well-dressed city people and peasants. Some fell in line.

Telling Stella to stay in, I ran out. On the Ilitsa, which is Zagreb's main thoroughfare, I caught up with the tail end of the parade. Vehicular traffic was stopped. The street was choked with people. "Work and bread! Work and bread!" The words had a menacing rhythm. Those on the sidewalks cheered the marchers. Windows opened and office-workers and housewives took up the cheering.

"I wonder where the gendarmes are?" I overheard some one say.

A moment later I heard some cries behind me. I turned, felt a sharp shove in my back, and found myself on the ground, a woman on top of me. "Gendarmes!" cried the woman. I got from under her and rose in time to see forty

or fifty uniformed and helmeted men—bestial-looking creatures—charge the marchers. The gendarmes held their rifles
by the barrels and swung them over the ragged crowd. They
had given them no warning. They hit them on the shoulders,
breaking their collar bones. Before the mob scattered into
the doorways and side streets, several lay across the tram-
way tracks. The gendarmes dragged them off like sacks
of potatoes and traffic was resumed. From the time I was
knocked over (I assume by a gendarme) and the time when
the tram cars moved on, perhaps no more than a minute
elapsed.

The incident was the speediest, most efficient piece of
terroristic brutality I have ever witnessed.

VI

The third or fourth day after our return from Slovenia I
was again given the cold shoulder in Zagreb. No one
stopped to talk to me as they had been wont to before.
Some passed by, obviously pretending they did not see me.
In the coffee-house where Stella and I went for breakfast,
a man whom we knew well looked past us. The waiter gave
me a dirty look.

I was puzzled and disturbed. Returning to the hotel, I
found a friend of mine waiting for me and he showed me an
article in the Belgrade newspaper *Vreme*, a regime organ,
in which I was quoted to have said that, traveling about the
past ten months, I had found everywhere villages full of
happy, prosperous peasants who were enthusiastic for the
king and his present regime—and more to the same effect.

Of course, I had never made any such statement to
anyone.

My friend said: "Just keep calm. They want to discredit
you with the anti-regimists, so they will not tell you things.
But you should worry; you know enough. . . . They are
very stupid in Belgrade. They don't realize that by printing
false interviews and causing you these annoyances they are

helping you to write a book which will damn them. . . .
Some of the people here in Zagreb who don't know you so
well as I do naturally can't be entirely sure you never gave
such an interview. They have been tricked and betrayed so
much. The general mood of the country which we have developed under the dictatorship is such that no one entirely
trusts anybody."

The thing was very unpleasant. The next day I heard
that regime newspapers all over Yugoslavia had reprinted
the "interview" and, later, that it had been reprinted also
in two Serb papers in America. I thought of demanding
that *Vreme* publish a denial from me, but, talking about it
with my friends, that proved inadvisable. I was leaving the
country in a few weeks, and the regime, if I antagonized it,
might confiscate all my notes for this book, which filled a
small trunk. That had happened to an English writer only
a few months before. The American consul in Zagreb ad-
vised me that if the Yugoslav authorities chose to take my
notes or otherwise annoy me, he could not protect me. Besides, my Croatian publisher was afraid that if I made the
denial the government might confiscate the unsold copies
of my books. So I decided to make no denial. "Everything
will come out in the wash." And, anyhow, within a few days
nearly everybody in Zagreb who cared to know knew I had
not given the "interview."

VII

We stayed in Croatia till mid-March. . . . A little snow
fell. . . . Hitler was forging into full power in Germany.
Terror reigned there which was a hundred times worse
than what was going on in Yugoslavia. In Zagreb everyone
became very depressed. "Hitler . . . Hitler." Those eager
for socio-economic and political changes in Europe in general which might react favorably on Yugoslavia and the
Balkans were saying, "This puts the clock farther back for
all of us. Nothing worse could have happened." Some said,

{ 289 }

"Maybe this will hasten on a new war—then chaos, revolution—then a new order. Maybe that is the only way."

Zagreb was a bleak place—a center of a nation's agony.

Every other day or so, taking the automobile which the Returned Emigrants' committee had arranged to be at our disposal, we drove to some village and learned the things I describe early in this chapter. But we learned other things.

The well-to-do peasants had plenty to eat—more, much more than enough, for, as in Slovenia, they could sell almost nothing. In one home in Turopolye, one of the solidest sections, near Zagreb, they invited us to stay for dinner and we ate—unsalted turkey! They had scores of turkeys, geese, ducks, chickens, pigs for which there was no market, hence no money for salt. In nearly every village the same story— no sugar, no salt; in many houses, no petroleum, no matches. In villages of from 500 to 2,000 people I was told that all the peasants together did not possess $30 in cash, and these were so-called *imuchna sela* ("prosperous villages") —*i.e.,* till recently fairly well-to-do.

All the villages, while seemingly self-sufficient, were wholly unsound in their economy from the viewpoint of a progressive civilization or people living there. In a typical, though rather large, village in the Podravina region, north of Zagreb, I was put in touch—by a mutual friend of ours in Zagreb—with an acute middle-aged peasant, who was a local leader (secretly, of course) of the leftist element in the Peasant Party. He had had a few years of schooling and read everything he could get. He gave me the following picture of his village:

"Our population (using round figures) is 2,500. We have 400 *gospodarstva*" (families or homes which exist as independent economic units). "We have 2,000 acres of soil, of which 300 are not cultivated because occupied by buildings or otherwise unavailable. That leaves us 1,700 acres, or about four acres per family. Which is not enough. To live at all, even according to our standards, a family of five or six should have at least eight acres to cultivate. But, since some of us have anywhere from twenty to forty acres, most of the families have not even four, and a great many, aside from the ground their shacks stand on, have no soil whatever. . . . In other words, in this village of 2,000 souls and 1,700 fertile acres, two-thirds of us don't belong, economically speaking. Two-thirds of us are not really peasants, but village proletariat who barely exist—paupers dependent on the resources, the charity of others. . . . Once upon a time one could go to America and with one's earnings there support from five to ten persons back here. Now America can't take us any more. Our emigrants are returning to share our misery. We are as caught in a trap. There is no more room for expansion, for new villages. Thanks partly to Raditch, most of the large estates have been divided.[1]

"Another matter. . . . In this village, which, let me say, is one of the best in Podravina, we have (using round numbers again) 500 horses, representing a capital of 500,-000 dinars. These animals eat up every year all the hay and oats we can grow on 800 of our 1,700 productive acres. . . . Now, for the money we have invested in horses we could buy three or four modern tractors. Moreover, if we did not have the horses, we could turn the 800 acres now in hay and oats to corn- or wheat-growing, which in good times would yield us 2,000,000 dinars a year—enough to buy ten new tractors and other farm machinery and pave our village streets, which now are rivers of mud, and modernize our old houses."

"Well, why don't you get busy and do that?" I asked, although I knew my question was foolish.

He grinned. "Because we are dumb peasants. . . . But no, not really. The truth is we are caught in a rut of traditions started in the old days when we were serfs and

[1] This condition of over-population in peasant villages exists not only in Croatia, but, with variations, in about 200,000 villages elsewhere in the Balkans and eastern Europe.

subjects of foreign rulers. We are backward because our masters for a thousand years did everything to keep us backward. We use horses and oxen because we have always used them. It is hard for us to break with our old ways. We need some one to help us, encourage us, energize us from above; if necessary, to force us into progress. As the system now is, no one is interested in us, in our surplus population, our village proletariat which starves and shivers and rots in these shacks you see all around. No one in authority is interested in attacking our bad economy at the roots. We ourselves can't move also because we are weighted down by all sorts of local problems, confused by petty jealousies, endlessly frustrated by depression and wars which hit us every once in a while and ruin everything we have tried to accomplish. . . . They say we have been "liberated"; now we are part of Yugoslavia; but Belgrade is no better than was Budapest or Vienna—the government is interested only in exploiting us, turning our natural resources over to foreigners, and pulling us into the army."

"But what of the future?" I asked.

He grinned again, shrugged his shoulders. "Maybe Stalin will fix everything."

"What do you mean?"

He thought awhile. "Of course, I don't know what is going to happen exactly. We are part of the European mess, world mess. Maybe there will be another war. It is almost sure to come; everybody says so. Then we peasants—I think peasants everywhere—will revolt. There are about one hundred million of us here in the Balkans and north of us. Most of us are Slavs, like the Russians. . . . Sometimes I daydream and imagine the Red Army starting from Moscow a million strong. We join them—then to the devil with all this! We become a part of Russia—independent republics within a great union. All Slavs together and anyone else who cares to come in with us. . . . Sometimes I really think something like that will happen some day. It may take years. Maybe ten, twenty years. When it happens, it may be worse than it is now for a while. A million of us may have to die, but, *boga ti,* we are dying anyway—degenerating, fretting, feeling miserable; working, producing, without improving our lot. We are the beasts of burden of the civilization, as they call it: and some of us are getting very tired of our circumstances."

"You think Raditch, were he alive today, would agree with you?"

"Raditch woke us up, organized us, made us conscious of our power. He changed all the time. Today he would see that Russia alone is doing things. There is misery in Russia, but misery for the sake of progress, the future; to save herself from Western imperialism. Russia is like ourselves, a backward, peasant country, but she is building industries of her own to absorb her surplus peasant population, supply her needs of manufactured goods, save her natural wealth for herself. We need that. We need it in a hurry, or our rulers in Belgrade will give the French and English all the wealth in our mines and forests. . . . Sometimes I wish a new world war would start tomorrow. It would be terrible, but perhaps the last war—the beginning of the end of all that is now. Indeed, war may be our only chance. It will put arms into our hands."

"Are you a Bolshevik—a Communist?"

"I don't know what I am. I told you how I think." He showed me some underground pamphlets he kept hidden in cracks of a wall in his barn. Some of them were issued by the Communist Party.

I asked him, "Does Dr. Machek"—the present leader of the Peasant Party; in prison, as I write this—"think as you do?"

"I don't know, but I hope he is not far from my views."

"Are there many peasants like you in this village?"

"Who think exactly as I think? . . . Four or five. Then there are about a dozen who are beginning to think as we do. They are the old-time Raditchites. Even our priest is with us; he is a young man. He says he is a Communist.

When the time comes, he can swing two-thirds of the village. The paupers are ready to swing to us any day we want them. They have nothing to lose. The same is true of at least one-third of peasants who owe the government and the banks more than their properties, depreciated in value due to the depression, are worth. They have nothing to lose. Our only opposition here are a few *kulaks*, as they call them in Russia. . . . Of course, now we must keep low. But a time will come. We must wait. We can wait, oh, a long time, if necessary. We have resisted tyranny and injustice for a thousand years; what is ten years more? Or a hundred?"

He asked me, when I returned to the United States, to send him some pictures of American farm machinery "in action" which he could use for propaganda purposes among the intelligent peasants in the village.

VIII

In Zagreb, between visits to villages, I met a number of interesting people who were more than local or national figures.

One of these was Miroslav Krleza, a Croat writer, who, although little known as yet outside the Slavic countries of eastern, southeastern, and central Europe, incontestably is one of the most powerful contemporary writers in the world, almost equally effective as playwright, poet, novelist, short-story writer, essayist, and pamphleteer. A man still below forty, he has Dostoevski's genius as an intuitive psychologist, is a Marxist ideologically, a stylist of elemental force. Several of his books were confiscated by the government. Incidentally, he is the only serious writer in Yugoslavia who makes a living solely by his pen.

Another was Mme. Milka Ternina, who in the '90's and early 1900's probably was the most eminent exponent of the soprano parts of Wagner. Thirty years ago the opera-going world of the Continent, London, and New York was at her feet. In 1899 men drew her carriage through the streets of Bayreuth. In 1906 an accident resulted in a serious nervous affliction on her face and she retired from the profession to strict privacy in an old house in Zagreb, which is near her native village. A woman of great simplicity and dignity, she said she could not understand why I should want to see her. "I am just an old woman." She had just past her seventieth year and was not very well. She recalled her successes in the Metropolitan Opera, but thought no one in New York remembered her any more.

Two others I met were men of great significance in Yugoslavia, and, indeed, international figures still playing vital rôles in the world. I deal with them separately in the ensuing two chapters.

CHAPTER XV

A Peasant Genius

SOON AFTER OUR ARRIVAL IN ZAGREB, MAXO VANKA arranged for us to meet Ivan Mestrovitch, generally considered the world's foremost living sculptor and no doubt one of the greatest figures in the realm of art since its beginnings. He makes his permanent home in a modernized old palace in the mediæval section of the town.

Prior to making his acquaintance we had seen, I think, nearly every piece of his work scattered over Yugoslavia, including the famous Racitch Memorial in the village of Cavtat, near Dubrovnik; the several monuments in Split, and his own as yet uncompleted mausoleum at Otavitse, his home village in the Dalmatian highlands, where we had also met his seventy-four-year-old peasant mother. We had seen, too, the photographs of several hundred of his sculptures in England, France, Czechoslovakia and the United States, including the immense "Indians" in Chicago.

After we met him, we enjoyed the hospitality of his home on several occasions. His wife, Olga Mestrovitch, is a woman of deep loveliness that transcends beauty; she and Stella "clicked" at once and became fast friends.

On a couple of occasions I sat with Mestrovitch and his cronies in their favorite coffee-house on the Ilitsa, listening to their gossip, banter, discussion of politics, art, women, and God. One evening, when he happened to be in a talkative mood and his dark, centerless eyes shone through the smoke of his eternal cigarette, I listened to his curiously brilliant and picturesque stories and descriptions of life in his beloved Dalmatia and Zagoryé for hours, and could have listened all night.

Once I watched him sit still and silent as stone hour after hour in a roomful of people, looking immeasurably bored and weary, physically and spiritually. The next day, in his own house, we listened to him sing old Croatian folk-songs half the night. He sang them at once with great gusto and infinite tenderness—the same folk-songs that had served as a basis for most of the compositions of Haydn, who was also a Croat of peasant birth.

Mestrovitch and I had several talks, mostly about Yugoslavia. Often I was not sure what he was driving at, for off and on a strong peasant-mystic streak in his mental make-up and even stronger political considerations put a befuddling Byzantine vagueness into his talk. Some of his views and ideas seemed to me downright silly, unsound, mediæval. At times he exasperated me.

But always, from the moment we came together till we parted, I was clearly and continually aware of being in the presence of a formidable personality—a man of fierce and authentic power which was intrinsic of his whole make-up—a creative dynamo—a force not merely in his field of art, but, during the last two decades, in European politics—a factor in the life of Yugoslavia as no artist, whatever his medium, had ever been in any other land.

II

Mestrovitch is an indigenous product of the Yugoslav part of the Balkans. He could have appeared nowhere else. With all his virtues and faults, the one as numerous and pronounced as the other, he is intensely representative and expressive of that country—or, at least, was at its beginning. He is as thoroughly Balkan and Yugoslavic as, for instance, Sinclair Lewis is American.

His parents were poor, struggling Croat peasants (not Serb, as usually stated in America and English prints) in the tiny, forlorn hamlet of Otavitse, twenty-odd miles inland from Shibenik. They were uneducated, but theirs was the rich "heart culture" and the historic, poetic, and religious background of Yugoslav peasantry. They were members of a race in which endless centuries of oppression and persecution—on the part of the Byzantine, Turkish, Venetian, Austrian, and their own rulers—have bottled up much primitive creative energy.

Already as a young woman, when Ivan was a little boy, his mother knew by heart nearly a thousand folk-songs, poems and tales, most of them then still unrecorded in print, and many of which took hours to sing, recite, or tell from start to finish. She sang, recited, and told them to her children, who also heard them from other people in Otavitse. Most of those tales, songs, and poems were parts of the great Kossovo epic. They were an essential part of the cultural and spiritual side of the village where Mestrovitch spent his boyhood. They became a part of him. In fact, nothing in his later life impressed itself more powerfully upon his mind and spirit than the Kossovo legends.

Ivan's father (now dead), besides being a humble tiller of the soil and raiser of sheep, was also a mason, stonecutter and wood-carver. He taught the boy even before he was ten to make figures of wood and stone, which in the vicinity of Otavitse is extremely soft limestone, lending itself easily to carving with a knife.

In his mid-teens, while watching his father's sheep and cutting their portraits in stone, Ivan was discovered by an Austrian mining engineer temporarily in Dalmatia, who some time later, in 1901, helped him to enter the Art Academy in Vienna. There his talent swiftly developed. In 1902 he exhibited in the Austrian capital, in 1904 in Belgrade, the next year in Zagreb. In 1907 he went to France and became a pupil of Rodin's, who soon thereafter declared him his superior—"the greatest phenomenon among the sculptors."

All this time young Mestrovitch worked on the idea of producing a colossal monument to the heroism and suffering of his race since the battle of Kossovo. He wanted to put into stone his mother's songs and legends. On the Plain of Kossovo he proposed to erect a great edifice on the order of the Delphic Temple which should enshrine the national ideals of the Yugoslavs; a temple which all his fellow nationals, regardless of religion, could freely visit and draw patriotic inspiration from the stone figures of the main characters in the Kossovo legends that throbbed in the uppermost layers of his consciousness and vitalized his creative power.

The idea began to take shape under his hands. His famous Kossovo Fragments, about fifty in number, were shown at Zagreb in 1911 and later in the same year in the Serb Pavilion of the International Art Exhibition at Rome.

In those sculptures—in several of which he attained, though then still in his early and middle twenties, a Michelangelesque grandeur of conception and strength of execution—he put into startling artistic forms much of the saga, the intense drama of the Yugoslav people's centuries-old national tragedy, idealism and aspirations for freedom, unity, self-realization, and self-expression within a country of their own. He crystallized that idealism and those aspirations in such a way that the great world outside the strife-torn and meagerly understood Balkans on whose good-will and sympathy depended their fulfillment could not help taking respectful notice of them. His vast figures of Kralyevitch Marko, the Serb Mother, the Maiden of Kossovo, Tsar Lazar, and the other legendary characters spoke the language of the Yugoslav *guslari* in a way that anyone could understand them. They were endowed with all the spiritual dignity and strength of the epic.

When out of the fullness of his racial background Mestrovitch produced those sculptures, the world became conscious of a new artist of the highest order. However, so far as his race was concerned, the chief value, at least the chief immediate value, of his sculptures was not as art, but as propaganda—the most glorious propaganda any artist ever made for his race.

The Kossovo Fragments once and for all exploded the idea, which the German and Austrian imperialists had spread about in Europe, that the Balkan Slavs were an inferior barbarian breed, without culture, hopeless from the viewpoint of civilization and unworthy of freedom or the rich and beautiful country they inhabited.

So far as the future Yugoslavia was concerned, Mestrovitch appeared in the nick of time.

At the 1911 show in Rome, his pieces created a great stir, and in the ensuing three years were exhibited in half a dozen other European centers.

Then—1914—Sarajevo—the war.

In 1915 the British government, amazed by the heroism with which the tiny Serb and Montenegrin armies withstood the terrific onslaughts of the Austrian and German military machines, invited Mestrovitch, then only thirty-two, to exhibit his Kossovo pieces in the Victoria and Albert Museum at South Kensington—an honor till then reserved for sculptors no longer living. This coming on top of his triumphs in the preceding few years on the Continent, easily made Mestrovitch the most discussed artistic figure in the world.

Although in the midst of the greatest war ever, the cultural, political, and journalistic England went agog about the dark, quiet-seeming, moody young "Serb" sculptor, his strange, beautiful work, and the fierce power behind it. Books, pamphlets, hundreds of articles were written interpreting the phenomenon. Lecturers found it profitable to go on tours all over England delivering hundreds of talks on Mestrovitch, Serbia, the Yugoslav idealism and aspiration, explaining why and how Sarajevo occurred; that behind Sarajevo was a terrific and legitimate urge to freedom and independence on the part of a people that had been abused and exploited by other races for centuries.

In producing the Kossovo statuary, Mestrovitch's original intention was not so much (if at all) to create political propaganda in foreign countries, but art, which, by its quality as such, might make tangible to his own people the essence of its centuries-long hope and struggle for freedom. None the less, as I have suggested, at that crucial moment of world's history, 1914-1918, the chief value of his art to his nation was as international propaganda.

In 1915-1916, partly in direct consequence of Mestrovitch's masterpieces, Serbia became as highly regarded in London as was Belgium, and Great Britain turned into a stanch supporter of the Yugoslav idea—the idea of making a large independent state of Serbia and such parts of Austria-Hungary as Slovenia, Croatia-Slavonia, Voyvodina, Dalmatia, and Bosnia-Herzegovina. Then France, already mildly favorable to the idea, joined Britain in that support; in 1918 Woodrow Wilson became strong for it—and, the war over, Yugoslavia came into existence.

There were other Yugoslav nationalists in France, England, and the United States who worked toward that idea, but without Mestrovitch's note-compelling art they in all probability would not have won the Allies and the United States so thoroughly to their cause. And it is incontestable that but for Mestrovitch entire Dalmatia, which is 98 per cent Slavic, would have been given to Italy.

III

When Stella and I first met him, Mestrovitch was going on fifty—a stocky, short man with a large, swarthy, but very attractive Slavic face. He is bald and has a soft black beard, beginning to be streaked with gray. He looks every inch an artist. Studying him, I thought he could be anything, do anything. At one moment his eyes are utterly weary, deep, tender, suffering; his full lips drooping, his soft voice tired. Then, suddenly, he says something or smiles, revealing his very white, strong teeth, and his whole personality livens up.

At various times I saw in him a mystic, an adventurer, a Christ, a devil, a lover, a child, a seer, an ascetic, a Rabelaisian, a cheap politician and opportunist: a multitude of people, good and evil, but—basically, essentially—always an artist, a genius, vast, with unlimited possibilities; also, though living in a palace, always a peasant, without formal, systematic education, sometimes plain stupid, his mind pulled by mystic concepts and temporary personal schemes and egotisms in various directions; but often, too, infinitely wise, shrewd, intuitive, practical, close-to-the-soil, profoundly realistic, especially in purely human, intimate situations.

The man possesses incredible strength. He has a huge torso, powerful shoulders, the hands and wrists of a section worker. In his studio, which forms a wing of his house, he frequently works twenty-four hours at a stretch at the hardest physical and creative labor imaginable. He has been known to work thirty-six hours, stopping only for a sandwich or a drink. Vast sculptures, which would take most sculptors (if they could do them at all) months to execute, he finishes in two or three days; then is utterly exhausted, but completely recuperates in as many days, during which he sees or talks with no one. He has over six hundred pieces of work scattered all over the world, but most of them perhaps are still in Yugoslavia.

Though anything but handsome, he is very attractive, especially to women, and will remain so if he lives to be ninety, which he probably will. In his home life he is as happy as a man of that nature could ever be. Olga Mestrovitch is a devoted, understanding, self-sacrificing wife. They have four children.

Apart from his family life, however, as I write this, he is anything but happy. Yugoslavia, the political result of his art, has been in deep socio-political agony since its inception. When I was there, that agony, which I merely suggest in this book, was worse than ever before. And Mestrovitch's life is closely tied up with the political affairs of his country. As one of its leading originators, he has been playing politics with the ruling group. For five years now he has been one of the foremost supporters of the Belgrade regime. In 1929 he indorsed the dictatorship. At first it was natural for him to play the game with Belgrade. He wanted to. Now, being what he is, it is practically unavoidable that he support the regime, whether he actually wants to or not. He is at the mercy of the "big shots." His economic circumstances are most unfortunate. He has invested the earnings from his art in Zagreb real estate, and as a landlord he is practically compelled to play the game, for the Belgrade regime has the power to ruin economically anyone it sees fit to ruin. This situation now is aggravated for Mestrovitch by the depression.

Besides, the Belgrade politicians have him where they want him in another way. Promising to eventually afford him the means to complete his projected temple on the Plain of Kossovo (in which they, of course, have no honest interest), they—that is, the government—bought his superb Fragments and stuck them into a warehouse-like building they chose to call a museum; but, instead of giving him a lump sum, they arranged to pay him for the statuary in annual instalments. The idea of this was to keep him in line. Should he withdraw his support of the regime, which now is an all-powerful dictatorship, instalment payments would cease.

There are other reasons why he supported the Belgrade hegemony at first. One is that, although infinitely wise in some things (now and then), he is fundamentally an ignorant man in political economy and practical politics. Another reason is that he has become somewhat of a city man. He loves the peasants, the poor *raya* from which he has sprung, but, it seems to me, only in an abstract, artistic way. In this he is a typical Balkan peasant who rises in the world.

Still other reasons for his supporting the Belgrade outfit are more or less patriotic, unselfish. Off and on, I think, he honestly believes that for the time being Yugoslavia under King Alexander is as well off internally as could be expected. He remarked to me that the Italians and the Germans had also had long inner struggles before uniting into solid states. Then, too, Yugoslavia, with her present diplomatic connections, has powerful foreign enemies and is perennially in danger of attack; so Mestrovitch believes that it is best to leave the country in the hands of King Alexander, who is a capable military man. To salve his conscience as a decent human being (for he is that, too) and as a Croat, he indulges in mental somersaults trying to make distinctions between the king's person and his rule. He appears to say that Alexander is a fine ruler, but his rule is bad.

When I saw and talked with him, Mestrovitch obviously was in a deep quandary within himself, full of inner conflicts, very uncomfortable. He had numerous enemies in Yugoslavia. Most of the younger artists—who are leftists, close to the social problems of the people, but whose artistic abilities come nowhere near his—despise him for his wobbly, ignorant reactionary politics (which he appears to consider "liberal"; at least that is how one of his friends described them to me). Croat nationalist-separatists, who exist only in Zagreb, are against him for the same reason. Regimists hate him because he is not 100 per cent for them and lives in Zagreb instead of Belgrade, thus augmenting the former city's cultural prestige and not increasing the latter's. Republicans dislike him because he is a monarchist. Communists loathe him because, instead of doing sculptures of sweating peasants, starving proletarians and such heroes of the class struggle as Bracan Bracanovitch, he wastes his time and talent on endless Christs, Madonnas, and nude women. Intelligent peasants in the villages shrug their shoulders at the mention of his name. A student, son of a peasant who considered himself a peasant, said to me, "Mestrovitch has gone too high for us to follow him. He has become one of the gentry. Now he looks down on us peasants with a mingling of love and contempt. He believes we are incapable of ruling ourselves, but thinks we are fine otherwise—at least when one contemplates us artistically. We are picturesque, dramatic—why?—because we're poor. He wants to keep us that way, though if you accused him of that

{ 304 }

he probably would deny it. . . . Mestrovitch was a factor in the creation of Yugoslavia, which was a progressive step in human affairs, but he is not a consistently progressive spirit. I think the radicals are justified in attacking him. . . ."

Mestrovitch brooded a great deal while I was in Zagreb. I knew that in his inmost heart he was against the regime, and he knew I knew it; so, in talking with me he indulged in vagueness. I urged him to speak out clearly against the racketism of the Belgrade regime which operated to create a deep discord between the Serbs and Croats. A clear statement from him, I implied, would be of great importance. It would electrify the country, stiffen the people's resistance to organized injustice and sadism. He might be exiled; but what did he care? If he needed money, I suggested to one of his friends who I knew would tell him, he could earn more in America or England in one year than he had earned in Yugoslavia the past decade. His friend replied, "He can't live anywhere else than in Yugoslavia, preferably here in Zagreb or in Dalmatia. With all his faults (I admit he's not perfect) he really loves this country—perhaps not intelligently, as you seem to suspect, but too much for his own good. When he goes to his exhibitions in Paris, London, Prague, or New York, he is always lonely, miserable there. He returns as quickly as he can. His life is here. He knows that everything he has in him he owes to his country, with its rich and complex background. Of course, he is miserable here, too; he suffers a great deal; but he is never lonely."

IV

Some one else in Zagreb described him to me as "a personification of Yugoslavia." He was that in 1919, but I think is no longer today, except in a very small way. He holds in him all the influences of the past still active in the country today. He is essentially archaic, unmodern, a man of the past.

He is deeply religious, but his religion is a mixture of mediæval Christianity and Slavic paganism. Philosophically, he is a twelfth-century mystic. In 1926 a Zagreb review, *Nova Evropa,* published an essay of his on Michelangelo, in which one comes upon ideas such as this: "Love for eternity is sacrifice, and sacrifice is the search for the eternal. Evil passes, and good passes, but bliss is eternal, and eternity is God."

Politically, as I have shown, he is an opportunist, careful, fatalistic, an enemy of social experimentation. He distrusts human nature. He distrusts the masses. He appears to believe in the necessity of extreme suffering in order to keep humanity spiritually on its toes. In dozens of his works he glorifies suffering, and since the easiest way to have people suffer is through economic poverty, he is no great enemy of forces which produce poverty.

Personally, he is human, all too human; always interesting, too interesting. He is hooked to the influences of the past and his own narrow interests. In socio-political matters, although, as his friends insist, he is a "liberal," he is always closer to reaction than to progress. He is a monarchist. He is "personally loyal" to King Alexander, as he declared in a recent statement published in Zagreb. He is against the growing number of men and women in Yugoslavia and other countries who want to break with the past, liquidate various archaisms, and gear themselves to the future. He has made no protest against the terror and sadism in Yugoslavia; hence one is justified in assuming that he is in favor of people being tortured in prisons if that will keep them from attacking the *status quo* and the sacred things of long ago.

In several of his sculptures, especially those representing womanhood and motherhood, he is a pure artist dealing with eternal things. They are technically perfect, minglings of various styles from the ancient Greek classic to the ultramodern, yet withal individual and original. Studying or merely enjoying their profound beauty and universal qualities, one temporarily forgives Mestrovitch all his political and personal shortcomings. One loves his works; one loves him for his artistic genius and power. Then one thinks of the following words by Lenin, as quoted by Gorki: "[Great music] affects your nerves, makes you want to say stupid nice things and stroke the heads of people who could create such beauty while living in this vile hell."

CHAPTER XVI

"Doctor Hercules"

ALMOST EVERYWHERE IN YUGOSLAVIA WE CAME IN contact with splendid human beings; most of these, however, were humble people, unknown in the country at large. Of the prominent men I really liked and admired only one—Dr. Andriya Stampar, a public-health expert who, in the last decade, developed in Yugoslavia a system for looking after the people's health which, to my mind, is one of the most dramatic and noteworthy achievements in Europe since the war.

I know of no character in real life, past or contemporary, with whom I could even distantly compare this son of ordinary peasant parents, born forty-four years ago in a tiny village in Croatia. I met him several times in Zagreb. At first, when I was with him, listening to him, studying his colossal and withal charming personality, I thought of Sondelius, the public-health evangelist, disease-fighter, and general uplifter in Sinclair Lewis' novel, *Arrowsmith.* Later I began to think of him as a sort of twentieth-century Hercules with an M.D. degree from the University of Vienna who, instead of the Augean stables, had cleaned up in an amazingly short period vast disease-ravaged regions of his country.

His story seems to me as exciting as any fiction or film thriller.

Two years ago Dr. Stampar fell victim to intrigue on the part of his political opposition in Belgrade and now is no longer officially connected with the dramatic movement for national health he has started and built up in his country. None the less, the man is one of the great successes of post-war Europe and by far the soundest individual of any prominence in the Balkans. In fact, I believe that in soundness he has few rivals in the whole of present-day Europe.

II

Early in 1919, a few months after Yugoslavia had come into existence, Dr. Stampar, then just thirty, was made the head of the Department of Public Hygiene in the Ministry of Social Institutions at Belgrade. Prior to that he had been an obscure young physician in Croatia.

Like most Croats of humble origin, he was an idealist almost to the point of being naïve, not to say slightly fantastic. Private practice held no appeal for him. He constantly bewailed the fact that only 20 per cent of the world's population derived any benefit from the science of medicine. That fact, indeed, bulged in his mind as a major tragedy of the human race. In Yugoslavia probably not even 20 per cent of the people received any benefit from the marvelous results of modern medical research. "Most of the good there is in medicine," he used to say (and still says today), "is locked up in laboratories—or practically so, so far as the masses of people are concerned." He believed that medicine, as splendid as it was in laboratories and professional journals, was mainly unsound, not to say absurd, in its strategy and tactics against disease. In his mind, the foremost duty of medicine was not merely to try to cure individuals after they succumbed to it, but to prevent disease.

His appointment as chief of the Department of Public Hygiene was the best thing that had happened in Yugoslavia since its inception. I say this advisedly and without reservations.

Coming to Belgrade, Dr. Stampar found himself in charge of a loose organization of district medical officers whose official duties were incidental to their private practice and, in fact, consisted chiefly of sending occasional reports, based on guesswork, to the Ministry on the state of health in their areas. For his office he was assigned a room barely large enough to contain his huge person, for he is six feet-five and of massive built. He was given a desk, two chairs, and a cuspidor, no staff and no funds. His salary was the equivalent of thirty-five dollars a month.

With this means he was supposed to cope with the conditions that throbbed in his consciousness as Yugoslavia's outstanding problem. These conditions were the legacy not only of the World War, but of a dozen wars and centuries of misgovernment and neglect in the greater part of the country formerly under various foreign rules.

In 1919 there were in Yugoslavia 20,000 cases of typhus; in 1920 nearly 4,000 cases of smallpox. Tuberculosis was increasing. Every year there were from two to three million cases of malaria; in fact, in some districts of South Serbia and the Dalmatian highlands from 60 to 100 per cent of the people were acutely malarial two-thirds of the year. The death rate due to this affliction was immense. Child mortality was enormous.

In his naïve idealism, Dr. Stampar believed that his job as public hygiene chief was to "clean up the country," destroy the disease-producing conditions, and teach the people how to keep it clean and how to live. He ached to get started right away, but that was impossible. Belgrade swarmed with opportunists whose paramount interest in fighting one another for high government jobs had no close relation to national welfare. They laughed at the gigantic young Croat medico whose idealism propelled him about the capital in search of money whereby he could start his Herculean clean-up.

In 1920, however, the young man succeeded in procuring a small appropriation which enabled him to hire several other young doctors and send two of them to Germany and France, to study sanitary methods in those countries.

It took him four years to convert a sufficient number of powerful politicians in the Belgrade government and Parliament (for Yugoslavia then was still a parliamentary

monarchy) to secure the necessary funds for the organization and work he had in mind; and in the ensuing seven
years—from 1924 to 1931—realized his plans, not completely, but in their main essentials.

That Dr. Stampar succeeded in this is due in very great
part to the Rockefeller Foundation, which, early in his
struggle with the indifferent or hostile politicians, commenced to take a deep interest in his aims and finally put
at his disposal a considerable sum of American dollars, with
which he built a great research headquarters in Zagreb and
thus impressed the government in Belgrade. In fact (if
one may speculate a bit), it is possible that without the support of the American institution at that time Dr. Stampar
could not have started his epic work in 1924, or if he had
begun it, could not have carried it out as he did.

The organization he built up in that period is imposing.

When he became hygiene chief, there were in the whole
of Yugoslavia only a half-dozen small buildings in various
stages of neglect and dilapidation, ostensibly dedicated to
public sanitation and health, but actually lacking in proper
personnel and equipment. Today there are scattered through
the country over 800 buildings, large and small, all devoted
exclusively to public health, equipped with the most up-to-
date instruments and appliances, and run by trained men
and women—physicians, dentists, chemists, sanitation engineers, midwives, nurses—most of whom remain loyal, if
not to Dr. Stampar personally, to the idea he had instilled
in them before he ceased to be their chief.

Some paragraphs back I have given a few figures of
typhus, smallpox and malaria cases in Yugoslavia immediately after the war. They were higher than in any other
country in Europe. Today a case of smallpox is rare in
Yugoslavia. Typhus is completely stamped out. Tuberculosis and child mortality are decreasing. The cleansing of
the malarial districts in South Serbia and the Dalmatian
highlands has been so effectively conducted the last six years
that in certain places where the incidence used to be 80 per

cent of the population it is now reduced to 10 or 15 per cent. Mortality from malaria is declining yearly. And there is reasonable hope that—unless Dr. Stampar's system is either destroyed by another war or crippled by the withholding of appropriations on the part of the dictatorial régime now in charge of Yugoslavia—malaria will be entirely banished from the country within the next decade.

III

The central point in Dr. Stampar's philosophy and method is that—in a country such as Yugoslavia, at any rate—the doctor should seek out the patient, and not wait for the patient to come to him. Disease should be attacked at the root by the application of what he calls "social medicine," and by "social medicine" he means the ascertaining of the causes why a certain person or group of persons, locality or district, is visited by this or that disease, and its permanent removal. To this end the coöperation of the afflicted community is essential. This is not difficult in a country where the standard of education is high. Among the Balkan peasants, often incorrectly described as simple, it is not easy; for their characters, the result of centuries of mistreatment and misgovernment, are twisted by rancor and distrust. Here and there, as mentioned in preceding chapters, people still practice magic and believe in taboos. Hence the second point in Dr. Stampar's system is education. The doctor must be a teacher as much as a healer, patiently instructing the people in practical hygiene and showing them how with care they may almost entirely dispense with his services.

An obvious corollary is that the doctor must not depend on fees for his livelihood, but must be paid by the state. Here Dr. Stampar earned for himself the enmity of a great number of private practitioners throughout Yugoslavia; and they were an important part of the political opposition which finally succeeded in having him removed from authority. But before he was removed he created a huge organization in which the above doctrines were rigorously applied, and which consists of three main categories of institutions operated under the general policy of the Department of Public Hygiene in Belgrade.

First come the central health institutes in the capitals of the nine provinces. These, in charge of the provincial directors of hygiene, are centers of administrative and scientific work. They comprise departments of bacteriology and parasitology, social medicine and health propaganda, and sanitary engineering. Here tests are made, serums prepared, statistics gathered, special circulars and pamphlets written and printed, and the larger plans drawn up for fighting disease and cleansing unhealthy districts of the province.

Then come the eighty-odd district institutes, in charge of district hygiene directors, comprising sections for mother-and-child welfare, social (venereal) diseases and tuberculosis, school clinics, dental offices, small bacteriological laboratories, museum of hygiene, bathrooms, and special departments to meet conditions and problems peculiar to that region. The district institutes come in close contact with the people and their problems. Besides the director, the staff consists of two or three additional doctors, a dentist, a sanitary engineer, several nurses, and other assistants. All of them together maintain a constant control over the local health situation.

And, finally, there are more than six hundred village health stations, which are closest to the problems of community hygiene and personal health. I visited scores of these stations all over the country. They are outposts and skirmishers, so to speak, of the district institutes. They consist simply of well-equipped dispensaries in charge of trained nurses. They usually have small "museums" with wax figures showing diseased parts and instructional pictures and placards. Some of them have also movie-projection machines and once a week health films are shown. Four or five shower-baths with hot and cold water and plenty of soap and towels are available to the village population. Twice or three times a week the village stations are visited by a physician from the district office. A dentist comes once a week. All examinations and treatments for any disease or injury whatsoever are free of charge and conducted with as great courtesy and consideration for the patient as he would receive at the hands of any private doctor.

There are numerous other institutions, usually connected with the central health headquarters in the various provincial capitals. Of these, perhaps the most important and interesting is the School of Hygiene attached to the central health institute in Zagreb, and located in a splendid building erected with the money put at Dr. Stampar's disposal by the Rockefeller organization. It is for training personnel of all kinds, including doctors, in the science of hygiene as it is understood by Dr. Stampar.

Not the least important of the activities in this school are the courses for young peasants, in which the pupils are taught the general principles of hygiene, first aid, practical instruction in agriculture and veterinary science. They are young men and women picked from the villages for their character and intelligence, and are intended to form a vanguard in the war against disease and pathological social conditions of all sorts. They become pioneers of health work in their own homes and coöperate with the personnel of the nearest village health station. Many of them develop into veritable evangelists of hygiene.

The Zagreb school has on its staff a group of trained young women—"sisters"—who spend most of their time in distant villages giving courses in cooking, housekeeping, and child care.

In Split and in Skoplyé I found special anti-malaria organizations—"shock troops" of bicycle-riders and horsemen who go into the out-of-the-way, neglected places with boxes of quinine pills, which they distribute among the people free of charge. Millions of these pills are distributed yearly, to say nothing of quantities of other drugs and medicine.

At Skoplyé I attended the graduating exercises of the 1932-33 class of midwives. Thirty-three young women received their diplomas and appointments to distant villages. The director of the school delivered a speech in which he called them, and later swore them in as, "soldiers in our war against infant mortality and womb diseases."

In South Serbia, where the Byzantine and Turkish overlords, as already mentioned, had denuded the mountains in order to supply Egypt, Constantinople, and Asia Minor with lumber and charcoal, I saw men at work on mountain ridges planting young trees under the supervision of sanitary engineers from the central hygienic headquarters at Skoplyé. "This," it was explained to me, "is also one of Dr. Stampar's ideas. He perceived already in 1920, when he first visited South Serbia, that we could never hope to completely eliminate the malarial mosquito (which even now causes 300,000 cases of the disease every year) so long as there are no forests in the mountains to hold back the rain water which now rushes in torrents into the valleys and forms swamps where the mosquito breeds in tens of millions, and where we can't totally destroy him with crude oil and other such comparatively superficial means. Dr. Stampar believed from the beginning that we must attack the problem at the root. We must make forests grow again."

Everywhere, but especially, of course, in the disease-ridden regions, I came upon sanitary engineers—some of them trained personally by Dr. Stampar and all of them imbued with the spirit of the man's philosophy—who were stirring up the peasant populations of the villages to "get busy and clean up." I listened to them patiently explain to the people—in many places illiterate and half degenerated from centuries of malaria and exploitation and neglect on the part of the Venetian, Austrian, or Turkish rulers—why it was necessary for them to gravel their muddy village

{ 315 }

streets, dig drainage canals in the mosquito-breeding swamps near their communities, take the manure piles from in front of their thresholds and the goats and sheep from their living-rooms and kitchens, enlarge their windows, and so on.

I saw them organize men and women into labor gangs which, under their supervision, then accomplished the most urgent tasks of sanitation. Where drinking-water was unhealthy, they induced the villagers to dig new wells or brought water into the community from further up the creek or river, or from a well which they tapped or discovered for them. If the village was too poor to buy new pumps and pipes, they supplied them with them; for in all likelihood the peasants' poverty and backwardness were due to centuries of unsanitary living.

In an ancient, poverty-stricken, and hitherto neglected hamlet stuck in a ravine in the Dalmatian highlands I attended the dedication of a new sanitary cistern. The new well had been dug by the villagers at the instigation of a sanitary engineer from Split. His office had supplied the cement, the cistern, and the pipes. Prior to that the women of the village had been compelled to carry water, which was not fit for drinking, in small flat barrels strapped to their backs, from a creek three miles off. Now, of a sudden, their water-supply was right in the village, which in their minds was nothing short of a miracle. I never heard such an outcry of delight or saw such an outpouring of gratitude as at the dramatic moment when the first spurt of clear cold water came out of the pump in the presence of the entire population assembled for the occasion. Tears rolling down their wind-burnt faces, men and women knelt on the stony ground and raised their big, gnarled hands in spontaneous thanksgiving. One of the peasants afterwards said to me, "So far as anyone of us knows, this is the first time since our village came into existence that anyone from the outside world came here and was interested in doing something for us. Heretofore the only man who ever visited us was the tax-collector, who often came with a gendarme. Now this cistern—it's too good to be true!"

IV

Dr. Stampar's rule is that wherever there is disease the people of the district or village must be interested in stamping it out. If they are not interested they do not deserve to be helped. But he holds that if it is pointed out to them that the malaria or typhus which has ravaged their locality for years can be stopped or reduced by draining their land or putting in a better water-supply, and that the government will furnish the plant and the pipes, provided they do the rest, the chances are they will be interested and ready to undertake the work.

A great deal depends on the extent to which the health officers and their aids succeed in winning the confidence of the people. Hence it is necessary for every member of the public hygiene service to be instructed in the psychology of the Yugoslav peasant in the various regions.

When Dr. Stampar first began his war against malaria, for instance, it frequently happened that the people refused to accept quinine or any other medicine or aid. They could not believe that the government—any government—would give them anything for nothing. Hitherto, whether it was under Venice or Turkey or Austria, the function of the government, so far as they were concerned, had been merely to tax them, call the men into the army, and generally exploit them. Now they were told that they had been "liberated," that they were under a new government, which was a Yugoslav government; but they didn't put much faith in the rumor. They couldn't conceive of a good, friendly government. They feared these pills were some sort of trick. If they accepted them from this man, next week another man was liable to appear, perhaps carrying a gun, and demand they fork up some (to them) enormous sums of money for the medicine, which, if they took it, might do them more harm than good. As for accepting a new cistern for the village, that was out of the question. In offering it to them the government was sure to have some deep-laid plot against them. "It was years," Dr. Stampar told me, "before we managed to overcome that sort of thing. Now such distrust is rarely encountered by the doctors and sanitary engineers and their assistants of the Public Hygiene Service."

By 1927 the village people in all the neglected sections of the country welcomed the doctors and sanitary engineers and their aids as though they were saints and angels come from On High. They accepted the quinine and, in their gratitude, often kissed the hygienists' hands. Heeding their advice, they graveled the village roads, began to drain their lands, enlarged the windows of their dwellings, built sidewalks, sanitary backhouses, and concrete platforms for manure, and so on.

News of these marvelous "people from the city" who traveled about on two wheels or on horseback, and some of them in amazing horseless and oxless carriages, and distributed health among the poor folk free of charge in the form of tiny white pills and beautifully painted new cisterns, and who spoke in a way that peasants could understand them, reached into the most remote mountain settlements, hundreds of kilometers from the railway, connected with the civilized world only by narrow rocky trails. People from far-off places who had never before heard of hygiene or modern medicine came to the provincial headquarters in the city to ask for advice and assistance in small operations of sanitary engineering, and Dr. Stampar's organization was equipped to provide this sort of support.

In the villages where health stations were established, the doctors, who came there once or twice a week, and the nurses, who lived permanently in the neat white new buildings, became extremely popular with the people. The shower-baths were great fun. The dispensaries and mother-and-child welfare service were a blessing no one could have dreamed of a few years ago. The motion pictures were a miracle. In fact, everything connected with this *hegijena* idea was more or less a miracle.

And everything was free. If one became sick or cut one-self or developed a toothache, all one needed to do was to go to the station and be fixed up. The doctors were jolly fellows; they joked with everybody as though they were not great and educated men. Pregnant women were visited once a week by "sisters" in beautiful white uniforms, who told them what to eat and how to take care of themselves. These "sisters" were the most marvelous creatures in the eyes of the villagers. They had many wonderful ideas about pre-paring good simple dishes and improving the appearance of one's house. If a child happened to be sickly or under-nourished, the "sister" asked the parents to bring it to the health station and let the doctor look it over. Then the doctor would send it to a special children's sanitarium in the city, and two or three months later the baby would be returned fat and chubby. And it cost nothing.

It was natural that, early in Dr. Stampar's war on illness and backwardness in the villages, the women became greater enthusiasts for his program than their husbands, but the men did not lag far behind. "Now," I was told, "millions of our peasants are shaved on Thursday. Formerly they shaved only once a week, on Sunday before going to church."

V

While creating this organization and putting it to work, Dr. Stampar traveled all over Yugoslavia. He is a man of boundless energy, capable of twenty-four and even thirty-six hours of the most strenuous work at a stretch without sleeping or eating. He does not smoke, drinks nothing stronger than water, and eats only the simplest food. If necessary, he can hike or ride horseback all day. And so, from 1920 to 1931, he visited every town, village, hamlet, and settlement in the country, barring none. He discovered communities which were not even on the map.

Although, as I have suggested, a colossal personality, he is essentially a simple man, utterly free of pretense, basically a peasant. Speech comes out of his mouth in a rhythmic roll with beautiful cadences. Talking even with an educated person, he seldom uses a word that the most backward peasant cannot understand. He is a master of simple impromptu speechifying. Raditch-like, he often talks in parables. Somewhat of a demagogue (in the best, most innocent sense of that word), he always says the right thing. He can flatter the peasant while telling him his lacks.

With his great bald dome of a head and a big moon-face, he is not handsome, but has a winning smile and a free and easy manner which invites everybody to come to him and be friends. A natural, unquenchable optimist, he laughs a lot. His laughter comes out of the depths of him as a vast melodious rumble punctuated by thin, sudden squeals, the laughter of a peasant.

Such a man, considering the great work he was doing, could not help becoming a hero in the minds of millions of men and women the country over. Imbued with his ideal, the doctors, sanitary engineers, and nurses told the peasants about their great chief. And so wherever he appeared he was instantly surrounded by crowds of eager, grateful, worshipful peasants. He did not discourage this adulation. It was a form of recognition and encouragement from the very people he loved most. Besides, he needed support from the masses to stay in office and continue his work.

Taking advantage of his popularity, commercial photographers printed thousands of his photographs and within a year there wasn't a village in the formerly unsanitary parts of Yugoslavia where several homes did not have Dr. Stampar's picture framed and hung on the wall. I saw it myself in numerous peasant houses. In one hut I visited, a tiny oil-light burned in front of it as though it were the picture of a saint and prophet.

All this naturally perturbed certain powerful politicians in Belgrade. The man was getting too popular, too strong. He was dangerous. Constantly expanding his program and activities, he was becoming half the government. Feeling his popularity and strength with the masses, Dr. Stampar went farther and farther. He wanted a health station in every village and asked for larger and larger appropriations for his work, and the Parliament, realizing how popular he was with the people, voted him almost as much as he asked, though afterwards the sums were frequently reduced by the budget bureau.

He protested against the Ministry of War's policy of sending young men drafted into the army from healthful to disease-infested regions, and *vice versa*.

He requested the Ministry of Forests to reforest the barren mountains in Macedonia in order to eventually eliminate the mosquito-breeding swamps. When the Ministry of Forests did nothing about it, he went into reforestation himself.

When he came into office there were nearly a million wooden plows used by the poor peasants of Yugoslavia. Dr. Stampar figured that they were poor (and hence pathological in one way or another) partly because they used wooden plows, with which they could not plow deep. So he requested the Ministry of Agriculture to help the poor peasantry get steel plows and other more modern implements. The Ministry of Agriculture was slow in getting ready; so he himself ordered his doctors and sanitary engineers in the villages to urge and help the peasants get better implements—with the result that now in Yugoslavia only about 100,000 wooden plows are still in use.

The opposition to him increased. Besides the politicians,

there were the already-mentioned private medical practitioners who hated him, although his giving free treatments to peasants in no way cut into their incomes, for before he established the village health stations 95 per cent of the peasants had never visited a doctor. Drug-store proprietors ganged up against him, even though before he began to distribute quinine and other medicine free of charge the overwhelming majority of peasants had never bought a penny's worth in any drug store.

But while Yugoslavia still had a properly elected Parliament, Dr. Stampar and his work were comparatively safe. The majority of the members of Parliament, mindful of their voters back in the villages, supported him. Then, in 1929, came the dictatorship (of which more in the next chapter), and almost immediately Dr. Stampar's authority was reduced. A whispering campaign was started accusing him of Communism. He vehemently denied he had any interest in Communism; only in hygiene and public health. He was trying to do merely what he thought was common sense and necessary to the welfare of the country. Anonymous letters were written to the Rockefeller Foundation in New York, slandering him. The Foundation, however, continued to support him.

In 1930 he was relieved of his duties as chief of the Public Hygiene Department and made an inspector, with no authority whatever. In 1931, when only forty-two years of age, he was pensioned "for the good of the service."

There is no telling what this blow would have done to the man if he did not have his natural peasant strength, humor, and optimism. For a year and a half he intermittently roved over the country like a wounded titan and tried to lose himself in his devotion to his family.

In 1932 he was elected vice-chairman of the Committee for Hygiene and Public Health of the League of Nations and given a year's job to roam over Europe and tell doctors and sanitary engineers in Greece, Germany, Czechoslovakia, Hungary, Spain, Poland, Bulgaria, and Rumania what he had accomplished in Yugoslavia. As I write this, I hear he has been sent to Nanking to help organize a war against disease in China. He speaks several languages and is glad of these opportunities to serve mankind at large; his heart and mind, however, are really in the malarial swamps and God-forsaken villages of Yugoslavia.

The work he has started goes on, but slowly, lamely, on appropriations which are lower every year. Many departments of it are being gradually discontinued, while King Alexander's dictatorship uses up most of the budget to maintain one of the largest military machines in contemporary Europe and a terror system which holds it in power.

In northern Croatia I visited a village called Sigetec, where half of the population is afflicted with goiter. The condition is due to certain bio-geographical causes. The director of the government salt monopoly in Belgrade has been appealed to repeatedly in the past two years to put a small quantity of iodine in the salt distributed in that locality, which would tend to combat the goiter condition; but in vain. "Were Dr. Stampar still in authority," one of the doctors at the Zagreb central institute said to me, "we would have gone into the iodined-salt business by ourselves. As it is, we can't do anything about it. Every second child born in Sigetec develops a goiter."

I saw Dr. Stampar, as I have mentioned, several times in Zagreb, but he did not complain to me, not really. He laughed a great deal. Most of the credit for his achievement he ascribes to the Rockefeller Foundation and his assistants on the scenes of action. He is the perennial peasant-optimist. "Why, just look at me," he said, laughing. "I'm young—only forty-three—in my prime—in fact, just a baby! I'm healthy. I'm strong. I'll live to be a hundred. What has been done in the villages can't possibly be destroyed—not all of it, anyhow. The people themselves won't let it be destroyed. Some day, perhaps, I'll get a chance again to continue what I have begun. Now I have lots of time to think, and I have new ideas—'bigger and better,' as you say in America."

I told him that a month or so before I had seen a light burning before his picture in a peasant hut.

"You don't say!" he exclaimed. He almost cried, but instead he laughed again.

CHAPTER XVII

I Meet the King-Dictator

EARLY IN MARCH, AFTER THE DIVERSE IRRITATIONS IN Zagreb, Stella and I definitely decided not to stay in Europe the entire year. Our feeling of discomfort increased day by day. Both of us were very tired. Traveling, meeting new people at every turn, listening to their troubles and tales of horror, and growing more and more indignant over the social and political situation as it had come to our cognizance—all these things were physically and emotionally exhausting.

For a few days I thought I would not return to Belgrade. I was assured His Majesty would receive me toward the middle of the month, but momentarily my attitude was "To the devil with him!" I had several notebooks of information about him from reliable sources. But the gentleman in the government press bureau, who thought I should see how charming the king really was, wrote me, insisting that I return to the capital. My Croat friends also urged me to go back. "After all, he is the most important individual in the country, the 'soul' of the *diktatura*. . . . You would go to see Mussolini or Stalin or Hitler, wouldn't you, if you had a chance? . . . Whatever anyone may think of him, Alexander is a considerable figure. . . . Remember this is the Balkans and we are living in an era when anything is possible. Almost anything may happen to him within the next few years. Nicholas of Russia—Wilhelm of Germany —Charles of Austria—Alfonso of Spain—who knows, Alexander may be next. . . . You owe it to yourself as a writer to see him. . . ."

So in mid-March we returned to Belgrade and I announced myself to the Minister of the Court, who received me coldly and, almost without looking at me, said I would be received in two or three days. I left his office without shaking hands. Subsequently I learned that everybody in the press bureau and the Royal Chancellery was not eager to give me the audience, but the group maintaining that I would be impressed by the royal charm finally prevailed. What side the Minister of the Court was on I don't know. . . .

Two days later a soldier brought me a formal letter from the Marshal of the Court, who was a brigadier-general, informing me His Majesty would receive me at eleven A.M. on March seventeenth in his residence at Dedinyé, which is a fortress-villa perched upon a little hill four miles outside of Belgrade. A court automobile would convey me there.

At a quarter to eleven on the appointed date I found myself in a vast, shining limousine, speeding through Belgrade. At the sight of it, every soldier and gendarme along the way snapped to attention. If I did not laugh, it was because I was worried some would-be regicide might mistake me for Alexander. I wondered if the glass on the limousine was bullet-proof. Very probably it was.

In less than ten minutes we were at Dedinyé, which reminded me, both inside and out, of the late Rudolph Valentino's "Hawk's Nest" estate in Hollywood, where I had been years before. Two handsome soldiers stood rigid at the entrance. An adjutant in a foppish uniform received me and, bowing me into a small waiting-room, begged me to wait till I was summoned.

Promptly at eleven another adjutant, full of stripes, medals, and what-nots, appeared, bowed, and begged me to follow him. I did so—down a short, handsomely carpeted corridor; through a large room, rather too elaborately furnished; through a smaller room, where another army officer stood near a door and knocked.

"Unutra! (Inside!)"
The officer opened the door and I walked in.

II

Among the few remaining crowned heads in Europe, Alexander is one of the youngest and the only absolute ruler. Most of the others, from the British monarch down to Albania's Zog, are either mere figureheads or mannikins of powerful rulers of other countries. There are almost no restraints upon Alexander's supremacy from any quarter in Yugoslavia. I met people in Belgrade and elsewhere who maintained that he was virtually a prisoner of a group of Serb generals and high-powered capitalists (all of them in cahoots with the imperialistic interests of France and England), who compel him to serve as executive officer of their diverse rackets. One man said to me, "If Alexander abdicated, he would be dead within a week, no matter where he might flee. They"—meaning the agents of the inner military-economic group in Belgrade—"would find and kill him. He is in much the same position as are your big gang chiefs in America." But most people in Yugoslavia put no credence in this theory. I don't, myself. Alexander holds complete and conscious authority over all important and many of the less important phases of life in his country because he wants to hold it and is supported by individuals in Yugoslavia, France, and England, to whose advantage it is that they support him. He is the "big shot" of Yugoslavia accountable to no one but history.

His dynasty is one of the most recent in origin, and he is one of the few kings in Europe (the only one in the Balkans) whose nationality, on both his father's and his mother's sides, is the same as that of the majority of his subjects.

His career is one of the foremost "success stories" in the contemporary world. In 1915, when tiny old Serbia, of which he was Crown Prince and Regent, had just been occupied by the Austro-German armies, he arrived at Scutari, Albania, after a ten days' ride over mountain passes, with nothing he could call his own but a weary, hungry horse, a saddle, a soiled uniform, a sword and a pistol belted around his waist, and a tooth-brush, a cake of soap, a towel, and a comb in his saddle-bag. Today he is the head of a state nearly four times the size of former Serbia and the richest man in the Balkans. His civil list allowance is over $1,000,- 000 a year—ten times higher than the salary of the President of the United States; in fact, higher than the pay of any other ruler in the world, crowned or not, except the Mikado of Japan—and that is only a part of his income. When he arrived at Scutari in 1915, with him were only one staff officer and one private. Today his bodyguard, paid by the state, consists of 40,000 officers and men; a full division with infantry, cavalry, light artillery, and aviation.

Aside from military training, Alexander's formal education is incomplete, but he is extremely clever in many branches of knowledge and endeavor. He is a genius at Balkanic political intrigue and a resourceful military commander, with considerable record in the field. He is a man of much force and physical courage. Toward his active antagonists he is ruthless. When I saw him, he had over 2,000 of them in prisons.

Ten years ago he married a daughter of Queen Marie of Rumania, who, unlike her mother, is a simple, modest, almost ordinary woman. She has borne three sons. Her position in Yugoslavia is no enviable one. In Belgrade I heard whispers she was "afraid." Thirty years ago a king and queen were murdered in the royal palace in Belgrade. So far two attempts on her husband's life have been made.

Alexander is not handsome; nor is he the contrary. He is five-feet-nine and slight of build. His carriage is military, his movements and gestures are easy and agile. His slowly sloping brow, heavy eyebrows, slightly hooked nose, prominent chin are typically Balkanite. He is dark-complexioned and has a short mustache. His dark hair, parted on the side, is graying at the temples. His mouth is rather sizable; his lips are pale, thin, and tense. His dark-brown eyes, deep in the sockets and with slight shadows under them, have a look which may mean almost anything.

In civilian clothes, he cuts a poor, almost ludicrous figure, so he never wears them, except on rare occasions when he goes hunting. He looks well on horseback. When he received me he had on a simple, much-worn officer's uniform, the royal insignia on his shoulders, and a small decoration under his chin.

For the first few minutes when I met him, I was inclined to believe most of the favorable things I had heard about him. He was charming when he greeted me and asked me to sit down with him. His smile was, to all seeming, genuine. After about ten minutes with him, however, I commenced to feel his charm had little, if any, depth or sincerity, that it was all a very dexterous act.

But if one considers his heritage and the influences which played on him in his formative years, one cannot help marveling how he can even act charming.

III

Alexander is a product of the Balkans and "the King business." For centuries past his forbears have waded in blood. The most important dates in his own career have to do with conspiracies, palace revolutions, regicides, wars, executions, assassinations, shootings in the Parliament, organized terror on a large scale.

The founder of the dynasty was Black (Kara) George, so named by the Turks because of his dark visage; a one-time swineherd and swine-dealer from Topola, a village south of Belgrade, who, late in the eighteenth century, became a *haiduk* chief—half patriot, half bandit—against the Turks. Black George conducted his patriotic banditry on a big scale and, in addition to amassing much wealth, liberated great sections of Serb territory from the Sultan; whereupon his fellow patriots and bandits made him king.

A man of sullen, violent temper, he was frankly a despot. He stood for no criticism of, or interference with, his plans and doings. In dealing with his opponents, either in politics or business, he employed the most drastic methods. He admitted having killed with his own hand over a hundred men, including his own father and brother. He was at his best in mortal combat. After he became a ruler and the Turks left him alone for a while, his tendency was to create and seize economic advantage for himself.

He was Alexander's great-grandfather.

Early in the nineteenth century another up-and-coming ex-swineherd and swine-merchant, Milan Obrenovitch, overthrew and slew Black George, delivering his head to the Sultan, in exchange for which the Sublime Porte consented to his assuming the rule of Serbia.

Thenceforth the history of Serbia has been a matter of long wars with Turks and Bulgars and an endless feud between the Karageorgevitch and Obrenovitch dynasties. Kings, queens, and pretenders to the throne have been murdered, each by some one acting in behalf of some member of the other dynasty. Each dynasty had its followers among politicians and army men. The masses of people, of whom neither the Karageorgevitches nor the Obrenovitches were characteristic, had nothing to do with these bloody politics. It made small difference to them which dynasty ruled. Both were equally bad—till Peter Karageorgevitch came to the throne.

The last regicide in Belgrade occurred in 1903, when a band of army officers calling themselves "The Black Hand" murdered King Alexander Obrenovitch and Queen Draga in their palace, and tossed their bodies onto the street, then forced the Parliament to call the then oldest Karageorgevitch, Prince Peter, a grandson of Black George, to assume the crown.

The incident, which outraged all of Europe at the time,

was almost a normal thing in Serbia; from the viewpoint of the country's future, all but necessary. Alexander Obrenovitch and Draga had practically sold Serbia to Austria and for years the royal palace in Belgrade had been a rendezvous of Balkan and Central-European corruptionists, intrigants, and libertines. The killing of the pair was, within the Balkan tradition, the easiest, most effective way out of a terrible situation, which was beginning to affect the masses of people.

"The Black Hand" was, in the Balkanic sense, a genuinely patriotic group. Their motives in butchering the corrupt, degenerate rulers were as pure as anything can be in the Balkans. Some of them were socialists of a sort and considered themselves idealists. They had the backing of civilian socialists.

The leader of the gruesome plot was one Dragutin Dimitriyevitch, nicknamed "Apis," who eleven years later, still acting as a Serb patriot, organized the Sarajevo assassinations of the Austrian Archduke Franz Ferdinand and his wife, thus precipitating the World War. There were a dozen or more other officers in the 1903 affair. Here I shall mention but one more—Peter ("Pero") Zivkovitch, a lieutenant of the Royal Guards, whose part in the plot was to unlock the door of the royal apartments, admitting the conspirators.

I mention "Apis" (now dead) not only because he was instrumental in bringing the Karageorgevitches back into power and precipitated the war which led to the expansion of Serbia into Yugoslavia, but also because he played an important rôle in Alexander's career apart from that; and Lieutenant (now General) Zivkovitch for the same reason.

IV

King Peter, father of Alexander, was, for a Karageorgevitch, a singular individual. A man of warm humanity and broad intelligence, he was rather splendid even as a king. He had a passion for decent government and the common people's well-being. That this can be said of him is due, perhaps, chiefly to the fact that from his fourteenth to his fifty-ninth year he lived mostly outside the Balkans and was strongly influenced, first, by the rather thorough education in the humanities he received in Switzerland and France, and, subsequently, by the powerful currents of liberal thought in western Europe in the second half of the nineteenth century.

For a time Peter lived in Cetinyé, where he married a daughter of Prince (later King) Nikita. In six years Zorka bore him five children, then died. Two of the children also died, leaving a daughter, Princess Yelena, and two sons, Princes George and Alexander.

Unwilling to sponge on old Nikita, Peter returned to France and later to Switzerland, and in those countries intermittently earned his living by teaching foreigners French, writing articles for newspapers, and translating from French and English into Serbian, till he was called to the throne. One of his translations, to which he wrote a sympathetic introduction when it appeared in book form in Serbia, was John Stuart Mill's essay, "On Liberty."

Too poor to give his children a liberal education, he yielded to Nikita's urging to let him ask the Tsar of Russia to take all three of them on his court and give them what education was to be had in St. Petersburg. So far as Yugoslavia, then still in the womb of time, was concerned, this was the worst thing Peter did in his life.

In St. Petersburg, living, so to speak, on the crumbs off the Tsar's table and attending the Imperial Military Academy, where every third student was a grand duke whose ancestral estate probably was larger than entire Serbia, young Alexander, destined to become the ruler of a great new state, observed the power, manners, and organization of the Tsar's court and Russia's nobility. There he also studied the Tsarist ways and means of ruling a country. There the potential Karageorgevitch and Nikita qualities of his nature developed to the full. . . .

Peter, characteristically, received the news of his elevation to kingship from his barber in Switzerland, who, on his entrance into the shop, bowed halfway to the floor and addressed him, "Your Majesty."

"What do you mean?" asked Peter, surprised.

"Has Your Majesty not seen the morning papers?"

"No."

"The Parliament in Belgrade yesterday elected you king."

"Are you sure? Don't you mean president?"

"No, Your Majesty, king."

A few days before, following the murder of the Obrenovitch (with which, by the way, he had had no direct connection), Peter had sent word to Belgrade that, since his ideas were definitely liberal and democratic, he desired, if the Parliament wished to make him head of Serbia, to be elected president, not king. But the Parliament had thought that making Serbia a republic would have been too drastic a step. The Russian Tsar, on whose good will some of the factions counted, might have been displeased.

Another reason, perhaps, why Peter, then nearly sixty, wanted to be president instead of king was that he did not believe either of his sons was fit to succeed him. Yelena was the old man's favorite child. She was a girl of great tact and diplomacy. When they were all together, she acted as a pacifier of her brothers, who always clashed. She was the oldest of the three—nineteen, when her father became king—and good-looking. Peter regretted she was not a boy, so he could proclaim her his successor. She married a Russian grand duke, whom the Bolshevists killed in 1918. Now she lives on the Riviera, a bitter woman. Her brothers have given her no end of pain. She hates Alexander, perhaps, more than the Reds.

V

When Peter ascended the throne, his oldest son George, who was sixteen, automatically became crown prince. Alexander was a year younger. Aside from both being Kara-georgevitches, the boys had little in common. George was mild and charming one minute, sullen and dangerous the next. When he became an officer he fraternized with common soldiers, then, suddenly flying into a rage over some trifle, whipped them. Once he ordered a cavalry troop into the Danube. He rode through Belgrade sitting backward in the saddle. He showered gifts on his servants one day, kicked and cursed them the next. He had a great range of interests and in some matters was brilliant. He had a weakness for artists, loved their society, gave them money when he had it, and sent a number of them to Paris and Vienna to study.

Alexander, though also of a highly nervous and violent make-up, could control himself. A schemer and go-getter, he was tight in money matters. Once he had made up his mind to do something, he never stopped till he accomplished it. Women and drink were never important in his life. He could bide his time, be subtle and discreet, though occasionally, too, he was indiscreet to the point of recklessness and brutality.

Already in his late teens, he was wont, in conversation with some of the officers of the court, to contemptuously refer to his father, who believed in parliamentarism and the soundness of the common people, as "the old woman." The only way to rule, he maintained, was the Russian way. The *raya* behaved as it should only when it was poor. The Serb peasant, while great in war, was little better than the Russian muzhik. . . . Recently, in fits of candor and indiscretion, Alexander has expressed similar views. One hears them discussed in whispered conversations in informed circles in Belgrade and elsewhere in Yugoslavia. . . .

For a few years after Peter's ascension to the throne the

dominant clique in the Serb army was the liberal, democratic, semi-republican "Black Hand," which also had a powerful influence on the general political life of the country. Alexander, of course, had no use for this group. Surreptitiously he started to play with a reactionary clique called "The White Hand," which, following the murder of the Obrenovitch pair, had been all but disbanded. By the time he was twenty he had a considerable following. He drew to himself officers who formerly had been neither Black nor White. He even pulled a few from the inner circle of "The Black Hand," among them Peter Zivkovitch, with whom he established a close personal relationship.

The officers figured it was good politics for them to line up—for the time being, secretly, of course—with Alexander. Peter was old; George was bound sooner or later to do something whereby he would forfeit his right to the throne; and Alexander, with the terrific concentration in his nature of the most formidable qualities of Black George and old Nikita, coupled with his self-control, was practically certain to be a king some day.

They figured correctly.

In 1909 George killed his valet in a fit of rage and, in consequence of the scandal, was forced by the Council of Ministers to sign away his right to succeed his father, and Alexander, then in his twenty-first year, was declared crown prince. One account, fairly well authenticated and retailed as true in Yugoslavia, has it that the servants in George's apartment had been paid to annoy and irritate him, so that he was in a violent temper most of the time and finally killed the valet.

The loss of the throne was no serious matter to George. Receiving an allowance from the government, he continued in his mad way. He went to Paris and had a gay time with his artist friends in the Latin Quarter. When in Belgrade, he often acted crazier than he was. To all who would listen he told true, garbled, and totally untrue stories about life on the court, till Alexander, on coming to power, had him interned. When I was in Yugoslavia, George, now forty-six, was a prisoner in a villa near Nish, in central Serbia, guarded by a detachment of his brother's trusted gendarmes.

VI

After Alexander was made crown prince, the conservative "White Hand" came aggressively into the open, while the old king, then in his seventies and ailing, continued to support "The Black Hand," some of whose members still held to republican and socialist ideas. For five years, including the two Balkan Wars in 1912 and 1913, the struggle went on between the two groups of officers and court politicians, the two political ideas and temperaments, the king and the crown prince, father and son.

Alexander's power grew steadily. Not only was he a subtle politician, but he proved himself a good soldier in war and was personally charming. He mixed with junior officers and common peasant soldiers. His manner and speech were democratic. He had what we in America call a sharp sense for publicity, and he said and did things, in camp, on the march, and even on battlefield, which made the army talk of him in romantic, legendary terms.

In public he always deferred to Peter, for whom, as I say, he had no respect. That was good politics: for the people, realizing that at last they had a ruler who sincerely cared for their interests, loved and admired the old man. The people did not know there were sharp differences between father and son. Peter suffered in silence.

Members of "The Black Hand," notably "Apis," realized that when Alexander, whom they thought they knew inside and out, came into complete power, their fate would be sealed. After the last Balkan War, when Peter was frequently ill, their position looked desperate. Most of them, unlike Zivkovitch and a few others, were too sincere in their ideas to go over to "The White Hand." As the latter's influence increased, the "Black Handers" were desperate as individuals and as an organization.

In their desperation—according to persons in Belgrade who were "on the inside" of Serb politics just before the war and with whom I talked—they suddenly revised their program and took for its central point the so-called Yugoslav Idea, which aimed to unite with the Serbs into one state the Croats, Slovenes, and Moslems of Bosnia, then under Austria and Hungary. In this they were prompted also by growing Austro-German anti-Slavism and aggression in the Balkans.

They thought that, if they succeeded in bringing about the creation of a large Yugoslav state, the political situation in the new country would be too complicated for Alexander and his clique to control it and put in effect their ideas of government. They thought, too, it appears, that the Croats and Slovenes might help the Serb republicans to establish a great Balkan democracy with a republican form of government. Their motto was "Unity or death!" To realize their program, they proceeded, under the leadership of "Apis," in the traditional Balkan manner. They knew the Yugoslavs could be united only in consequence of a great war. Logically (from their viewpoint), they produced Sarajevo. For brevity's sake I simplify, perhaps oversimplify, the matter; but there is no doubt that the desperation, early in 1914, of "The Black Hand" in its struggle against Alexander and his faction, was an important factor in the Sarajevo incident, which precipitated the war and, four and a half years later, the creation of the dreamed-of Yugoslav state.

Two weeks before the Sarajevo assassinations, Alexander, supported by "The White Hand" and some powerful civilian politicians, had shoved his father aside and made himself regent. He was then not yet twenty-six years of age.

VII

To say, as has been said, that Serbia was "crucified" in the war is no exaggeration. The country was conquered and the conquerors brought in typhus and other diseases which in two years killed over 20 per cent of the civilian population. Belgrade was destroyed. Cattle, horses, farm implements, and even house furnishings were taken out of the country to Austria, Hungary, and Germany in thousands of train and barge loads.

When Austria declared war on Serbia, the Serb army, which had just gone through two terrible, though victorious, wars, was about 400,000. Within a year that number was reduced to 40,000 officers and men. Most of them, in rags and barefooted, carrying old Peter in a basket, escaped to Albania and thence made their way to Corfu and Saloniki. There was fear the enemy would wipe out the entire male population left in Serbia; so the remnants of the army took with them 30,000 young boys who, if the war ever ended, might continue the race. The bones of over half of these boys are now dust in the Albanian mountains.

Perhaps no people in the world's history suffered such agony and survived it. No nation ever demonstrated a greater stamina or valor.

Regent Alexander, like his father, shared the nation's agony and participated in its heroism. He endured hardships as no other ruler or general in the World War. He emerged from the war a popular hero of his people, admired and respected by persons of other nationalities—journalists, officers, diplomats, doctors, and relief workers in the Balkans, most of whom, of course, knew only of his war record.

But the other side of Alexander's nature continued to function even in his country's darkest hours. He felt fairly confident that the sovereignty of Serbia would eventually be restored. When toward the end of 1916 it appeared that, in case of an Allied victory, Serbia really would bulge out into a great Yugoslav state with Belgrade as its capital,

Alexander and his henchmen worked and schemed to fortify his already highly advantageous position as regent of Serbia.

Most officers who were members of "The Black Hand," of course, perished in battle, but not all. Several came with what was left of the army to Saloniki. Among them was "Apis," then a lieutenant-colonel.

To get rid of "Apis" and other "Black Handers," Alexander's clique of generals and politicians organized a conspiracy. Of a sudden, late in 1916, the Allied forces in Macedonia, with headquarters in Saloniki, were electrified by the news that an attempt had just been made on Regent Alexander's life by members of a secret society in the Serb army. Years later it was conclusively established that no such attempted assassination had occurred; at the time, however, the story rang true. There followed the so-called Saloniki Trial. "Apis" and scores of other officers suspected of membership in "The Black Hand" or of however mild antagonism to the regent and his inner circle, were court-martialed. Four, including "Apis," who had been most instrumental in returning the Karageorgevitch dynasty to power, were sentenced to death and executed; most of the others were dismissed from the army and exiled. . . . The stunt was reminiscent of Black George; only it was subtler than anything Black George could have done. . . .

For a while, I am informed, even Peter, feebler and more miserable daily, believed "The Black Hand" had tried to kill Alexander. Subsequently he learned the truth; but, king in name only, he was powerless to do anything about it. In Belgrade one hears of stormy incidents between father and son in Saloniki and, later, in Belgrade.

The masses of people, however, knew nothing of what went on behind the scenes of their national tragedy. When the war ended and Yugoslavia came into existence, Alexander was the most popular man that had ever held power in that part of the Balkans. He permitted Peter to be called "Liberator," but he got most of the homage. In the first years after the war he moved much about the country. A deft actor, he was charming to all; simple, democratic everywhere, with just enough pomp now and then to impress those who liked to be impressed. He kissed peasant babies throughout the kingdom. He stopped his car, went into the fields, chatted with peasants, patted them on their backs, joked with peasant women, tasted their bread, became godfather of their children. All of which was part of the strategy and tactics of his will to power.

His father lived, neglected, in a dilapidated house outside of Belgrade. Svetozar Pribicevitch, then an important minister of the government and now one of Alexander's most bitter enemies living in exile, tells in a book, recently published in Paris, of his visit to the old king shortly before his death in 1921. In a bare room, Peter lay on a bed without sheets, only a rough army blanket over his body, his bare feet sticking out from under the cover. His only servant was a soldier. He didn't want to be taken to the palace. Then, "The king is dead! Long live the king!" . . .

VIII

When he became king, Alexander was thirty-three and at the height of his popularity; but under the constitution then in effect he had no power save that he was commander-in-chief of the army, and he took full advantage of this latter fact.

"The White Hand" was in control of the army and he always managed to have as Minister of War one of his trusted Serb generals. He had the backing of the French General Staff and French capital interested in Yugoslavia for important military and economic reasons, and in a few years built up a great war machine based upon iron discipline. He made his friend General Peter Zivkovitch commandant of the Royal Guards, and together they raised that force to 40,000 picked men. In the last ten years 12,-000 carloads of war equipment have rolled into Yugoslavia from France and Czechoslovakia. This equipment is stored in vast arsenals at strategic points, but most of it is in Kraguyevats, south of Belgrade.

On the top of a hill outside of Belgrade Alexander built himself a small fortress-villa, Dedinyé, and around the hill were erected rows and rows of barracks for the infantry, cavalry, and artillery regiments organized to guard his person. The lawn in front of the villa was made large enough for an airplane to take off, and rumor has it that under the building were dug secret chambers and passageways.

The people of the new kingdom had little political experience. When the country was organized, the highest positions in the government were filled by old-time politicians, mostly Balkanites of the type of Nikola Pasitch, or younger men who had suffered great privation in the war and now wanted to get as quickly and close to the trough as possible and seize for themselves and their friends and relatives every economic advantage in sight.

The Parliament, with its two dozen parties, was a circus and a madhouse. The party leaders were for the most part demagogues and pushers whose common aim was to become ministers and get to the trough.

With wisdom, tact, and firm insistence on moderation, a man in Alexander's position, with his immense popularity among the masses, could have forced or induced the Parliament to do its work intelligently, kept adventurers and grafters out of office, and thereby made it possible for able and decent men to get into politics.

But Alexander was not that sort of king. A great-grandson of Black George, a grandson of Nikita and a sympathetic student of the tsarist methods of government, he chose, while creating his military machine and building his personal fortress, to temporarily keep out of open politics and secretly play—as he did for seven years—one party leader against the other: Serbs against Croats, Croats against Serbs, Slovenes against both, Moslems against Orthodox Christians, the latter against Catholics. He changed ministers every few months. In seven years there were twenty-odd complete changes of government—and in seven cases out of ten, as soon as a minister became an ex-minister he went into business and built himself a palace in Belgrade or retired to the Riviera. All this produced inefficiency in government offices and increased the ineffectiveness of the Parliament. *It created a spirit under which the various racial and religious groups became more attentive to their differences than their resemblances. It stirred the demagogues, including Stephan Raditch, to more and more irrational and scandalous behavior.*

Playing secret, subtle politics with corrupt ministers and would-be ministers, Alexander, with his Machiavellian cunning, had no difficulty in raising his personal allowance from the government to over a million dollars a year, and acquiring estates and castles without paying for them. Nor was it difficult for him to become shareholder, in most cases without investing a penny, in some of the country's leading industries, banks, public utilities, and newspapers, from which he now draws—*via* a system of straw men—an annual income exceeding that of his civil-list allowance. The bulk of his money he has been sending, since 1922, to banks in other countries. He has become a controlling power in the Rumanian oil business.

With this sort of thing going on, Belgrade became a veritable stronghold of corruption and inefficiency. Members of Parliament, egged on by the king's agents or of their own accord, called one another bad names while in session, and engaged in fist fights. By the middle of the last decade the Parliament reduced itself to an international scandal and a joke.

This was what Alexander wanted.

The situation reached its climax in the murder of Stephan Raditch on the floor of the Parliament. The killer had been in closest contact with the court for years and the first thing he did after the shooting was to report to the Minister of the Court in the royal palace, and was surprised and indignant when the latter had him arrested. He was tried and given a term in the most comfortable prison in the country, and the best informed people in Yugoslavia believe he had been prompted to do the shooting.

The incident horrified the country and entire Europe—which, again, was what Alexander wanted.

Suddenly, on January 6, 1929, immediately after an incognito trip to Paris, where he secured the support of the French Government (then under Briand), he issued a manifesto abolishing the Parliament and the constitution, over which he had no legal power and which, six years before, he had solemnly sworn to defend and preserve, and, surrounded by his junta of corrupt generals, politicians and racketeer-capitalists (all of them allied with foreign interests in Yugoslavia), leaped to the saddle as Dictator. He declared that this act was dictated by "My conscience and My love for My fatherland" *in order to preserve the unity of the Serbs, Croats, and Slovenes!* . . . "In proclaiming this decision of Mine to My People I order all authorities in the State to act in accordance with it, and I command each and all to respect it and to submit to it."

Half of the people, having no hint of the real situation in Belgrade during the previous years, were glad the Parliament was dissolved. In their ignorance and simplicity, they trusted their heroic and charming king, who had been so great in war and now so frequently appeared among them in the most democratic manner. They did not know that in the past few years he had done more than anyone else in Yugoslavia to disunite the three branches of the nation. The other half submitted to the dictatorship because that was all they could do. The king-dictator had behind him the army, the only power in the state which was equipped for fighting. There was significance in the fact that the King made General Peter Zivkovitch, of the Royal Guards, his prime minister. To the foreign press the king-dictator and the premier declared that the dictatorship was only temporary. Alexander said that, as his father's son, he believed in parliamentarism with all his soul. Zivkovitch likewise maintained that his ideal was parliamentary rule. As soon as possible, perhaps in six months, they insisted, a new democratic form of government would be established.

But six months went by, then a year passed, and Alexander and Zivkovitch, working hand in hand, made no move to reinstate democracy in a saner form. Their regime became more and more dictatorial and tyrannical. When ex-Minister Pribicevitch proposed to publicly appeal to the king to keep his promise and suspend the dictatorship, he was arrested and, though in poor health, exiled to a remote malarial village. That he did not die there is due to President Masaryk of Czechoslovakia, who intervened on his behalf.

Less known politicians were clapped into prisons, along with thousands of peasants, workers and intellectuals who dared to come out in favor of democracy and the liberal or radical form of government. Political parties were outlawed. Scores of opponents to the dictatorship were assassinated in the streets of the principal cities by secret government agents. The press was under a severe censorship. Terror was general.

The king-dictator took upon himself all authority, including that over the National Bank, the state monopolies (salt, sugar, tobacco, and matches) which are Yugoslavia's principal economic factors. Under his direct, personal control came also the state mines, forests, railroads, the postal department and the telephone and telegraph systems. His ministers were mere clerks. The most important economic resources of the country were at his disposal, and he used them to further intrench himself. Besides, he received large loans from France, some of them secret, some in the form of guns and munitions.

Former members of parliament, who a year ago used to abuse one another, met and, comparing notes, discovered that their antagonism had been the result of intrigues emanating from the court.

By 1931 it became obvious that Alexander had planned to establish absolute rule from the beginning, very probably even before he became king; that, when he established it, he had not intended to return the country to any sort of constitutional form of government; and that now, with all the force and resources of the state at his command, with all the sadism in the country organized to keep down the liberal and radical opposition, it might be some time before the people—the majority of whom are passionately addicted to principles of liberty—would succeed in regaining control of their government.

IX

The night before I went to Dedinyé, a former minister of the government, now in passive opposition to the *diktatura*, visited me in my hotel room. "You will meet an interesting man," he said; "a man of great ability and capacity for work. He probably is the hardest-working ruler in Europe today. When in Belgrade, he is at his desk from eight in the morning till ten in the evening. He even supervises the housework both in the town palace and at Dedinyé. Often he makes the menu for the day. The Queen can't move, can't receive anyone, without his permission. . . . He revels in all the license of sovereign power. Everything goes through his hands. No instructor in any secondary school can be transferred or elevated to a higher grade without the royal signature. It's a disease with him, this craving for direct personal authority. . . . A tyrant. Nikita all over again. . . . He is ambitious for fame. The fame of another person within Yugoslavia he considers an insolent invasion of the royal prerogative. As soon as a man achieves eminence in politics, he finds ways and means to do away with him. He likes only yes-men who know how to keep themselves subdued, in the background. He is spiteful, ungrateful. He uses a man, then tosses him aside. That was his practice before he made himself dictator. He makes promises when it is necessary for him to make them, but seldom keeps them. He trusts few people, and those not always or in everything. He has a staff of personal spies. Some of these are important officials in the government and the army who confidentially report to him on other officials. Beside them, there is, of course, the regular espionage organization—15,000 secret agents whose sole or principal duties are to spy on and terrorize the political opposition. All of them are on the state payroll.

"And speaking of the state payroll reminds me that last spring, just before you came to Yugoslavia, he lowered his own civil-list allowance five per cent; the government, it seems, was having a hard time balancing the budget. The press was ordered to print that fact on the first page. Of course, no mention was made that he was still getting over a million dollars a year. A week later, however, he transferred all the employees of the royal household to the state payroll. The English governess of the royal princes, for instance, was put on the payroll of the Ministry of Enlightenment as a teacher. . . .

"He is a stranger to real wisdom, but possesses a profound cunning. Long before he became dictator, he prevailed on industrialists—or, rather, I should say, fellow industrialists—to build no factories in Belgrade. He wants no industrial proletariat in the capital. Too dangerous. He told the capitalists to build their plants and mills *across the river*, in Zemun and Panchevo, which now are our largest industrial centers. The only proletariat allowed in Belgrade is connected with railway and river transportation. . . . Some say that the "White Guard" Russians, who came here with Wrangel, gave him that idea, but I think he was quite capable of thinking of it himself.

"You have heard the rumor that he is a sick man, with serious organic disorder in his digestive system which now and then causes him great agony and, with overwork, brings him to the verge of collapse. Actually, his illness is only an acute nervous condition, which, however, greatly affects his moods and thus interferes or influences his work, including some of his most important decisions.

"This nervous condition perhaps is the weakest spot in his make-up. His moods, frequent enough to make them important, are apt to be extreme. One day he rages against some particular opponent to his rule, or the people because they do not appreciate what he is trying to do; for now and then he is sure that everything he does is for the benefit of the country. Two months later he is apt to weep hysterically before some person, who later tells about it, and insists he is trying to do well by the country and can't understand why people don't like his efforts. Most of the time, however, he has excellent control of himself."

The day before my visit to Dedinyé an official of one of the ministries in Belgrade said to me, "There is no doubt that the king believes his kind of rule with him as ruler is the best rule Yugoslavia could have. He thinks the friendship of France and England is valuable to Yugoslavia. But for them, Italy would have attacked us long ago; which is true, of course. . . . He is against Communist Russia and is only too glad to serve the anti-Communist powers of western Europe; but at the same time that he serves them he uses them, just as they use him. It works both ways. They know they could have no better man in charge of their military, diplomatic, and economic interest in Yugoslavia. . . . I am against him (secretly, of course!), but I am willing to admit that, since his becoming dictator, he has done some things that are good. For instance, he put efficiency into government offices. . . . I believe that most of the time he considers himself a patriot in the good old Balkan traditions of his forbears, Kara George and Nikita. Everything that is wrong with the country and his regime he blames on the perverseness of the people, the demagogues, and outside influences, such as the present world-wide economic crisis. I understand he hates the United States, blaming the severity of the depression on Herbert Hoover, whom he holds also responsible for the fact that Germany ceased paying reparations. . . . I believe that in some departments he sincerely strives to do good according to his lights; only he is very egotistical and bull-headed; thinks too much of himself and of money, too little of the rest of us."

Another of Alexander's weaknesses, much discussed in Belgrade, is his superstitiousness. He frequently consults clairvoyants. Shortly after the war, an old woman in Macedonia is said to have told him he would be assassinated when he opened the new Parliament building; which no end of people in Yugoslavia insist is the chief reason why the new Parliament building, immediately behind the royal palace, is still unfinished, although it was started twenty years ago. This old woman's prophecy is widely considered also as one of the causes of Alexander's violent anti-parliamentarism.

He is in constant fear of assassination. Every few months, I was informed, usually in connection with the nervous spasms in his intestines, he becomes extremely panicky, trusts no one, and sometimes for weeks at a spell sleeps in a different room or a different palace each night. He remembers the 1903 regicide. He knows his fear of assassination is discussed everywhere; so every once in a while, to show he is not afraid, he suddenly appears on the main thoroughfare of Belgrade, pale and rigid, accompanied only by one of his adjutants, apparently unguarded; but it is becoming generally known that for hours before hundreds of secret agents, in various disguises, are scattered up and down the avenue.

X

My audience with Alexander was no pleasant experience. He seemed cordial enough in his greeting; he was polite, democratic. He asked me how I liked Yugoslavia; where all had I been? I ventured to remark that the country was beautiful. Which section had impressed me most? I said that, as a native of Slovenia, I was naturally partial to Slovenia, but Dalmatia was lovely, too; Montenegro was startling; Bosnia and Herzegovina were impressive in their own ways; South Serbia was the most interesting; Shumadia and parts of Croatia reminded me of certain regions in America. He listened and seemed interested. "Slovenia is very lovely," he said. "I look forward every year to spending a few weeks at Bled."

I said that the people of Yugoslavia were a fine, proud race, and he nodded. Then there were long, to me very awkward, pauses in our conversation, and we looked at one another. I sensed his unfriendliness, his eagerness to be rid of me. He knew I had declined his Order of the White Eagle. He doubtless had received conflicting reports on what I might write about Yugoslavia. He had been urged to see me. It was a nuisance, a waste of his time.

I remarked that, going about the country, I had observed poverty. He winced a little and said, unsmiling, "Yes, it is this world-wide depression. It began outside our borders and now is affecting us rather severely. It is true the peasant cannot sell his product as readily as a few years ago, and he hasn't much money—*a sit yé, sit yé!*—but he's full, he's full!"—meaning he is not hungry.

Another pause. We eyed one another.

He apologized he had not received me earlier and said he was very busy. It was a hint, but I stayed ten or fifteen minutes longer, about twenty minutes in all. I felt a satisfaction in keeping him from his work. Just then, as I had been told by a reporter an hour before, he was personally directing the debate on the budget in the sham Parliament of his yes-men he had established in 1931 in response to pressure brought upon him by France and England. He was ordering some of his puppets to orate, lamely and stupidly, of course, against the regime, and others to brilliantly reply for the regime.

Finally, still very charming, Alexander Karageorgevitch rose. It is his regal custom to ask visitors whom he considers friendly if they have a wish he can grant, or to give them of his own accord an autographed photograph or a package of specially made court cigarettes. He did not ask me if I had a wish, nor did he give me anything.

It probably was fortunate he did not ask me if I had a wish. The day before, browsing in a musty second-hand bookshop, I had bought for three dinars (five cents) an old paper-bound copy of King Peter's translation of Mill's "On Liberty." The book was all dog-eared and soiled, and as such symbolical of liberty in Yugoslavia. Before leaving my hotel to go to Dedinyé, I had put it in my inside coat pocket, playing with the idea of saying to Alexander, if opportunity offered, that I was a collector of rare and curious publications and desired to have his autograph on his father's best-known translation. When I saw he was not going to ask me if I wished for something (which I had been told he might, although I had refused the order), I thought for a moment of asking him for the autograph, anyhow; then changed my mind. I planned to be in Yugoslavia another week and wanted to have as few additional annoyances as possible. Also, I wanted to cross the Yugoslav border with all my notes for this book.

We chatted awhile longer. Alexander asked me when I expected to publish my book on Yugoslavia. I said, "About this time next year." I could not bring myself to call him "Your Majesty." He said he read things printed about Yugoslavia in foreign prints, but none of the writers betrayed the least understanding of what they were writing about. I said I had noticed that, too, and would try to remedy that situation so far as it was in my power.

He looked at me. I looked at him.

When was I leaving Yugoslavia? I said in about a week. From what port? Trieste. .ⁱ. . Then he shook my hand, said he was glad to have met me, wished me *sretan put*, and, expressing no hope to see me again, hurried back to his telephone to continue his budget debate.

On my part, although, as I say, the audience was no pleasant experience, I was glad to have met him, too. Riding back to Belgrade in the royal limousine, I had a very strong feeling about him. He was a man of the times, in the same category of strong-arm rulers with Mussolini, Hitler, Pilsudski, and the rest of the tyrants and dictators. He was a cog in the new political system of post-war Europe, helping to hold together a crumbling civilization with gangster methods. He was a figure in the dreadful European nightmare that seemed rapidly and inevitably approaching its climax—another great war, to be followed (as nearly everyone with whom I talked appeared to believe) by general upheavals of the masses. At the moment he had the whole country "on the spot"; he might stay in power one, two, five or ten more years; but the future was clearly and definitely against him and his kind.

Conclusion

CHAPTER XVIII

Back to America

IT WAS A LITTLE OVER TEN MONTHS SINCE OUR COMING to Yugoslavia. In that time we had experienced the country as perhaps no person had ever before. We had seen, heard, smelled, tasted, and felt it almost from one end to the other, and reacted to it both mentally and emotionally. And by now, as already suggested, the adventure had become a great strain on both of us. We could not relax. Stella was full of real and imaginary worries. She was afraid I might have a nervous collapse. I had lost fifteen pounds. Even in sleep my whole being was taut, rigid. I awoke in the middle of the night thinking of the young men exiled to the malarial villages in Old Serbia, or something similar. What made things worse was that the rumors of the imminence of a new war continued. When I contemplated the probability of a new world conflagration, simultaneously loathing and desiring it (desiring it because I thought that might give the people a chance to revolt), it was all I could do to control my feelings.

Leaving Belgrade for Slovenia after my audience with King Alexander, we were obsessed with the idea of getting out of Yugoslavia and out of Europe as soon as possible. The United States, with its nation-wide "bank holiday" and its 15,000,000 unemployed, was no paradise on earth, yet our being American citizens, traveling on passports issued by the State Department in Washington, was something very precious. A few days before we had definitely booked passage on a ship sailing from Trieste to New York on March 29th.

We arrived in Lublyana on the 19th. No one in Carniola

knew we were leaving right away. My people in Blato and our friends in Lublyana believed we would stay in Yugoslavia until May, a full year. I thought it was best to tell my family suddenly, casually—and that was what I did. I said I had just received word from America about an urgent matter (wholly imaginary) which required my being in New York by mid-April. We would leave Yugoslavia in four or five days.

"Why so soon?" said my mother. "The ship, you say, doesn't sail till the 29th. If you go to Trieste on the 28th, it would be early enough, wouldn't it?"

I said I had some business to attend to in Italy. But the main reason why I wanted to go at least a week before sailing was that, should I have some trouble with the Yugoslav customs guards and gendarmes at the border on account of my notes for this book, I would have time to attend to it. Also, it was harder and harder to control myself. I trembled with apprehension for my four brothers, three of whom already had notifications where to report in the event of a general mobilization. My head whirled with what I knew was going on all over Yugoslavia, in Germany and elsewhere. Barbarism, barbarism ——

But, somehow, during those last few days Stella and I spent in Blato and Lublyana, we were all very gay. We laughed a lot, a little hysterically, no doubt. Anxious that no one should get in trouble with the terroristic authorities on my account, I steered clear of any talk about the political situation. Instead, I told of the funny things Stella and I had seen or experienced in our travels. I pretended that to go back to America was little more than going to Zagreb or Belgrade. I said I would come home again in two or three years. I was as casual as I could be. To please my mother and sisters, I ate more than was good for me.

One evening we went to our last party in Lublyana and took leave of most of our literary friends in Carniola. To the others we said good-by through the newspapers.

Saying good-by to my people in Blato was hard.

Mother said, "Now maybe we shan't see you for another nineteen years." She looked sad.

I laughed, "But, Mother, didn't I tell you I'll come again in a few years?"

"*Bog dai no!*" she said. "May God will it so!" She held my hands and swayed a little. She stood on the same spot in front of the house where she had stood when I first went to America and when I returned. We embraced. There were no tears.

"Take care of yourself, Mother," I said. "Don't work too hard."

She smiled. "You take care of yourself, too."

I said I would and shook hands with my father, Uncle Mikha, Cousin Toné and his wife, Yulka. Yulka was big with child, due to give birth in two or three weeks. "Too bad you can't wait till then," said Toné. They had asked me to be their first-born's godfather. I had nominated my brother Stan to be my proxy at the christening.

I said good-by all around the village. Stella did the same. My brother Yozhé had taught her to say in Slovenian, "*Bom vesela ko vas bom spet videla!* (I'll be glad to see you again!)"—which made a great hit with all the villagers. "We'll be glad to see you again, too," they said, laughing. "Come soon!"

A young peasant from a near-by village came to say good-by to me. He drew me aside and told me how the people up and down the valley were still telling the legend about Mr. Guggenheim and me. "Now, when you get back, tell him all you know," he said as we shook hands. "Write the whole truth, even if that will make it impossible for you to come home again as long as this regime lasts."

The train left Lublyana for Trieste late in the afternoon. My brothers and sisters came with us from Blato. A few minutes before we pulled out, a crowd of Lublyana literati and students appeared on the station platform. Most of them were my friends. They all seemed very marvelous, sincere people. We shook hands again, exchanged a few jokes, remarks. We laughed some more. *"Do svidenya!* (So long! Till we meet again!)"

Then we were off.

I was terribly sorry for all of them—my brothers and sisters, my friends—most of the people in Carniola, in Yugoslavia. Their rich, beautiful country was a trap. Entire Europe was a trap for the plain people of most countries. . . . What future was there for my young brothers? These young writers and students? To be subjects of a terroristic ruler, then be killed in war against the subjects of some other dictator, unless they and their potential "enemies" found a way of getting rid of their tyrants and changing the whole politico-economic system of which the tyrants were a part. . . .

There was a touch of spring in the air. The birds were flying back from the south. Carniola looked very lovely, though not so lovely, of course, as it had been in May the year before. Near the track, as our train sped Trieste-ward, we saw a peasant plowing. He looked like my brother Stan, tall, husky, bent over the plow-handles. There was a great dignity in his task. Why couldn't the world be organized to permit him to plow and produce in peace all his life? As we passed him he reached the end of a furrow. He glanced up and waved. . . . I had an enormous lump in my throat.

THE END

Critical Comment

on

"Laughing in the Jungle"

by

Louis Adamic

"No one can quarrel with Mr. Adamic's wise conclusions, with the high spirits of his report on American life as an immigrant found it, with the appealing simplicity and healthiness of his nature. He came here when he was fourteen years old, and the simplicity and frankness of his nature, the realistic honesty of his attitude toward men and events he seems to have brought with him. What he learned in America was how to write. He writes well, with a strong clarity and an easy eloquence. He emerges from this book a good guy."
—*William Soskin in the N. Y. Evening Post.*

∞

"Mr. Adamic has an abiding sense of human dignity, and to my mind he touches greatness as a story-teller. . . he is no mere autobiographer. It is through other men's struggles, through their conflict of values, that we catch, fleetingly yet clearly, his own adventure. This seemingly unconscious technique of mirrored self-portraiture is done so almost perfectly that it is the reader who limns the portrait of the artist."—*Benjamin Stolberg in the N. Y. Herald Tribune.*

∞

"Adamic has a magnificent authenticity which makes his writing very moving. He is a literate Bohunk who is still a Bohunk; an American proletarian who tells a story with the directness of a hobo beside a camp fire. He is singularly creedless, without a touch of Mary Antin sentimentality or of class-conscious propaganda. He tells what he has seen, in stories."—*Lewis Gannett.*

∞

"I was entirely charmed with the book. Not only is the material interesting and a valuable contribution to one's knowledge of one's country, but I find the story clear and convincing and with a very pleasing quality. There is penetration in his point of view. I hope it has the success it deserves."—*Mary Austin.*

"Adamic has this distinction—unique and delightful. He is a realist who can laugh. It is refreshing to read after a man who doesn't blink the truth nor wince at the facts that make the truth, and can still fight and hope and laugh. I am delighted with the book."—*William Allen White.*

∞

"A vitally interesting book, an important book: the sanest account of an immigrant's experiences we have ever had; the only one I know in which the raw matter of fact has been given a twice-truthful statement by a man who exhibits, instinctively, the restraint of an artist."—*Evelyn Scott.*

∞

"It is by all odds the best story about and by an immigrant that I have ever read—and I read every word of it with unflagging interest."—*R. L. Duffus.*

∞

"A grand book . . . the music and color of life on its lower levels."—*James Stevens, author of "Paul Bunyan."*

This book is composed in Linotype Caslon Old Style, a careful adaptation to machine composition of the type designed by the first English type founder, William Caslon. After two centuries it is still unrivaled for grace, strength, and legibility. The format is by A. W. Rushmore. Set, printed and bound by the Haddon Craftsmen for the publishers, MESSRS. HARPER & BROTHERS, *New York and London*